PRAISE FOR

The Lost Daughters of China

"An evocative memoir that will not only attract parents or would-be parents of Chinese baby girls but . . . also touch the hearts of us all." — *Chicago Tribune*

"A wonderful book. Evans's discussion of the economic and cultural pressures that affect Chinese families is well researched, intelligent, and balanced. Moreover, she provides a thoughtful view on what parents must convey with regard to the dual legacies of the adopted child."

— AMY TAN, author of *The Joy Luck Club*
and *The Bonesetter's Daughter*

"Perceptive and moving." — *Publishers Weekly*

"There has been much press about rescuing (adopting) baby girls from China's oppressive sociopolitical climate, but little about the women and men who are losing their daughters. Here, Evans gives us a whole story, both moving and jarring. This is the book I have been waiting to see."

— JAN WALDRON,
author of *Giving Away Simone*

"A bittersweet journey. *Lost Daughters* takes a brutal look at the Chinese bureaucracy and a confluence of harsh realities—the Chinese government's strict population policy of one-birth-per-couple imposed in 1980, the culture's traditional reliance on male heirs, plus untold hardships and emotionally wrenching circumstances known only to a birth mother." —*The Dallas Morning News*

"Clear, interesting, thorough, fair and important. What's finally most impressive about Evans's feelings for her daughter is how they have led her to care about all the other little Chinese daughters who have lost their birth parents, and about the 'lost mothers' who feel compelled to give them up."

—*San Francisco Chronicle Sunday Book Review*

"In this balanced account of the extraordinarily complex issues involving the lost daughters of China, Evans is respectful of the Chinese, of adoptive parents, and of the rights of women. She is a wise, great-hearted woman who writes from both a personal and a cultural perspective. As I read this book, I thought of many friends who would love it. I believe you will love it too."

— MARY PIPHER, author of *Reviving Ophelia*
and *Another Country*

"[Evans] eloquently assesses the conditions that force couples to abandon their off-spring and chronicles the emotional anguish that accompanies the decision to give up a child. Full of questions and insights about family and the morphing of cultures, this book is essential reading for those interested in adoption, population policy, or the politics of domestic arrangements."   —*Library Journal*

"A fascinating statement about the cultural phenomenon of unwanted girls in China, viewed through the lens of a Caucasian adoptive parent. In this book, the personal and the political intersect in important and enlightening ways."
                    — CLAIRE S. CHOW, author of *Leaving Deep Water*

"An important read for all who care about human rights and the lives of women and girls."   —Women's Press website

"Finely crafted and deeply felt . . . Evans is surely right that the issue of China's 'lost and found' babies will grow in cultural and political significance as the number of adoptive families in the United States rises. A compelling story, *Lost Daughters* is highly recommended to anyone curious about the subject."
                    —*Population and Development Review*

"Breathtaking—an unforgettable story. *The Lost Daughters of China* describes not only the tragedy of social engineering, but the healing power of a mother's love."
                    — IRIS CHANG, author of *The Rape of Nanking*

"Evans views China from an honest and unflinching feminist perspective that has garnered praise from many Chinese women. She gives us the joyful tale of an adoption entwined with the sobering reality of millions of girls missing or uncounted from China's population. Touching and engrossing."
                    —*Red Thread*

"Powerful and important. *The Lost Daughters of China* is not simply the journey of a child, a man, and a woman, but a history of cultural mixing at the end of the millennium."
                    — BELLE YANG, author of *Baba: A Return.*
                    to China upon My Father's Shoulders

"Substantive and moving."
                    — MAUREEN CORRIGAN, NPR book reviewer,
                    in *Leave Me Alone, I'm Reading*

The

Lost

Daughters

of

China

Adopted Girls,

Their Journey

to America,

and the

Search for a

Missing Past

Jeremy P. Tarcher/Penguin
a member of Penguin Group (USA) Inc. · New York

The
Lost
Daughters
of
China

Karin Evans

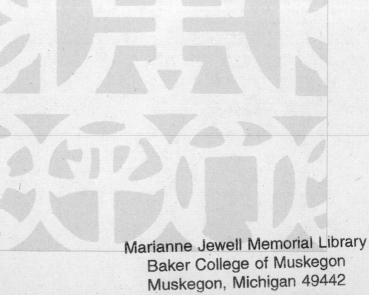

JEREMY P. TARCHER/PENGUIN
Published by the Penguin Group
Penguin Group (USA) Inc., 375 Hudson Street, New York, New York 10014, USA •
Penguin Group (Canada), 90 Eglinton Avenue East, Suite 700, Toronto, Ontario M4P 2Y3,
Canada (a division of Pearson Canada Inc.) • Penguin Books Ltd, 80 Strand,
London WC2R 0RL, England • Penguin Ireland, 25 St Stephen's Green, Dublin 2, Ireland
(a division of Penguin Books Ltd) • Penguin Group (Australia), 250 Camberwell Road,
Camberwell, Victoria 3124, Australia (a division of Pearson Australia Group Pty Ltd) •
Penguin Books India Pvt Ltd, 11 Community Centre, Panchsheel Park, New Delhi–110 017,
India • Penguin Group (NZ), 67 Apollo Drive, Rosedale, North Shore 0632, New Zealand
(a division of Pearson New Zealand Ltd) • Penguin Books (South Africa) (Pty) Ltd,
24 Sturdee Avenue, Rosebank, Johannesburg 2196, South Africa

Penguin Books Ltd, Registered Offices: 80 Strand, London WC2R 0RL, England

Most Tarcher/Penguin books are available at special quantity discounts for bulk purchase for sales
promotions, premiums, fund-raising, and educational needs. Special books or book excerpts also can
be created to fit specific needs. For details, write Penguin Group (USA) Inc. Special Markets, 375
Hudson Street, New York, New York 10014.

Library of Congress Cataloging-in-Publication Data

Evans, Karin.
    The lost daughters of China : adopted girls, their journey to America, and the search for a miss-
ing past / Karin Evans.—Rev. ed.
        p.   cm.
    Includes bibliographical references.
    ISBN 978-1-58542-676-8
    1. Orphanages—China.   2. Abandoned children—China.   3. Chinese—United States.
4. Intercountry adoption—Case studies.   I. Title.
    HV1317.E93   2008   2008028756
    362.734082'0951—dc22

Printed in the United States of America
10 9 8 7 6 5 4 3 2 1

Book design by Carla Bolte

For all lost children, everywhere

Contents

亲爱的小玉：

叫我阿珍吧，就象我们传统的叫法。你可以有我倒杯茶。

怎么跟你说呢？发生在你身上一切的一切都使我很难抑制住自己的热情。我在中国生活了廿七年。可以说是嫉妒得很顽强似的，而我被列为你有某种缘份。难奇怪的？因为你是从中国批领养的。长江的水在我们以血液中流淌，黄河的泥沙堵的我们的骨架。当我还看着我们如绿叶繁茂。最重要是我们都是女性。中国女性就象老话中说的象草一样生长不衰就是被践踏过。我们有一种共同的不甘心，从这个角度来看待我们就和我们的辈姐们一样。

你就如我的辈姐的一样。

……如果你有疑问。有什么论文那都是女孩子，有什么命运

Calligraphy by Anchee Min

A Letter to All the Lost Daughters of China

Anchee Min

Call me Aha-yi, aunt. I am introducing myself to you the way we do in China. You may have the honor to serve me tea.

How would I begin? I don't get emotional easily. I lived in China for twenty-seven years; life has toughened me up, and yet I must confess that I am deeply moved by this book. For a strange reason I feel connected to you, orphans adopted from China. The Yangtze River runs in our blood, and the time dust of the yellow-earth culture frames our bones. The straight lacquer-black hair. Yes, we share a lot. Most important, we are all females, Chinese females, the kind an old saying describes as "grass born to be stepped on."

We are in the battle together. You are my nieces.

Aunts in China are mean, at least mine are. It is because they are obligated to tell you the truth. It's their role in the family. They tell the naked truth to their nieces and nephews. Parents and grandparents spoil the children because they would do anything to avoid hurting their feelings. But aunts are expected to care for the children in a different way. And now, if you don't mind, I will perform my duty.

Let's start with the whys. Why is it the girls who are lost? Don't take it personally. Please understand that Chinese women are cultivated to suffer. Giving away a daughter to someone, a childless sibling or a great-aunt who is in need of caring, was considered a virtue. Girls were presents, companions, kitchen-hands, bed-mates, baby-making machines. Also, the tradition makes a mother feel ashamed for not being able to produce a son. China is an agricultural country where hard labor is a means of survival—a man can carry three hundred pounds of soil while a woman carries a hundred fifty. See my point?

When I was about five, my mother was pitied every time we went out. It was because she had three daughters. "Look, a string of crabs!" My mother didn't feel sorry for herself. Despite the fact that she finally gave birth to my brother, she and my father made me the family's favorite. "On purpose," my father con- fessed later on. "I don't want you to get any idea that girls are no good. And I don't want your brother to get any idea that he is better because he is a boy." Well, my parents are educators, while the majority of their countrymen are peasants.

In 1995, I was in China helping launch a movement called Mothers, Save Your Daughters. It started with a report in a paper called *China's Communist Youth League.* It was an in-depth study. There was a story about a couple who murdered five of their infant daughters in the hope of gaining a son. The news shattered me to the point that I didn't want to return to Amer- ica. I wanted to help promote education in rural areas. I believe that if only that couple had had education, the killing wouldn't have happened. They were peasants and illiterate; they were not in touch with their consciences.

There are struggles, of course. How could a mother not struggle after she carried you months in her body? You might be the result of her hesitation. She couldn't do it; her heart opposed her and her hands shook. So she thought of an alternative. If a child is strong enough to endure, she might escape her fate.

Each of your birth mothers was not sure, but she wanted to do her best for you for the last time. She might have traveled as far as her money allowed her, to a richer area and a busier market where she would lay you down and hide you inside lotus roots or celery leaves. I am sure she would watch from a distance, hiding herself behind a crowd or in a bush. There she would experience a kind of death. She would suffer until someone picked you up and yelled. She would try, try hard not to answer the call—*Whose child?*—not to run toward you. She would bite her lips until they bled. For her, you will forever be a "broken arm hidden in her sleeve."

"Many women break their nerves that way," one foster mother I spoke with in Anhui province told me. "There are nutty-looking women who sneak around my house from time to time trying to locate the daughters they abandoned. They don't say anything. No questions. They just wander around like ghosts. I tell them that it's no good to linger on the pain. Let the past be gone. These children are going to live."

Oh, how I wish your Chinese birth mothers could read this book. They would be comforted, relieved, and released from nightmares that haunt them. As a woman who grew up in China, I identify with their despair, the despair of being deprived of understanding.

I believe that I have said enough. I couldn't say it any other way. Forgive me. The hope is that you are in America and you are loved. You are in control of creating your own future. I wish you all the best.

The

Lost

Daughters

of

China

Introduction

Suddenly they were everywhere, the little girls from China. Found forsaken in their homeland, whisked out of orphanages by American parents, they were growing up across the United States. In the New York metropolitan area alone, there are now thousands of these adopted daughters, strolling through the American Museum of Natural History or running into one another in sandboxes and Central Park. In Los Angeles, they are building castles at the beach. In Chicago, they are ice-skating and going to see Georgia O'Keeffe's paintings. In Atlanta, there are now several hundred households with daughters from China.

In Chattanooga, Tennessee, and Portland, Oregon, and Houston, Texas, more children from China are growing up. In the San Francisco Bay Area (where the local count exceeds three thousand), they are gathering at a fancy Chinese restaurant to observe the Autumn Moon Festival, wandering outside to gaze at the moon and honor the memory of their birth parents. A Chinese-born girl from Guangdong province was growing up in

Ohio's Amish country. In one admittedly unusual family in the deep South, an American woman and her fifty-four-year-old mother traveled to China together and each came home with a Chinese daughter.

In 1997, my husband and I joined this subculture of East-West families when we traveled to southern China, walked into a social welfare home for children, and were handed an astonishingly beautiful year-old baby. In the year 2000, we began the process all over again. In the summer of 2001, we flew across the Pacific again to bring home a second daughter, almost three. Once again, we experienced a journey of transformation. We were instantly twice as busy, twice as blessed.

With those meetings, we became participants in a major cross-cultural story of our time, part of a human interaction in which people journey halfway across the globe in search of a child, where the lives of lost girls in China are linked with the lives of waiting parents from the West in a fateful moment of bureaucratic matchmaking. It's a phenomenon that spans the gaps of distance, culture, race, language, economics, and heritage. It is a tale of twenty-first-century cultures mixing with each other in an unprecedented way. While we settled our children into their new lives, thousands and thousands of other families across the United States and in numerous foreign countries were also introducing adopted Chinese daughters (and a few sons) to a new life with a new family.

For more than a decade, the China adoption trend had continued to build. China's adoption program, with its centralized operations, regulated fees, and relatively smooth protocols, emerged as a model for other foreign nations, The pages of American newspapers—whether in Mesa, Arizona, or Plain City, Ohio—regularly included one story after another of little girls from China coming home to new families. From the small number of Chinese children adopted by Americans in the 1980s and early 1990s, nearly 4,000 Chinese children were adopted in 1997 when we came home with Kelly; more than 5,000 when we came home with Franny. By 2005 the number of Chinese children adopted by Americans yearly had peaked at 7,906, before the Chinese government slowed things down with a new set of rules.[*][1] By 2008, close to 70,000 children from China had come to the United States. Those adopted in other countries brought the total to well over 100,000 little girls who'd left China, adopted by foreign parents. Little girls from China were growing up all over the world—in Australia, New Zealand, Sweden, Iceland, Italy, Mexico, Argentina, and numerous other countries, including sizable numbers in Canada and Ireland. The biggest group outside the United States was in Spain.

Sometimes I try to imagine a group photograph that would capture the magnitude of this event in history: 70,000 girls, ranging in age from less than a year old to college age, enough to fill a stadium. Photograph them in Central Park from high overhead in a helicopter, perhaps, all the girls hand in hand, stretching from one end of the park and back again, maybe farther. Or picture them smaller, as so many of them have been photographed—babies on a couch in China, bobbing one against another. For some reason, whenever I think of such overwhelming numbers of babies or children, I do "couch

---

[*]The latest regulations and subsequent rules for foreign adoption can be found on the Families with Children from China website (www.fwcc.org) as well as on the website of the China Center of Adoption Affairs (www.ccaa.org). In the decade since we went through the adoption process, there have been numerous changes in the rules, and there will likely be more.

math." In this case, ten babies to a couch would mean a group shot composed of seven thousand couches. It's still beyond imagining. But the numbers are a fact, and the experience has touched hundreds of thousands of people if you add up the children and parents alone.

In the 2004 U.S. presidential election, an adopted child from China came close to hanging out in the White House. On the Democratic convention floor, nominee John Kerry could be seen lifting up a small girl wearing a Chinese silk dress—his niece. During the 2008 Beijing Olympics opening ceremonies, Jenny Bowen, adoptive mother of two girls, and the founder of Half the Sky Foundation, a nonprofit that serves the children in China's orphanages, was selected to be one of the torch bearers. She was running, said Bowen, for all the girls who remained in China's welfare institutions, and for all the children orphaned in the Sichuan earthquake. Musician Lucy Kaplansky adopted a child from China and released an album called *The Red Thread*. An eleven-year-old adopted girl living in Milwaukee, Jade-Lianna Gao Peters, was the voice of the new Nickelodeon TV Chinese culture show for children, *Ni Hao, Kai-Lan*.

Yet another little girl from a Chinese institution wound up on television, sitting on Katie Couric's lap. This was one of many East-West miracle stories. First, an adoptive mother of three, Kate Haroldson, who lives in Sacramento, California, went to an orphanage in Fenyi to adopt her youngest daughter. "Of course a half a dozen kids ran toward the gate as we entered." One of the children was Gong Lu, a four-year-old girl who was suffering from a massive disfiguring facial tumor on her nose, a hemangioma. Haroldson went to work, contacting Love Without Boundaries (LWB), which provides medical help to kids in China who need it. She also e-mailed Dr. Lisa Buckmiller, who often traveled abroad with LWB to treat children. "I asked her if she knew how to get this sweet girl help." Buckmiller, a pediatric vascular surgeon at Arkansas Children's Hospital, agreed to help the child.

Love Without Boundaries raised the money and Gong Lu was brought to Little Rock, accompanied by her orphanage director. The little girl told her doctors, "After the surgery, I hope to be a beautiful girl. Then I would like to go to school like other children." She added, "I want to find a good father and mother who can adopt me."

The surgery was a life-changing success. NBC got wind of the story and little Gong Lu went on television and charmed Couric. But the tale wasn't over yet. The doctor and her husband, Richard Hinkle, began the process to adopt Gong Lu. Though it took a while, as it tends to do, they succeeded. Today, Gong Lu likes to be called Anna. She lives in Little Rock, where she goes to school, and is the joy of her family's life. In the fall of 2007, Buckmiller took her daughter with her on a medical mission back to China. They visited her orphanage, and Anna helped interpret for her mother.

From Mandarin-immersion preschools to average American playgroups, from California's Berkeley High School to New Hampshire's Phillips Exeter Academy, children adopted from China were growing into their new lives. They excelled, they struggled. It was a wide-ranging group of children—some adopted as infants, some much older; some from institutions, others from foster care; some with special needs, some not. They'd come from numerous provinces all over China, from the thick of the urban bustle, to the dusty quiet of remote villages.

It was also a diverse group of adopting families. In Washington state, blind adoptive parents adopted a blind child. In Albuquerque, a couple confined to wheelchairs adopted a child with special physical needs. A child born in China was adopted by a father who had grown up in the Navajo Nation in the American Southwest and a mother who was Chinese American. Another was adopted by a Hollywood star. Girls from China became bat mitzvah; others made their first communions; one sat with her parents in a Buddhist meditation class.

When Chinese president Hu Jintao made his first state visit to the United States, in 2006, part of the greeting committee at a stop in Everett, Washington, was composed of four girls adopted from China. They presented the president and his wife with flowers and welcomed them in Mandarin.

As the children came to new homes, the adoptive families began to create a substantial relationship with China, keeping in touch with former caretakers, exchanging photos and letters, taking trips back to their children's first homes, raising money for the children left behind in the welfare institutions.

So numerous now are the children adopted from China—daughters of couples, of many single mothers, of some single fathers—that they form a substantial subculture of small immigrants, a kind of nationwide sisterhood. It's not surprising that just about everybody I meet these days has a friend or a friend of a friend who has adopted, or is hoping to adopt, a little girl from China. In our own house and neighborhood, in distant countries, back and forth across the Pacific, this East-West community continues to build.

Much has happened in the girls' lives, in our lives, in the adoption community, and in China, since we first walked into a Chinese orphanage on that fateful fall day in 1997, and then made a second momentous journey to China four years later. In the early years it was the parents who formed playgroups, organized reunions, and tried to think about what this all meant. Before we knew it, it was the children's turn to explore their own lives, come to their own conclusions, and turn to one another, or to older adoptees, for support. For the older girls it was time to choose their own paths through the issues that have come with this historic mixing of human destinies.

A decade after we adopted our first daughter, adoption itself was experiencing growing pains in China, as evidenced by the tightening of rules for foreign applicants. The Chinese government's overhaul of its adoption policies in 2007 resulted in some substantial changes. Though adoption went on, the numbers began to fall off and the waiting times stretched out. The demographics of the adopting families began to change, since certain Chinese American families were now given preference, single parents of either gender were ruled out completely, and other new criteria for adopting parents were put in place. The rush to China for children was, if not quite over, substantially altered and slowed down.

Simultaneously, a big wave of the girls who had been adopted in the early years were growing into teenagers. More and more were in high school. A few had started college. It was an unprecedented and powerful cohort. As they came of age, some unique emotional landscapes and new vantage points for looking at this human drama opened up.

In an average month now, some four hundred more small girls are flown across the Pacific to begin new lives in the United States. They will grow up as the daughters of teachers and football players, secretaries and school principals, novelists and political consultants, film actors and physicians, full-time moms and full-time dads. If all continues to go well, by the end of this year, some five thousand more Chinese girls will make the journey from China to the United States.

For adopting parents, the trip to China will come after much waiting—by 2008 as long as two or even three years—plus piles and piles of paperwork and plenty of official scrutiny from agencies within the United States and the People's Republic of China. This will culminate, if all goes well, in a referral, by which applicants' bulging dossiers are matched with a Chinese child. With that match, the adopting parents will be given the sparest information about their new daughter: her institutional address, a small photograph perhaps, a birth date (which may be a guess), a few vital statistics (height, weight), a medical assessment (which may be cursory), and a name, chosen, usually, by the orphanage.

For Americans picking up children in the social welfare institutions of China, this particular avenue of international adoption often represents a final miracle, after the frustrations of infertility, unsuccessful medical intervention, perhaps, or the forbidding costs of domestic adoption. For the orphaned girls and boys of China, international adoption offers a way out of the institution, a chance at a new life—but life in a culture vastly different from that of the land of their birth. The children themselves will have chosen none of this, of course. A Chinese government bureau, in combination with foreign adoption workers, will have placed their fates in the hands of American strangers.

The fact that China could provide so many foreign parents with children, nearly every one of them a girl, was a reflection of a darker reality. The world's most populous nation, desperate to keep its population down, had in the past several decades become a nation of lost daughters. A confluence of harsh realities—the Chinese government's strict "one-child" population policy introduced in 1980, the culture's traditional reliance on sons, plus untold hardships and emotionally wrenching circumstances known only to birth parents—will have forced these little girls from their families. The children who are placed with adopting families represent only a tiny fraction of those found abandoned throughout the country or of those girls missing altogether from China's population as a result of many factors, including selective abortion of female fetuses.

The majority of children adopted from China have no known histories to look into, should they ever want to trace their pasts. Most birth parents leave little information, if any. For all the benefits of adoption into a loving family in the West, there is a loss of roots each small girl must deal with as she grows into adulthood, coming of age halfway across the globe, having in most cases lost the thread that might someday lead her back to relatives in China.

As prospective international parents, my husband and I tried to prepare ourselves. We sought all the help we could—the insights of other adoptive parents, the support of friends and family. Yet how could we possibly be prepared for the life ahead, for the unknown terrain, and most important, for the eventual feelings about all this from our daughters themselves? Although I feel extremely fortunate to be able to share my life with my own adopted daughters, I also feel a great sadness when I think of the possible confusion and sense of loss they and the other daughters of China may feel when they are of an age and an inclination to want to know where they came from, and why, and from whom.

What would all this mean when our daughters were teenagers, living in a household in California with blue-eyed Caucasian parents, wondering what had gone on in the land of their birth?

Someday, I knew, I would need to tell my daughters what I could about life in China in the time they were born. I had a duty to understand what we'd all been part of, but I approached the subject cautiously, aware that I was no China scholar, nor even a neutral observer. Still, I wanted to learn what might have led to that moment in an orphanage when I first looked into the eyes of one beautiful child, and then another, who'd both wound up—until that instant—with no families of their own. I wanted to know what conditions could explain the thousands of bundles found lying alone in railroad stations and school buildings and along roadways all over China. I wanted to know what had happened in the lives of the mothers in that country that had led them to such desperate acts. What cultural, political, and social forces had made China a uniquely difficult place for this generation of female infants?

This book began as an inquiry into those questions, an exploration of this particular intersection between American and Chinese history. As a parent and as a journalist, I wanted to know what life had been like for my children's birth parents, and what my daughters' futures might have held had they stayed in China. I wanted to understand what life was likely to be like for the generation of adopted Chinese girls growing up in the United States. There was an important story unfolding here, a considerable human drama involving tens of thousands of children, their birth parents, and a growing community of East-West families.

For the world at large, this book began as an attempt to fill in the blank spaces in a profound human exchange. For my daughters, it was an attempt to tackle as many of the unanswered questions as possible, so that one day they would know something about the times in which they were born and the background from which they came.

The causes and conditions are enormously complex. As I have talked with people and worked my way through the available information, I have felt increasingly like the blind people in the old Chinese proverb, each of whom tries to describe an elephant by touching just one small part of the animal (It's a rope! It's a snake! It's a wall!). While facts (as well as we can pin them down) and various explanations may describe certain happenings in one place or another, no theory can possibly encompass the point of view of every man or woman in China. As just one measure of the complexity, there are hundreds of thousands of villages in that enormous nation, each with its own small, unique social fabric. Add to that the varieties of personal experience in a country with dramatically different geographic regions, numerous ethnic strains, great economic disparities, and more than 1.3 billion residents. No statement can apply to every community, no statistics can include every reality, no single explanation can account for every lost child. Once the human heart is involved, the mystery grows ever deeper.

By 2008, homeland trips were the latest adventures for adoptive families. Various groups, including adoption agencies and commercial travel ventures, and the Chinese government itself began offering excursions back to China. The youngsters and their parents could tour the Great Wall and the warriors at Xian and meet a baby panda at the panda preserve in Chengdu. In some cases, they could visit foster families or go back to the social welfare institution where they'd lived and reconnect with caregivers and directors and the children still there. Some institutions were even building special facilities for adoptive families who came back to visit. With every trip back to the province that a child once called home, or a trip to the institution, came the possibility that further information might be uncovered, or even that a birth family might materialize. What then?

Every Chinese daughter adopted into an American family has a story all her own, but in some ways all the stories are similar. One of the deepest ties possible between human beings, the bond between parent and child, torn apart on one continent, is rewoven on another. By telling my own family's story and by talking to others—adoptive parents, adopted children, China scholars, anthropologists, demographers, sociologists, psychologists, ordinary people from China—I hoped to piece together a portrait of East-West adoption. In the end, though, all I really know for certain is our small part in a series of events that are both sorrowful and miraculous, a profound mixing of Chinese and American lives in the twentieth and twenty-first centuries.

These words by author Betty Jean Lifton have stayed with me while I worked on this book: "As a writer I have immersed myself in other subjects, but have always returned to the adoption theme. Whether in fantasy or reality, it haunts us all, adopted and non-adopted alike. It is a metaphor for the human condition, sending us forth on that mythic quest that will prove that we are bonded to each other and to all the creatures of this world—and in the process, reveal to us who we are."[2]

As my daughters and their "sisters"—all the other adopted daughters of China—grow up, the journey continues. The next story is theirs to tell.

1

Journey to the East

Moon thin as water
And watery candlelight
Shine upon China
A sleeping silkworm
Exhaling a long long thread of silk
On a nine-hundred and sixty-thousand
  square miles
Mulberry leaf.

—*Li Xiaoyu, "The Silk Dream"* [1]

In the Pearl River Delta of southern China, the land is criss-crossed by water. Rivers, like long fingers, reach deep into the landscape from the South China Sea, and along their banks fertile soil would seem to promise paradise. The climate is subtropical and mild, rainfall is plentiful, and the fields are patchworked in muted tones of green. Farmers tend their rice in rolling terraces. Water buffalo stand placidly in the fields. Where there aren't rice paddies, plots of elephant-leafed taro and pole beans spring from the ground. Sugarcane grows in profusion, and there are mulberry trees, harboring billions of silkworms.

Long ago, these rivers helped open this part of China to the world. First Romans, then Arabs, then European missionaries and merchants all ventured upriver. By the late eighteenth century, the British had established a foothold with the East India Company, seeking China's wares. In the place they called Canton, British merchants put up their warehouses, pushing opium in exchange for Chinese silk, porcelain, and tea.

Today the provincial capital is not called Canton, as it was in the old days of Western imperialism, but Guangzhou. Foreigners still are drawn here, some by the welcoming entrepreneurial atmosphere, others for reasons of the heart. Waterways still spiderweb the delta in this part of Guangdong province, but the waters are grayer now and the air is hazier. And there are other rivers here, too—concrete superhighways, the first built in 1989—along which flow locally made goods, imported ideas, and an on-the-move populace. Freeways, some privately financed by business tycoons, link the now sprawling cities of the Pearl River Delta with one another, with bustling new trade zones, and with enterprising Hong Kong to the south.

My husband, Mark, and I were rolling along one of these highways on a mild fall day in 1997, viewing the changing landscape of China through a tour bus window. Just a few years before, it had taken seven hours to travel from Guangzhou to the midsized southern Chinese city of Jiangmen, where we were headed, but the new freeway had shortened the trip to less than two.

We sped along with the standard collection of Chinese traffic—overloaded trucks, underpowered scooters, swarms of bicycles and motorcycles, and an occasional European-made luxury car with tinted windows. Despite these modern intrusions, some of the terrain we passed through still looked ancient and serene, like a scroll painting of old China. Viewed from the bus window, a human being, small in the landscape, wearing a straw hat, stood beside a pair of yoked oxen. Rivers ran through the mist; boats motored languidly along the rivers. Here and there were old villages, made of red brick with tile roofs curving gracefully toward the sky.

When Jiangmen City came into view, it was wrapped, like most of urban China, in a cloud of haze, though less densely than Guangzhou. Traffic picked up and the bus slowed, rolling past boxy concrete structures and small factories. The road filled with increasing numbers of wobbling bicycles and skittering motorbikes. We passed a truck so full of pigs that, viewed through the slats, they seemed to be stacked double and triple; some looked upside down. Beside the highway, green vegetation gave way to dust, and the calm of the countryside was broken.

I was riveted on this scenery, noting its landmarks and trying to soak in the feel of it, curious about what lay beyond the village walls we had seen and behind the iron-grated windows we now passed. Somewhere in this landscape our daughter had been born. Whether she came into the world in the green of the countryside or the gray of the city, I didn't know. But Mark and I were on our way to meet her. Traveling toward a Chinese orphanage, we were about to become parents.

For one who waits,
A moment seems like an eternity.
   —Fortune cookie message, 1996

The journey that found us peering through a bus window at the landscape of southern China had begun nearly two years earlier, half a world away, when we first set foot on what turned out to be a very long paper trail. In January 1996, my husband and I walked into an international adoption agency and emerged with a thick folder of forms. We sat down and pondered a number of questions: "Please give a brief statement of your reasons for wanting to adopt a child. What is your profession? Education level? Income? If you've had experience with infertility, please provide details." We filled in the basics: One writer, one lawyer, both over forty (in my case, well past). Recently married, no children. Both previously married and divorced. Three siblings each. Good health, covered by health insurance. Pets? One aging, gentle Siberian husky and two cats. Hobbies? Cycling, gardening, reading, painting.

Why did we want to adopt? I wrote that I'd like to share my life and love with a child and be part of that "gift of wonder" that writer Rachel Carson celebrated in her book of that title. I said that I had lost a baby years before, an infant son who had suffered a cerebral hemorrhage at birth and died at three days old. I had thought of adopting ever since, but the circumstances had never seemed right until now.

Mark wrote that he, too, had long wanted children, but it hadn't worked out. He said that his hero in the father department was the lawyer Atticus Finch in Harper Lee's *To Kill a Mockingbird*. He described Atticus as a man who gave his children the utmost respect and loving guidance, and with great patience helped them understand and prepare for a world that could be harsh and unfair.

We began the process of adoption with high hopes and great anxiety. I didn't need an adoption agency to tell me I was seriously out of sync when it came to starting a family. My college friends were now sending their children off to college. Yet I had this clear, certain yearning, a longing I had tried to push aside for years after my baby died, busying myself with work and various projects. I had, as one cyclist friend put it, kept my head down and my feet moving. When, after more than a few disappointments, I found myself one day with a man who also wanted to adopt a child, all my old desires woke up. I was startled by their sudden appearance and intensity.

It took courage to call an adoption agency, to get my hopes up; to risk judgment on my worthiness at being a parent. But some door, long closed, had opened. Sunlight and possibilities filtered in. Why not? I thought.

We had heard that China had lots of babies available for adoption, and it seemed a better idea to us to try to adopt a child who was already without parents than to try to compete with a large pool of couples in America who were vying for a diminishing number of newborns. I'd lived in Hong Kong during my first years as a journalist and I was drawn to that part of the world. Something about the land and water, the sights, sounds, and smells, the people bustling through the streets, just agreed with me. I'd felt at home.

The adoption agency agreed that China was a good idea for us. There were numerous little girls available, the application and approval process tended to be faster than in other countries, and China at the time was more forgiving of older parents than were some South and Central American adoption programs. Moreover, the Chinese adoption program wasn't tainted by rumors of stolen children or babies for sale or black-market profiteers. The health of the children was generally good. China was, in fact, blessed by the relative absence of such modern ills as fetal alcohol syndrome or HIV infection. The children could be adopted at a young age—most at a year old or younger—lessening the chances of attachment disorder, and the care in the orphanages that dealt with foreign adoption was apparently good.

So we set forth. I comforted myself with the thought that maybe it would be better for a small orphan in China to have an older mother than no mother at all. "The Chinese respect what you are trying to do," the woman at the agency told me. Having passed our initial interview, we put down some money and walked away with our instructions. We were told the whole process would take about a year and cost around $15,000.

We next had to apply to the U.S. Immigration and Naturalization Service for "advance permission to adopt a foreign orphan." That required digging up our original birth certificates, marriage certificates, and divorce decrees; and getting fingerprinted for a background check by the Federal Bureau of Investigation. We also needed a home study by a licensed social worker, required by the State of California—as well as by the INS and the Chinese authorities—to certify that we were stable candidates as parents and would provide a safe and supportive environment for a child.

Since the INS form asked the question, one or two orphans?, we requested permission to adopt two children at once; we thought it would be good for the children to have each other. But the agency said this wouldn't be possible. China didn't allow foreigners to do this—except in the rare case of twins. Evidently, they felt it would be unfair to allow foreign parents to take two children at once when many of their own people were now limited by government policy to a single child.

It made a rough kind of sense, but then we found that once an American family adopts one child, they can adopt a second. They just have to start the entire process all over again, from start to finish, and pay a second set of fees. And the second time (adoption rules have since changed, so check the website of Families with Children from China, www.fwcc.org, for current regulations[2]), a family was required to adopt a child with "special needs"—some medical problem, usually correctable, that required attention. At the time, parents under thirty-five, or who already had children living at home, were also assigned a child with special needs. But these guidelines, we soon found, could shift depending on who was working with what agency, when, and in which province.

At the point we began, thousands of adoptive parents had gone to China before us and thousands more were waiting with us, drawn halfway across the world by a strange series of events. In the world's most populous country, babies were being found abandoned on a daily basis—nearly all of them girls. Some of the lost children wound up in state care. By the time Mark and I began the application process in San Francisco, many of China's institutions were filled to overflowing with abandoned baby girls, a small percentage of whom were making their way through the bureaucracy into the waiting arms of would-be parents like us.

The current wave of adoptions from China had begun as a trickle in the late 1980s. At first these arrangements were informal, individual affairs, which broke through the Chinese government's earlier reluctance to let non-Asians adopt Chinese children. A few Americans working in China managed to find abandoned or orphaned children, to more or less invent their own paperwork and make arrangements with the various layers of government. "I'd go to the police station and cry every week," said one American woman who was living in China in the mid-1980s and wanted to adopt a little girl who'd been left at a medical clinic at five days old. Eventually, the woman convinced both the Chinese and American authorities to let her leave China with the child, but it was a struggle.

In 1989, 201 children from China entered the United States, but the arrangements still were scattershot. Centralization came with the approval of a national adoption law, which China enacted in 1992, officially granting foreigners the right to adopt Chinese babies and setting up protocols for doing so.[3] Soon a number of U.S. adoption agencies were working with China, including veteran international groups such as Holt International Children's Services. By 1995 the number of Chinese children adopted annually by American parents was up to two thousand, and by the year 2000 it was more than five thousand.

The babies were usually between six and twelve months old by the time the necessary paperwork had been completed on both continents and the prospective parents had traveled to China to pick them up and take them home. Most were the small victims, it was generally believed, of the Chinese government's rigidly enforced population control—the so-called one-child policy.

In the United States, meanwhile, there were growing numbers of couples with infertility problems—six million by a 1998 count[4]—an increasing percentage of whom were now competing for a decreasing number of American infants available for adoption. The rate at which American women relinquish their babies had declined dramatically in the past few decades.[5] Given the availability of birth control and abortion in this country, the increasing number of single mothers who choose to raise babies on their own, and the number of childless people seeking healthy infants, would-be parents trying to adopt a newborn could find themselves facing tough competition, long waits, great expense (private adoption fees as high as $30,000, and more), broken agreements, and worries about the security of the legal adoption bond—fueled by several well-publicized cases of birth mothers attempting to take back their children. According to the Evan B. Donaldson Adoption Institute, for every person who succeeded in a domestic adoption, there were five or six others who didn't.

So, by the 1990s a growing number of people had turned to international adoptions—in Guatemala, Chile, Paraguay, and Ecuador; in Eastern Europe and Russia; and in Asian countries including Taiwan, Thailand, Vietnam, and South Korea, where there had been a long-standing adoption program dating back to the 1950s. But at the time Mark and I began our adoption process, China had the greatest numbers of infants available for adoption. Since an overwhelming majority of the would-be parents in the United States, whether they were pursuing parenthood through in vitro fertilization or adoption, said that they preferred girls,[6] China seemed a perfect destination for a large number of childless Americans. A few added another reason for choosing China: the absence of identifiable birth parents.[7]

By the late 1990s, at least a hundred agencies were involved in the business of getting Chinese children into the hands of American parents. They ranged from seasoned, large nonprofit Christian organizations to independent for-profit agencies to lone liaisons trying their luck at the baby-brokering business. There was by now a special adoption unit at the U.S. Consulate in Guangzhou, where a long line of adopting parents were interviewed each day so that their new children could be granted visas and the right to enter the United States.

Mark and I were soon answering dozens of personal questions. (Have you ever received psychiatric or psychological treatment? Have you ever been arrested, or have you ever had an arrest record expunged? What are your plans for child care?) We added up our assets, dug out our tax returns, asked friends to write letters of reference, requested letters of verification from our employers, and went to our doctors for the required checkups.

Within a few months we had a folder five inches thick, stuffed with forms and reports. We began to learn how much patience, acceptance, and trust was called for. Maybe it would all work out and maybe it wouldn't. As is usual with such a process, the recitation of our histories barely scratched the surface of our lives. But we dutifully laid out our stories on paper, expressing our great desire for a little being to pour our love into and to guide in the world.

There was no blank space on the forms for the few questions that would occur to us later as we felt our way through the bureaucratic maze: Are you ready to place the decision about whether you'll be able to have a child, and who that child will be, in the hands of strangers? Are you willing to pay hefty sums of money to people you've never met in order to make it all happen? Are you willing to open your lives to government agencies, domestic and foreign, to jump countless official hurdles, to document just about every aspect of your life, and to go through the agonies of waiting far longer than you thought, with very little assurance about anything?

Yes, yes, and yes, as it turned out.

We began a lengthy period of anticipation and confusion, joining hundreds of other would-be adoptive parents and becoming part of a subculture I never knew existed. We entered the world of the waiting.

"Why China?" people began to ask. "Because a little girl is waiting for us there," I said at first. But a lighthearted answer invariably led to a more weighty inquiry. How to explain all the lost, available girls?

Experts on China's lost girls frequently referred to an "epidemic" of abandonment when they talked about the problem.[8] Babies, female babies, it seemed, were found everywhere, every day. Babies in sunlight and babies in moonlight. Babies wrapped in newspapers, babies bundled in rags, babies in baskets, babies in boxes. Boys, too, were found occasionally and taken to institutions, but they tended to be children who suffered from mental or physical handicaps, and they were in the minority, less than 10 percent at most. Just how many of these lost children were there in all? No one seemed to really know.

I started writing letters to my as-yet-unknown daughter. All I knew at the time was that she'd be born somewhere in China, that she would wind up, for whatever reason, without a family, and that through some shuffling of destinies, our lives eventually would be woven together. At least, I hoped so. I had begun to think about her all the time.

I found a notebook at a fair run by a group of bookbinders. The cover was decorated with Chinese characters. I had no idea what they meant, which seemed an appropriate place to begin. I hoped whatever they said was in keeping with the spirit of writing to a tiny girl in China.

"Letters to an Unknown Daughter," I wrote on the first page. Each day I looked at the characters, wondering, and opened to a blank page. I began:

Dear Daughter, I'm beginning this journal of thoughts at a very uncertain point in your life, possibly months before you are even born, and I will have to start by offering you a loving explanation, rather than any clear facts, about our eventual coming together. The "you" I am writing to seems both elusive and strangely real. I can sense a spirit there as I write. The earthly details are hazy, of course. When we get together, you and I, I won't really know what you've been through—who carried you and gave birth to you, what she first whispered to you, how long she held on to you before having to make a deep, sad decision. I am certain the loss of you will linger with her all her days.

Among the collection of thoughts and reflections I have been gathering for you is this one: "Remember, there is a home we all come from, even before our mothers. We are all interconnected, parts of long-dead dinosaurs, the stardust of exploded stars." Those words came from the rector of the little church I attend. Her enduring message is one of reconciliation among people. She encourages all who listen to hold each other in our hearts, no matter what our external differences.

If I tell you that I was born in the western United States and you somewhere in China, those bits of geography merely narrow our landing spots on the globe. It's my conviction that life's great plan is bigger than any of us can imagine, and that you, wherever you are, and we, your future mother and father, are meant for each other, and that we will be inexplicably and finally joined. That's the light by which this "birth" story can be told.

We humans tend to place much importance upon our own particular threads of genetic inheritance. The urge for family continuity and inherited ties is a fine desire, of course, but I know that just as much love and devotion is possible among strangers who choose each other. I know it because I grew up with a father who adopted me.

If we each follow our strands back through time, they weave together—as Thomas Wolfe wrote in one of my favorite books, Look Homeward, Angel: *"Each of us is all the sums he has not counted: subtract us into nakedness and night again, and you shall*

*see begin in Crete four thousand years ago the love that ended yes-
terday in Texas."*

*I, too, believe that we each come with a common human heritage,
and that this inheritance is every bit as full when the facts of birth
are a mystery, as when they are better known. We're all intermin-
gled at some distant point, and our capacity for love means we can
all intermingle by choice. So many of the deepest ties are formed not
biologically, but through longings of the heart.*

You, from this moment on, are a child of the heart.

The adoption process was something else. The road between
us and the baby I held in my heart quickly became littered
with forms and demands for more forms. Unlike the vast majority of the population, who require no one's permission to
conceive a new life (at least not in this country; in China at
the time it was an entirely different matter), parents who are
matched with their children through adoption must first prove
themselves worthy—according to private agencies, state laws,
foreign governments, and U.S. immigration law. Their motivations are scrutinized, their backgrounds checked, their bank
balances added up, their living quarters surveyed, their psyches
probed. There can be additional obstacles: Some foreign governments, as well as some domestic agencies, allow single
mothers to adopt but not single fathers. Age can be a factor. The
laws of nature, plus a boost from modern technology, may
allow people to reproduce into their forties and beyond, but
adoption agencies can set a ceiling of forty or forty-five. And
there are other stumbling blocks that can be tossed onto the
path by particular agencies, social workers, state and federal
bureaucracies, and the sudden whims of foreign governments.

China, however, had so far welcomed applications from

foreigners of a different ethnicity—the vast majority of people adopting Chinese children were, after all, Caucasians—and was at the time accepting the applications of single parents of both sexes, and of people well into their forties, even into their fifties and sixties (although the adoption ministry balked when one American agency presented a candidate who was seventy. "We're looking for parents for these children, not grand-parents," said an official). A sufficient number of single mothers had adopted from China that they had their own national organization.[9] (Please note again that the information for our first adoption reflects the guidelines that existed at the time.)

Most people began naively, as we did, and waded through as best they could, opening their doors and lives to strangers, worrying that any misstep—Is the staircase too treacherous? Does the family dog look unkempt or untrustworthy? Is that student protest arrest still on my record?—might disqualify them. People who'd been through all this before assured Mark and me that, whatever hoops we had to jump through, it would be worth it. Once the child is in your arms, they told us, the or-deal dims. Just like labor and delivery. If you had to do it all over again, they told us, you would.

It was all unknown emotional territory, nonetheless, fraught with anxiety and confusion. But whatever we went through, it was nothing compared to the governmental intrusions into people's family lives that were going on in China just then.

Having had the optimism and the resources to make our way through the labyrinth, pay the fees, wait it out, and fly to China, Mark and I were living examples of the options open to people like us, whether we availed ourselves of high-tech med-icine, domestic adoption, or travel to a foreign country. Adopt-ing from China is a relatively expensive proposition, and though it takes considerable sacrifice for many families to come up with the money, and rules out many otherwise eligible but less prosperous people, the point is that thousands of Americans had been able to do it.

Americans who went to China in search of a child tended to be well-educated, financially secure professionals in their late thirties and forties. The average Chinese adoption cost between $10,000 and $20,000 in various agency fees in the United States and government fees and travel expenses in the People's Republic. A donation to the orphanage of $3,000 was required of all adoptive parents by the Chinese officials. In Guangdong province, the richest in China, that $3,000 could be equal to a couple years' worth of wages for a factory worker.

Mark and I, and others like us, had unprecedented freedom to go after something we deeply wanted, to push the boundaries a bit and reshape our lives, to tell our stories afterward. We could choose to have children rather late in life, and—if we could afford it—eventually return to China to adopt a sibling for our daughter. We could share the frustrations of the long wait with each other and travel in relative comfort.

In contrast, at the time, at least seventy million people in China, by the government's own admission, were so poor they lacked sufficient food and clothing. While some new American parents could stay in a four- or five-star hotel during their adoptive sojourn to China, the baby they took home may have come from a rural area where her parents lived in a one-room shelter with dirt floors and no electricity and where the price of a single night in a luxury hotel might constitute the family's yearly income.

While adoptive mothers like me may have gone through a couple of careers before they tried to have a family, women in

China had limited opportunities, and those who landed any kind of paying job were not likely to leave it. But perhaps the starkest contrast of all was this one: At the time we began thinking about a baby in China, Chinese women's reproductive lives were largely controlled by the state. Permission from the government was required in order to have a child; women who became pregnant without consent were often forced to have abortions, even late in their pregnancies. A woman who lacked official permission to bear the child she was carrying could quickly end up on the street—or worse. She could be hounded and heavily fined and her relatives harassed. If that baby was a girl, her husband and his family could disown her for giving birth to a child of the wrong gender. She could lose her job and her home.

While women in the United States could make an adoption plan for a child they weren't able to care for, Chinese mothers were caught in a cruel bind. "It's a crime to give up a child," a Chinese American adoption agency worker told me, "even if the family is so poor they cannot help the child. People will say the mother is very cruel and will not forgive her. Most of the women who abandon children do it in secret, hide somewhere, maybe move to another city. It's not a good thing to talk about in China."

Paradoxically, such hardships in China were the very factors that would eventually allow people like me to cross the Pacific when they dreamed of having a child.

Almost everywhere we went now—the fingerprint bureau, picnics in the park—Mark and I met people who were in the same process or who had already been through it or who knew someone else who'd adopted from China. A student in my art class told me about a friend of hers, a fifty-one-year-old single woman who had just brought back a toddler from China. The little girl had been in an orphanage until she was two years old, and apparently had learned to help with the laundry there. Home in America, this tiny person began pulling napkins and dish towels out of the laundry basket, smoothing them with her small hands into neat squares, and handing them to her new mother with an expectant smile.

At a party, I met another friend's adopted Chinese daughter for the first time. The little one was beautiful, eight months old, with bright dark eyes, shiny black hair with straight bangs, a sweet smile, and great interest in everything. Her eyes followed her new mother everywhere, even though the mother and daughter had been with each other only a month.

"You two look as if you have been together forever," I said, and it was true. The baby's new father said she still responded to her Chinese name, though they had given her a new first name. He thought that the sounds of her native language might soothe her, so sometimes he put her down in front of the television and turned on the Mandarin news channel.

I looked at these three—mother, father, and child—drawn together across thousands of miles, across culture and time, and I thought, What a happy ending. Not without its complications, I knew, including whatever had happened to the parents back in China. But if a little child can't be kept and cared for, how wonderful it was that she could end up in the arms of people who wanted her so much.

Within a month or so, having rounded up volumes of documents to verify just who we thought we were on this planet, Mark and I jumped the first big hurdle and sent off our application to the U.S. Immigration and Naturalization Service to seek their clearance. We were told to sit tight; it would take the INS six months or so to process our paperwork. No matter, I supposed, because we had more than enough to do in the meantime.

When Valentine's Day rolled around, my dear friend Frances, who was studying Chinese brush painting, sent a handmade card. With two elegant brush marks—a pair of red swooshes leaning toward each other, just touching—she formed a heart. A perfect symbol of adoption. I tucked the valentine into my notebook of letters to my daughter.

I was still writing almost daily letters to this unknown daughter of mine, but my picture of her kept changing each time we talked with the agency. At first they said we'd be assigned a toddler, most likely, because China preferred to give older children to older parents. We said we'd be open to a toddler. But then they checked again and said (according to the guidelines at the time) that since our combined ages added up to less than one hundred, we'd be eligible for an infant. Over time the answers continued to shift around, depending on when we called and to whom we talked. We tried to develop a more flexible picture of the child who might be waiting for us.

The majority of parents who apply to China, it seemed, requested a healthy infant. Those requests were usually honored, on the basis of some general guidelines that seemed to vary according to different times and different interpretations. At the time we applied, we were told that applicants who were over thirty-five with no children of their own were eligible to adopt an infant. Couples whose ages added up to less than one hundred years could adopt an infant, as long as one member of the couple was under fifty. Older parents were sometimes asked to take older children, though anyone of any age was free to request an older child.

As the weeks went by, I struggled to figure out where we were in the process. Although there were several major checkpoints on the route to approval—completion of an official home study, approval granted by the U.S. Immigration and Naturalization Service, and finally, dossiers sent off to China for clearance by the Chinese ministry concerned with foreign adoption—nothing seemed predictable. Time appeared to shrink or expand according to unexplained forces. An astonishing sea of paperwork, confusing regulations, slippery timelines, overworked bureaucrats having a bad day—all this stood between a baby, lying in a crib in an orphanage somewhere in China, and us, biding our time in San Francisco. We had lots of company, though. As more and more Americans had heard about babies in China, more and more had applied.

Was our daughter even born yet?

Two months into the process, we were probably at least eight months or so away from getting our papers sent off to China, where the adoption ministry could look us over and, if all went well, match us with a waiting child. So, I surmised, our daughter might just be coming into the world. Or, if we were eventually given an older child, she might be a year and a half now, with months to wait until we showed up. If she was already two or older, she might be folding laundry. It was hard to envision her. Every so often, Mark and I talked briefly about names, but each time we decided to hold off, to wait until we met her. If she was a toddler, she'd probably already have a Chinese name she was used to.

One night I woke from a dream, having seen a tiny face, and I felt as if I had caught a glimpse of her, whoever and wherever she might be. That vision, those dark wondering eyes, kept me going through all the paperwork and waiting. Eventually the social worker interviewed us several times, paid us a visit at home, took lots of notes, and said we'd hear back in a month or two.

While we were waiting for the social worker to render an opinion and for the FBI to clear our fingerprints, a British documentary called *The Dying Rooms* aired on American television, showing terrible scenes in Chinese orphanages.[10] A trio of British filmmakers had posed as charity workers, carrying a concealed camera, and gone into Chinese orphanages to investigate rumors of high death rates in China's institutions for lost children.

The scenes they filmed—of tiny girls tied, splay-legged, in bamboo potty chairs and of one little girl near death—captured the attention of human rights activists, raised the hackles of the Chinese government, and caused considerable argument among the community of Americans who had previously adopted children from China.

It was hard to know what to make of such information. The images were horribly disturbing, yet elsewhere were numerous accounts of healthy, happy children who had emerged from China's orphanages. What was going on?

Across the distance, I could only pray that our daughter (if we were to get one) was cared for and that she had the basics of food and warmth and someone to talk to her and touch her. The great feelings of attachment I had without anyone yet to attach to were agonizing. How could I shelter my tiny hoped-for daughter from disease or pain or sorrow if I couldn't get my hands on her?

Finally, one day in May, Mark and I came home from work

to find a big white envelope in the mailbox. The social worker's verdict! We carried it gingerly into the house and sat down before we opened it. Following pages of description about our families of origin, our hobbies and careers, our character traits and parental aptitude, were the magical words: "I recommend without reservation that this couple be allowed to adopt a child." A major obstacle cleared. I realized how much tension and fear I had been carrying around, wondering if we would pass muster. We celebrated. And we went on waiting.

I went down to San Francisco's new main library to begin some serious reading about China. There were groups of grade-school children working on the computers—blond kids, African American children, Asian boys and girls. It was good to see such a multicultural mix; I could imagine my own little daughter there someday, puzzling over some question on her homework. A display case held books and artifacts from China. I thought about the bare information I remembered from my own early schooling, which boiled down to vague recollections about the Yellow River, the Great Wall, silkworms, and mulberry trees. And, of course, the almost universal parental reminder about China's starving children who'd be happy to have the food I was leaving on my dinner plate. (In an interview I heard with one of the student leaders from the Tiananmen Square movement, he said his parents had told him about the starving children in America.)

I left the library with an armload of books on China, works by Jonathan Spence and Orville Schell and Bette Bao Lord and John Fairbank and Harry Wu, several collections of Chinese poetry, a book on calligraphy, and a volume by Lu Hsun, one of the most important writers in twentieth-century Chinese literature. Nothing at all about mulberry trees—or so I thought.

Later in my reading, I learned that Lu Hsun told a tale about mulberry trees that concerned adoption, actually a kind of abduction-adoption. According to an old folktale, slender-waisted wasps were said to steal baby bollworms off the mulberry trees, take them to their own nests, and raise them as wasps. Thus, children in China who are adopted are sometimes called "children of the mulberry bug."[11]

The accounts I read of the lives of Chinese women, whether contemporary or historical, offered pictures of unrelenting hardship. Bound feet, bound lives. Girls bought and sold. Infanticide. Lives of powerlessness and melancholy, reaching far back into history. "How sad to be a woman! Nothing on earth is held so cheap," wrote poet Fu Hsüan in the third century.[12] "Girls were a cheap commodity in China," wrote Adeline Yen Mah in her contemporary memoir *Falling Leaves: The True Story of an Unwanted Chinese Daughter.*

By summer, six months had passed with no word at all from the U.S. Immigration and Naturalization Service, and our anxiety was building again. After days of calling and getting no answer, I finally had some luck. The sole employee of the San Francisco division concerned with international adoption answered the phone. She looked up our papers and said pleasantly that they were being held up because there was a problem.

"A problem?" I croaked.

"I'll have to talk to your agency." That's all she'd say.

I felt a deep sense of fear and dread plant itself in my gut. Was this it—the U.S. immigration service would rule us unfit to be parents? I walked the short distance from my office down to the waterfront and sat and watched the seagulls. I was just itching to find out what was wrong, to fix things and get our papers moving. But what could I do? I sat and watched a huge container ship sail under the Golden Gate Bridge. It moved very slowly, led by a harbor pilot tug, and when it got into full view I could read the name: *China Moon*. My spirits were buoyed.

On the way back to the office I walked through an urban farmers' market and saw a Chinese man selling jewelry. On his folding table was a smiling sea-green "jade" Buddha on a rope, and when the man saw me looking at it, he put it around my neck. "It's good luck," he said. I went back to the office wearing my Buddha, my fighting spirit restoked. Just a few days later, the agency cleared up the problem—a minor bit of miscommunication, as it turned out—and before long the immigration service clearance came through.

Eight months after we'd begun, Mark and I were able to pack up all our papers and send the bulging dossier off to a U.S.–China facilitator, along with a sizable check. Some agencies handle arrangements, from start to finish, from the first paperwork to the trip to China. Ours handled all the U.S. details, then turned clients whose domestic paperwork was all in order over to a separate liaison who handled all the details on the China side. The China facilitator would take the paperwork to the next step, authenticating and notarizing all the documents, making sure everything was in order. His office would then translate everything into Mandarin and send the papers off to China. He'd handle all the arrangements from now on, letting us know when a child was assigned, and then escort us to China to pick her up.

Now it was this man, plus the People's Republic of China, rather than the conscientious social worker, the FBI, the State of California, or U.S. immigration authorities, who held our fates, as well as our future daughter's, in his hands. We were given a new deadline—six to eight months more until we might hear that we'd been approved by the Chinese government and had been assigned a child. We had to keep on top of things, someone said, or we might drift to the bottom of a huge pile. There were new pitfalls to worry about: every bit of throat-clearing or hint of strained relations between the United States and China; any rumbling of discontent in Hong Kong.

What had begun as a year's wait was now stretching into a year and a half. In adoption, there is no due date such as nature kindly provides for pregnant mothers, no periodic checkups or reassurances. We marked our progress by obstacles cleared, but no sooner did we leave one behind than another seemed to pop up. A few families who'd begun the process when we did had already been to China and back. But until we got that magical call from the China facilitator, saying a child was waiting, it was premature to think about getting our visas or time off from both our jobs to go to China. Waiting had begun to feel like a full-time career in itself, and there were no guarantees.

A friend sent a note of encouragement: "I am sorry you are having to wait so long," she wrote, "but maybe your little daughter hasn't been born yet."

Whether or not our daughter had come into the world by now, one thing soon became clear: we weren't heading for China anytime soon. At the moment, rumor had it, a huge document jam had developed in Beijing.

To calm my nerves, I took up qigong, the ancient practice from which tai chi emerged. Qigong is meant to enhance and maintain health. It means, literally, "cultivating energy," not a bad idea for someone my age who was hoping to tend to an infant or run after a toddler. In the beginning class, we learned how to "recover prenatal energy," as our instructor put it. "When energy changes, everything changes," said Master M. He had begun studying qigong in China as a child of five, learning it from his aunt, an expert practitioner who was killed during the Cultural Revolution. For someone who'd been through much hardship himself—perhaps because of it—my qigong master was a man of profound equanimity.

Since the paper chase had slowed down, I also took to tossing the I Ching to see what the future held. The ancient Chinese oracle—the popular modern book on the subject graced with an introduction by C. J. Jung—offers mysterious, engaging advice. One thinks of a question and then tosses sticks or coins that lead to one of the book's sixty-four readings. The "answers" come in allusively packaged chapters with esoteric titles: "Pushing Upward," say, or "The Taming Power of the Small." It's a reflective tool, meant to be mulled over. When I tossed the coins to ask what the future held for that hoped-for daughter in China, the I Ching answered with trigram number fourteen—*ta yu,* "Possession in Great Measure." That seemed an encouraging response.

Yet the wait went on, the sands shifted beneath our feet. At work, a friend who had a two-year-old and had offered me outgrown baby clothes kept dropping by and asking about progress. "By the end of the year," I had said at first. Now? It was hard to say since we weren't quite sure where we were. "The gestation period of an elephant," she said with a sympathetic smile.

I taped an old Chinese story on my bathroom mirror:

"Traveling at such a slow pace,
Do you think you can ever get there?"

A fast steed asked a lame turtle.
"Yes, as long as I keep going," said the turtle.
　　—From the Chinese saying "Bo bie quian li," or "A lame turtle goes
　　a thousand miles"[13]

It wasn't surprising when Mark said one weekend, "Let's go
to the dog pound and just look around." For a long time, we had
been thinking about getting a companion for Annie, our aging
Siberian husky. I knew from the first words out of Mark's
mouth that we were not going to go to the pound and just look
around. I had never successfully done that, ever. Both knowing
what we were up to, but not quite admitting it out loud, off
we went.

Behind bars, dozens of dogs sat forlornly on cushions in the
corners of their cages. At the end of one row was a little black
pup of uncertain origin, no bigger than a cat, nose between her
paws, looking bereft. She wouldn't come when we wiggled our
fingers inside the cage or called to her. A staff worker came up
and said we could visit with her if we liked, but first we'd need
to fill out the paperwork to see if we—déjà vu—met the criteria to be allowed to adopt a dog. I can't say how good it felt to
sail through five minutes' scrutiny and be handed a slip of
paper on which the desk clerk had scrawled, "OK to adopt."

The little black puppy was quiet and wary. The shelter volunteer said she had probably been abused because she was ter-
rified of people, men especially. She tentatively licked my
finger, then retreated to a corner. "Let's take her," said Mark. She
was just about human infant size—ten or twelve pounds—and
perfect for two baby-hungry people.

It was no mistake. During the long months ahead, I thought

often that God or the Buddha or whoever might be in charge knew what he or she was doing when this little creature came to us. Christened Maddy after English folk singer Maddy Prior, one of our favorite singers, the puppy walked up to our old husky, licked her a few times, and then lay down, and that was where she spent her days, curled up against Annie, alternately licking her face and trying to play. Maddy was also the perfect outlet for our frustrated parental urges. I walked in one day to find Mark on the sofa, puppy on his lap, lovingly brushing the long, tangled fur of her ears.

During all this time, when there was very little communication from the mysterious people working on our behalf, we eventually found some comfort from an unexpected quarter— the Internet. We discovered an information-sharing network for people who were waiting to adopt from China or who had just come back. It was the closest thing to hand-holding that we had experienced.

I would scroll through the site several times a day, gleaning tidbits, following the threads of discussions. People from all over the country broadcast good news and bad, posed questions, sent off bits of advice. All were in similar boats—awaiting a home study, or approval by the immigration service or a referral, having sent their papers off to China. Others had been looking at a little photo of someone for several months and were anxiously counting the days until the Chinese government said it was okay to come and pick her up. There was a warm spirit of encouragement among the people on the computer list, a generous sharing of information, and an occasional outpouring of frustrations.

A single father—Richard Smith, the man, in fact, who had started the Internet connection in the first place—posted a love letter to his new daughter on the site as he went off to China to meet her. Smith asked the other waiting parents to bear witness to his promise to always care for this little girl whom he planned to name Rebecca. A week after he brought her home, he wrote that she had been to the beach, looked at the ocean, and touched sand for the first time. She had also eaten ice cream and carrot cake and swung in a swing, laughing. "I know what it is to be reborn," Smith wrote. "I know what it is to love again."

The Chinese New Year was just a couple of months away and the Year of the Rat was about to turn into the Year of the Ox as we entered our second year of waiting. According to Internet rumors, China was reorganizing its adoption bureaucracy. While the various ministries regrouped, dossiers being processed by Beijing had slowed to a trickle. Soon the system would be up again and running; capable, the Chinese said, of moving applications along at a more efficient rate. But at that moment, the foreign adoption agencies that had been moving their paperwork quickly through were stalled. Somewhere between San Francisco and Beijing, evidently, we were caught with hundreds of other people in a monumental backlog.

Waiting began to do strange things to me, and somehow it seemed more and more appropriate to look to the East for comfort. I found some solace in an old fairy tale, a "good news, bad news" story called "The Lost Mare," which I stumbled on while leafing through my stack of Chinese reading material. Although there are many versions, this is the spirit of the story:

A boy living in northern rural China had a prized mare. But one day the horse disappeared. The boy was inconsolable, but his father,

a very wise man, said to him, "How do you know this isn't a bless-
ing?" Sure enough, a few months later, the horse turned up, bring-
ing with her a stallion. The boy was elated, but this time his father
cautioned him, "How do you know this isn't a curse?" Sure enough,
when the son took the stallion for a ride, he fell off and broke his
leg. When he complained, his father said, "How do you know this
isn't a blessing?" Sure enough, when war broke out with the neigh-
boring nomads, almost all the young men in the village were killed,
but the boy with the broken leg stayed behind and was spared. As
the father summed it all up, "Sometimes disasters turn into bless-
ings, and sometimes blessings become disasters. Who knows what
lies ahead?"

As the Chinese saying associated with this story goes, *An zhi*
fei fu? or "Who could have guessed it was a blessing in disguise?" Our U.S.–China facilitator was now extending the estimates for waiting times by months and months. We felt like jet
passengers held hostage on a runway. You've made it this far, but
you don't know when—or if—you will take off, and no one will
tell you the reason for the delay. Mark and I had clearly entered
into some unfathomable territory. Were we falling behind? If we
were, was that a blessing or a disaster, good news or bad?

I thought about the course of my own life so far. Some
events I had viewed as blessings when they happened clearly
looked like disasters in retrospect. And in hindsight my per-
ception of things I thought disastrous at one time had shifted
around, too, having woven themselves so thoroughly into the
fabric of my life that it was hard to tell now where the thread
of despair left off and the thread of hope began. As for the
present series of events, what we were learning every day was
how little of this process—or anything else in life—we could

understand, much less control. There were just too many unknowns.

The timing and protocol by which waiting parents were matched with Chinese children at the time seemed to vary enormously, depending on the ways particular agencies worked. A tiny picture and a health report could be sent months before travel approval was granted. Some people traveled to China on the strength of a phone call, having never seen a picture or received any written information about their child at all. Some applicants seemed to speed through the process; others met inexplicable delays.

I continued to seek assurance where I could find it. When I found a single baby bootie lying under the redwood tree in front of our house, I took it as a sweet sign of hope. When I complained about the agonies of waiting to a Buddhist teacher I'd been studying with, she suggested I spend some time with children right here, right now. "Some of them could certainly use the attention," she said.

It was wise advice. I soon found myself following a group of volunteers who were taking some "pet therapists"—bunnies, a miniature pony, a gentle dog—into a children's hospital. There is probably no better antidote to self-obsession than to spend some time in a ward where children are struggling with cancer and third-degree burns and brain damage from swimming accidents. Each time I walked out through those hospital doors, I felt incredibly blessed.

When that same Buddhist teacher announced plans for a daylong ceremony to honor children who had died, I decided to go, not only to remember my own lost son, but also to give some thought to the mothers and daughters of China, who seemed to be losing each other every day now. The priest conducting the ceremony is one of the few people I know who speaks openly of the emotions women go through after they have lost a baby, whether through happenstance or choice. At a Zen center not far from the Pacific Ocean, she periodically holds these ceremonies of remembrance and letting go.

Over the years, many women have come to share a burden they have often carried silently for far too long. (Men are welcome, too, but they don't seem to come.) The participants are for the most part American women like myself, blessed with opportunity, education, prosperity, options. Yet those who had lost children, particularly through abortion or placing a child for adoption, had often grieved the loss alone, if they allowed themselves to grieve at all. Though the conditions may have been less extreme, the decision certainly less forced upon them than what I had heard was true in China, they had often lost more than they had admitted. Memories and dreams haunted them, weighed them down.

In the United States at the time it was estimated there were six million women who had given up babies for adoption. A writer who has conducted interviews with dozens of these women had found that denial, grief, and anger were common states for them, as were nightmares, phobias, and depression. Those who felt they had little choice in the matter had high levels of unresolved grief.[14] Women who've had abortions had also suffered from lingering emotional aftereffects.

On the day of the ceremony, as we all stood in a circle, stepping forward one by one to light a stick of incense in memory of our lost children, there were tears and deep sighs. I thought about all the mothers in China who had also lost children—in all the same ways that the people gathered here had suffered loss—and who most likely had not had the chance to stand with other women, as I was now standing, and share their burdens of sadness or regret.

As one year changed into another, I went down to Chinatown in search of a statue of Guan Yin, the Chinese Goddess of Mercy and protector of women. It seemed a good way to welcome in the Year of the Ox—surely our daughter's year, and ours. What I found instead, sitting on a shelf with dozens of others, was a carved soapstone Buddha, a red sale sticker of $4.99 on his head. At first I thought all the Buddhas on the shelf were alike, but when I looked more closely, I saw that some were crudely carved, but this one was exceptional. Someone had put his or her heart into it—though I felt uncomfortable knowing how very little the artist could have been paid for the work. Still, I thought, someone can be forced to carve a Buddha, no doubt, but not to carve a Buddha with such feeling. Perhaps by honoring the object, I could also honor the maker, and so I bought it. It seemed a fitting symbol: Out of conditions I hadn't a clue about had come something of great beauty.

I added the Buddha to a little shrine I had made upstairs in our house, reminiscent of my time in Hong Kong. The collection had begun with an old Chinese temple box and another figure of the Buddha. I'd added the necklace I had bought down at the San Francisco waterfront on that day I was particularly discouraged. As our wait went on, I had added an Egyptian scarab, a silver lizard, two turquoise Zuni bears, a carved bone horse, a jade duck—until the scene had come to resemble a kind of Nativity tableau in which a bunch of creatures had come to pay respects to the Buddha. Two miniature Indonesian temple vases held freshly picked small blossoms, surrounded— just to cover the bases—by a tiny silver-and-turquoise Navajo child's bracelet, a laminated card with a Catholic prayer for motherhood, and one baby bootie, origin unknown.

I liked the spirit of the shrine. I thought it might attract the universal baby-giving spirits to look down on Mark and me and smile.

There was one object I did not bring to the gathering. Years ago in Hong Kong, someone had given me a little carved male figure on a silk cord, explaining that it was a good-luck talisman, worn by women in hopes of giving birth to a son. It was a nice bit of folk art and I had kept it over the years without much thought. Now, given what I knew about the fate of so many Chinese baby girls, I saw it in an entirely different light, and one morning I took it out to the backyard and gave it a simple burial.

That was in the early spring. Summer came with flurries of expectation but no word from China. I was getting a little better at living day to day. And according to the Internet reports, things were picking up again in China. Day after day came the postings from parents who'd just been paired with a child. "Referral! Referral!" they announced. News came that the group just ahead of the group Mark and I were in was preparing to leave. Then departure was delayed. Summer was waning. We gave up again.

On the Internet link, tempers were soon fraying. For a while there were grumblings over TV host Kathie Lee Gifford's rumored plans to adopt from China. Would her dossier move along more quickly because of her celebrity status? people asked. When that controversy wore thin, I amused myself by following the threads of the Barbie doll discussion. Some adoptive parents were trying to locate Asian Barbies for their daughters; others were boycotting Barbie because of the working conditions in the overseas manufacturing plants. And always, there were people sharing the frustrations of the long wait. Some already had a little picture of a baby who was waiting for them, but they couldn't get approval yet to travel to China to meet her.

By early September, the facilitator said it wouldn't be too much longer.

We didn't do any packing.

When I was twenty-two months "pregnant," on an evening in early October, the phone rang. "You have a daughter," said a man we'd never met, the U.S.–China liaison. "She's a year old, healthy, and weighs eighteen pounds. She's in a social welfare institute, outside Guangzhou."

You have a daughter. While Mark and I were gasping with disbelief, the man (whom I'll call Max[15]) offered some further information. Her last name, he said, was Jiang, meaning "river." Her first name was Xiao Yu; Xiao (pronounced *zhow*, but soft on the *zh* sound) means "little," and Yu (almost a *yer* sound) means "education."

"Little Education"? Perhaps he meant "Little Scholar"? But the phone call was brief—he had other families to contact—and there wasn't time to pursue explanations. The man said in closing that we could request a photograph of the baby, but advised against it because, he said, people can get attached to photographs and sometimes things change. We said okay; I'm not sure why. Maybe because we had so much news to absorb already. Maybe because we knew we'd soon meet our daughter in person. Maybe because we were too scared to get too riveted on a little face, even then.

"Get your visas," Max said. "We'll be leaving for China in two weeks."

Unfortunately, on that October evening, the phone rang twice. The second time it was my mother, the sound of defeat in her voice. She was calling from the hospital where my father had been undergoing a series of tests. My dad had cancer, she said, inoperable cancer, and was not expected to live. In a few moments, life as I had known it completely rearranged itself. It's uncanny how such life-shaking events like these can move together, tossing us high into the air with one wave, and dashing us down with the next—though it wouldn't surprise the Buddha, who described the normal course of life as "one foot in suffering, the other in joy."

At least one thing was clear: The minute we heard the news about my father's illness, we both knew what to name the baby. We'd add my father's name to her Chinese name. "Little Education" would be Kelly Xiao Yu. I hoped my father could outlive the diagnosis, that he could somehow hold on long enough to meet her.

I flew to Phoenix the next morning, praying there had been some mistake, but I found my father lying in a hospital bed and the news was worse than I thought. Although he was seventy-nine, it of course seemed too soon for my father to die, and it felt as if our life together had gone so quickly. My father was thin and suffering. He lay in bed, looking out the window at the cloudless Arizona sky. A morphine drip was in his arm and he wasn't eating. "I wish I could talk to the doctor," he said forlornly. The day before, he'd gotten the worst kind of communication that modern American medicine has to offer. A physician had walked into his room and summarily announced the biopsy result. "It's cancer," he said, then left before anyone could ask questions or swallow the verdict.

Today, though, Dad in his usual generous way turned from his own troubles to ask about our news from China, and to say how happy he was for me. "We're going to name her Kelly," I said, "for you." He reached for my hand and in a voice raspy from pain and medication, said, "I'm so proud."

I told him we'd be leaving for China soon to pick up our little daughter and carry her home, and I promised to bring her to meet him just as soon as possible. He looked out the window and said that would be nice.

During that next week, I sat beside my father's bedside and we talked when we could. When he was sleeping, I watched him and thought about his life and how desperately I was going to miss him. Time slowed. I felt as if we were underwater, moving through some murky, unknown passage. Within just a few days, it was clear that my father wouldn't live long enough to meet his namesake from China. "You know, I don't feel like I'm here anymore," he whispered. "I feel as if I am someplace else." He was slipping away and nothing could help.

How quickly my father was gone. On the last night he was alive, my brother and sister cranked his bed up as high as they could so he could see the full autumn moon outside the hospital window. He died within hours.

A few days later, my brothers, my sister, my mother, and I were standing in a cemetery, our heads tipped back, watching the airplanes my dad had flown in his years as an Air Force pilot dip their wings as they passed over his grave in a final salute. A few leaves blew across the grass and the planes droned out of sight. Taps sounded.

That was on a Monday. On Thursday, Mark and I were due to leave for China.

I was feeling dazed, stretched between sorrow and anticipation, stumbling through the necessary motions to fly home and get ready for the trip. I had wished so fervently that there would be time for the two Kellys to meet. My Chinese daughter was about to be the third generation in a chosen heritage. But I was left with only stories to tell her about my adoptive father, the man she'd been named for. My mother gave me a tiny pair of Dad's pilot wings and I put them away for my daughter, along with an opal ring he'd given me on the day he'd adopted me.

A friend who'd known my father thought it was wonderful we were naming our daughter after him. "Every time you say the name, you'll spritz her with love," she said.

2

From China with Love

When the evening lights are lit
It looks like sparkling trees
And silver flowers everywhere
And then the park is full of hearty
laughs.

> —*Tourist atlas of Guangdong*
> *province*

The trip to China turned out to be a passage beyond imagination, almost impossible to absorb, much less describe.
What would a travel brochure say? Join several dozen American
adults and eighteen Chinese diaper-clad infants (all seriously off
their schedules, some with rashes) in a diesel bus tour of southern China, including visits to a number of bureaucratic high
spots, traffic jams, and noisy restaurants.

The timing, so soon after losing my father, felt awful, of
course. And looking back, large chunks of the trip still seem
surreal. Diaper changes in midair aboard a bouncing vehicle.
Chaotic meals; grains of rice scattered everywhere. One infant
sitting placidly in her new mother's lap at a restaurant, a stray
noodle draped on her forehead. A required visit to the local
medical clinic where the babies got shots and screamed bloody

murder. A bunch of Americans with Chinese infants on a tour bus singing "Que Será Será" in the middle of a sea of traffic. "Will she be happy? Will she be rich?" Buddhist monks in a quiet temple, chanting prayers for us all.

The journey officially began with a confirmation letter from Max, our U.S.–China facilitator. "Wow! Finally!" it said. "You can pack and leave for China to meet your child, who has been waiting for you for a long time." There would be a few dozen people traveling together, we were told, heading for several different orphanages.

And so, we leapt into action—rushing to obtain a China visa and dusting off our luggage. While some people had been packed for months, I hadn't begun, afraid that making assumptions would anger the gods. All I had were my long, long lists of what to bring. Diapers, formula, baby clothes, baby medical stuff, lots more paperwork, including three years' worth of our tax forms, and several thousand dollars in cash. Complete medical kits for babies were mentioned, but I could not imagine using much of what was in them. "First, do no harm," I reminded myself, and settled on the basics—diaper cream, baby Tylenol, a thermometer.

Some people recommended we bring familiar snacks to make ourselves feel at home. Cheetos to China? We decided we'd rather try the local fare, and besides, we had enough to worry about just figuring out what to feed the baby. Soy formula or milk? From adopting parents who'd been to China came conflicting advice. Chinese infants tend to be lactose intolerant, we were told. Take the soy. Chinese orphanages use powdered milk formula, we heard. Take milk.

Mark said it reminded him of an old *Little Rascals* episode in which the kids learn that one of the mothers is expecting a fourth child. Since they've also just learned in school that every fourth child born in the world is Chinese, they figure that the baby will be Chinese, and this sets off a quest to the local laundry man about what to feed the child. We were as clueless as the rascals. So we took soy and milk—some of it in cans, which weighed a ton.

We bought the suggested sleepers, undershirts, and two outfits per day (guessing at what would fit an eighteen-pound baby), plus slippers and socks. We doubted she'd be walking, since we'd heard that babies from the orphanages often had developmental delays. Next on the list was a thermos, and a baby carrier of some sort. We also needed what the child psychologists called a "transitional comfort object" for the baby. I bought most everything at the local discount chain store and found that the thermos was "Made in China." So was the comfort object (a fuzzy Winnie the Pooh bear, copyright the Disney Corporation), and so were the baby slippers, my walking shoes, the two money belts, and the baby backpack.

It felt more than a little strange buying all these China-made objects and clothes to carry with me to China (in my China-made suitcase) with which to bundle up a tiny baby, one of China's own, and bring her home. It's a fact of life these days that so many of the material goods that fill American stores are made in China. By now I had done enough reading to have an idea of how low Chinese wages were, and what the conditions were like in some of the places turning out plastic trinkets for the insatiable American shopper. I had read Harry Wu's account of Chinese labor camps.[1] But it seemed a bit hypocritical to be politically correct in the discount store when I was about to be involved in a far larger transaction. And to be truthful, I was too concerned with my own plans at the time to think much further about such issues.

We left San Francisco at midnight, heading for Hong Kong. Eight hours into the thirteen-hour flight, crammed upright in a tiny airline seat, reeling with fatigue and stiffness, panic set in: What on earth were we doing? How'd we get here? Were we insane? We're going to China to bring home a baby? I was far, far too tired even to think about it. I actually comforted myself with the thought that when we got to Hong Kong, we could just forget China and this whole adoption idea, go trekking in Nepal perhaps, and fly home later. We could explain to family and friends that things just didn't work out, that they ran out of babies. The more I thought about it, the more strongly Nepal—or Bali!—beckoned.

When we finally reached Hong Kong, it was morning in the East and I'd either returned to my senses or lost them altogether. The now closed Kai Tak Airport was still in use at the time, and our plane made a nerve-jangling descent through a dense urban corridor, sweeping so close to the high-rises in Kowloon that it seemed as if its wings would snag the laundry drying on the balconies. But we swooshed through unscathed and were soon dragging our disheveled selves into the airport. In the baggage area, we met up with a few of the other families in our group. We recognized one another by the papers we were clutching—instructions from Max, our China liaison, our tour guide, our stork.

By the time we got to the hotel lobby, our group was nearly complete. We were probably a fairly typical cross-section of those who've adopted from China. The majority of us were Caucasian, but there were people of Japanese and Chinese descent as well. We ranged in age from just under thirty-five to over fifty. We had among us a songwriter, a truck driver, an engineer, an architect, a kindergarten teacher, a college professor, a policeman, a physician, a psychologist. There were couples and singles. One of our fellow travelers was two and a half, adopted from China herself, coming back with her family to adopt a baby sister.

We spent a few days resting up in Hong Kong, riding the Star Ferry, walking along the waterfront, having high tea in the lobby of the stately old Peninsula Hotel. Walking up Nathan Road in Kowloon, I had a flashback of a day more than twenty years earlier when I had walked up that same street with my friend Mei Li.

I was working in Hong Kong back then, and Mei Li was one of two beautiful sisters I knew from Shanghai. When the Chinese Revolution heated up, the parents thought the only hope for their daughters' future was to smuggle them out of China. Mei Li, then six years old, spent a year at home in bed, and the whole family conspired as the girls invented all the symptoms of serious illness, in hopes that they'd be allowed to leave for Hong Kong, ostensibly for life-saving treatment. The ploy eventually worked, and the two youngsters were put on a train and sent to relatives in what was then the British colony. But it took their parents another ten years to get out of China. And when the family was finally reunited, the daughters and the parents didn't recognize one another.

When I met her, Mei Li had long dark hair with a wild perm. She was pencil thin and apt to wear startling outfits—an ankle-length yellow T-shirt, for instance—when she walked around Hong Kong, often stopping people in their tracks. I remember a bird fancier following us down a narrow street, dangling an old bamboo cage from his finger, pleading with Mei Li to stop. "My bird can sing," he called out. "My bird can talk, my bird, my bird . . ."

The two of us prowled the back alleys. We searched for jade and we sipped chrysanthemum tea. One day Mei Li said she had a special outing planned, so we took the Star Ferry across the harbor, riding second class on the lower deck, where we could be closer to the water, hanging over the rail and breathing in the pungent undercurrents of Hong Kong—jasmine and exhaust fumes and fish.

We walked way up Nathan Road, farther than I had ever been, where we entered a huge concrete city of resettlement estates. We climbed five or six flights and entered a small apartment that smelled of incense. There, sitting at a low scholar's table, was a blind man. A renowned fortune-teller, said Mei Li. In front of him was the first copy of the I Ching I'd ever seen, a deep dip worn right through the pages on each side where his hands kept moving, fingering the words.

He began by asking us to sit and offering us tea, and then he ran his fingers over the bones of our faces. He spoke in Mandarin and Mei Li translated. At one point, she hesitated. "What?" I asked. "He says you'll have a baby boy but he'll never live under your roof," she said. At the time, I couldn't imagine what he meant, any more than I could understand how he gleaned anything from the book lying under his fingertips. But years later when my infant son didn't make it home from the hospital, I thought of that fortune-teller.

I don't remember what the blind seer told Mei Li. I know she must have told me, because she relished talking about such things, but I was probably mulling over my own news. Now I think he might have told Mei Li that she'd marry and have a daughter, and that she'd cut her hair short and leave Hong Kong. She had done the first three things when I last heard from her. By now, everyone I knew back then had moved on. How strange it seemed to return, so many years later, poised on the brink of an event I could never have foretold (and which even the fortune-teller somehow missed, which made me a little nervous when I thought about it).

The next evening Mark and I and our entourage boarded a plane in Hong Kong and were whisked to Guangzhou, on the Pearl River Delta in southern China, just eighty miles away. As we descended, we looked out into blackness, then into a blinking maze of neon. In the airport corridor we encountered a huge Marlboro poster. We went through various paper-stamping stops, and then our guides collected our mountain of luggage and herded us toward a tour bus.

We were soon cruising through the China night, cooler than Hong Kong, the streets congested, the storefronts lighted up. From the bus window, I saw a familiar face decorating the sidewalk trash cans. Painted in trademark red, white, and black, Chinese characters emblazoned beneath his goatee, was the Kentucky Fried Colonel.

It was past nine p.m. local time when our bus swung into the driveway of the hotel. We were given ten minutes to check into our rooms, wash our faces, and report back to the lobby for dinner. Being bussed to a restaurant did not sound like a happy alternative to flopping on the bed and trying to get our bearings, but we were a docile group. "Max is trying to get us on the babies' time schedule," said one of the veterans.

Our room on the twenty-fifth floor faced the street and a

bigger, fancier hotel across the thoroughfare. Each floor had a central desk, where smiling young women in brown uniforms dispensed huge stainless-steel thermoses of boiling water for tea (and soon for the infant formula we'd be mixing up). Out the window, half a block away, Mark and I could see the golden arches, one of the twenty McDonald's restaurants in Guangzhou. The largest one in the world at the time was in China, smack on Beijing's Tiananmen Square.

In between the two beds in our room, two armchairs had been wedged, facing each other, front feet tied together, thick towels laid down under a crisp white sheet to form a crib. In something like sixty hours, we were going to fill those two roped-together chairs with a child. We looked at each other. Could there be any more exotic maternity suite, any stranger way to "have" a baby?

We'd come to Guangzhou during the fall Chinese Export Commodities Fair, and the city was decked out for wheeling and dealing. The hotels were festooned with yellow-and-red banners, lanterns, and balloons. Young women in red dresses handed out free cigarettes to the businessmen. Serious-looking men in suits, most of whom seemed to be making use of those free cigarettes, filled the hotel lobby and elevators.

Back on the bus, we peered out at the China night. On one side of the hotel was a Chinese Friendship Store, an official outlet for Chinese products from jewels to silks to herbal remedies, and a dress shop called Reason for Being. On the other side was a Mickey's Corner shop. The traffic was incessant, an endless flow of buses and taxis and motor scooters weaving in and out like bugs surfing a concrete current. Cyclists on rusty bicycles darted in front of rattly two-ton trucks. Motor scooters wove through the crunch, more than one rider with a cell phone to his ear. On the sidelines, street sweepers walked impassively, swishing bamboo-and-straw brooms in the gutters.

Horns blared. It was all stop and start, with a near miss thrown into nearly every beep and lurch. Luckily the congestion kept the speeds down. From my bus seat high above the din, I watched a taxi cut off a motor scooter carrying a family of four—one child perched in front of the man driving, a second strapped to the woman passenger's back. The scooter driver screeched to a halt, put a foot down, looked behind him, started out again.

The restaurant nightclub was empty when we walked in, but a piano player gamely burst into a medley of Western tunes. As we sipped soup, he worked his way through some Stephen Foster, and then broke into an innovative version of "Happy Birthday," followed by "Auld Lang Syne."

I tried to get my bearings. It was October and we were in China. Perhaps some sleep would help.

I thought of another family I had spoken with who'd come to China earlier with a different agency. They'd flown through Los Angeles with a group of other parents-to-be, been delayed there for five hours before takeoff, flown on to Hong Kong, changed planes for China, and landed in two cities before they reached their final destination, all without a layover. After traveling for a day and a half with no sleep, they were bussed, bleary-eyed, to a hotel, where they expected to rest up.

But as their bus pulled up in front of the hotel, they saw standing in the lobby, peering through the window at them, seven women holding seven babies. The women smiled at the sight of the bus and rushed toward them. Clearly these babies were meant for them. But the interpreter was elsewhere, no one on the Chinese side spoke English, none of the Americans spoke Mandarin, and for a while no one could figure out whose baby was whose. All of this on top of jet lag.

Back in our hotel, we fell gratefully into bed, bone-tired and restless. All night long, the cacophony of the traffic went on. But from twenty-five stories up, the steady honking took on the sound of a million impatient crickets, chirping, mercifully, into the background.

In the morning Mark and I stared wordlessly at our makeshift cradle. Mark looked out the window at the brown blanket of haze covering the city and pronounced Guangzhou an environmentalist's nightmare. The air was heavy and dark. The World Bank had in fact just released a report that named Guangzhou and four other Chinese cities among the most polluted places in the world.[2]

We turned on the television to find a variety of amateurish shows designed to teach English to Chinese viewers. On the screen, Chinese patients showed up at Caucasian doctors' offices complaining of sore throats and headaches, and the confident blond doctor dispensed medicine and cautionary advice in a slowly enunciated British accent.

China's leader, Jiang Zemin, was in the United States just then, for the U.S.–China summit, and the news channel showed footage of his visit. Max had said that this was a momentous week for China and America. Jiang himself was an orphan, we learned, adopted at an early age by an uncle. He'd pledged to aid and support orphans. During one broadcast, for just a moment the camera lingered on a group of protesters carrying signs concerning the fate of Tibet. The screen abruptly flickered to a color bar test pattern.

We strapped on our money belts under our shirts—which made for an odd pregnant sense all its own—and wandered downstairs for breakfast. The hotel dining room seemed to be expecting us. There were bowls of Cheerios and platters piled with fried eggs. Minnie Riperton, followed by Elton John, was playing on what would eventually come to sound like an endless tape loop. In a small park across the parking lot, a group of older women moved in the slow dance of tai chi.

By ten, we were back on the tour bus and off for the day's paperwork. No babies yet. Max kept a firm grip on us. "Each day I'll tell you just what we'll do that day," he said calmly. "I won't tell you the whole thing. Today we'll go apply for the adoption certificate at a Chinese government office." With a smile he suggested we try to be happy wherever we went. "When someone's certificate is approved, everybody clap." Make yourself a joy to deal with was the message. No whining. No ugly-American acts. (There may have been reason to cajole us. According to a Chinese American woman who worked at the U.S. Consulate in Guangzhou, adoptive parents had handed her dirty diapers and otherwise behaved rudely to people they thought were "local" staff.)

The logistics were a little more difficult than usual right now, said Max, since the trade fair was on, and Guangzhou was crowded with businesspeople from all over the world. Waving a handful of papers over his head, he led us briskly on and off the bus, from one appointment to the next, marching ahead with his sturdy briefcase. He wore wire-rimmed glasses and a look of constant concern.

The first glimpse of our daughter came at the Guangdong Provincial Adoption Registry for Foreigners. Before we got off the bus, Max handed us each a piece of rice paper on which tiny red footprints had been pressed. Our baby's little foot looked lovely; small dots for toes, a high arch, a narrow heel. The lines on her sole looked like the rivers on a map of the Pearl River Delta. We all stared at the small impressions and then Max collected the footprints and took us inside. First we filled out more forms asking why we wanted to adopt a Chinese baby. ("Because we love Chinese children and Chinese culture" was apparently a good answer.) We were asked to promise that we would never mistreat or abandon our child. Mark wrote out our solemn vow on the paper they provided.

Then we were interviewed, our fingers pressed onto red ink pads and our prints recorded. We signed our names, a woman official stamped the papers with a red-inked chop, and everyone clapped for us. The woman looked at Mark and me and said, "This must be very joyful for you, a child after all these years." Yes, oh yes, we managed to say. With a smile, she handed us a burgundy plastic folder: our official permission.

When everyone's papers were finished and the room was abuzz with applause and camera flashes, Max finally passed out the photographs of our children, a postage stamp–sized color image of each little girl. For the first time, we saw our daughter's face, a tiny serious child with big brown eyes, wearing yellow pajamas, staring straight ahead at the camera. She looked beautiful and worried and somehow familiar. She had quiver marks in her chin as if she were about to cry. My knees went weak.

We celebrated our clearance by dining at the elegant old Pan Xi restaurant. The famed establishment is on a lake, with waterfalls, bridges, and numerous private dining rooms. Henry Kissinger and Zhou Enlai were said to have dined here back in 1972, during the historic round of U.S.–China talks. In the courtyard was a birdcage with pheasants and game hens and exotic fowl I couldn't recognize—all available to be cooked to order. Nearby were tanks containing turtles and snakes and unfamiliar-looking fish. A small cage held a sad-eyed creature with a long pink nose. A badger? A possum?

We ate dish after dish of dumplings and noodles, washed down by psychedelic orange soda pop and tea. The menu noted: "Pan Xi Restaurant wishes all guests achieve grand prospects and everything goes well after tasting Eight Immortals Dinners." Outside, a sign decorated with dancing children said, in English, ALL'S WELL WITH THE WORLD.

For the rest of the day, we toured the city. Everywhere bamboo scaffolding chafed against tall buildings under construction. Aluminum and marble towers thrust themselves into the gray air. More than half the world's high-rise construction cranes were on duty in China, we'd been told. Shiny black glass, granite façades, wild amalgams of style shot into the sky, boxing in the skyline. Guangzhou had come a long way since—as local legend had it—six goats had come from the heavens, bearing grains of rice to found the city.

From the tour bus, we looked into old narrow alleys, beside which large craters awaited the builder's hand. The city's traditional architecture—red-brick buildings with graceful glazed-tile roofs—was fast coming down, ground under the foot of the International Style high-rise. We looked down from an overpass to see the rubble that was once an old walled neighborhood, a *hutong*, a maze of alleyways, one-story tile-roofed buildings, and gardens. Ancient masonry lay in heaps, wiped out by the wrecker's ball. Though there had been some campaigns to save such places, the land is just too valuable. In Beijing, areas around temples or the Forbidden City might be saved, but in

Guangzhou, it didn't look as if much of the old world would last. A few international entrepreneurs were doing a brisk trade in antique architectural leftovers—tiles, doors, carvings.

The scenes we motored past were hard to comprehend, as if someone were clicking the remote control too fast, splicing one image into another. To the side of the road, where the bicycles clustered, I saw a young woman sitting down in the road, looking stunned. I could only guess that she had fallen, just seconds before, from the back of a scooter or bicycle. There she sat, as the rest of the world, including our bus, sped by. I watched her until she faded from sight, left behind, literally, in the dust.

One night as Mark and I lay in bed, loud rock music drowned out the traffic noises. We looked out the window to see strobe lights and a huge crowd across the street at the Garden Hotel. A new club was having a grand opening, we learned. Film stars had come from Hong Kong, and the hotel driveway was filled with limousines. The next day we ventured across the street to see what was up. The hotel had fancy terrazzo floors, what was touted as the world's largest bowling alley, and a buzz of commerce in the lobby. Copies of *Time* magazine with Jiang Zemin on the cover were prominently displayed in the news kiosk. In keeping with China's capitalist boom, Jiang's son was at that moment making a fortune in the telephone business.[3] An Italian suit in the lobby shop had a $3,000 price tag.

In the lounge that afternoon, no rockers were evident, just small groups of tea and coffee drinkers, talking rapidly to one another. Beautifully dressed women sat with expensively suited men. The air was thick with business fervor and cigarette smoke. Seventy percent of Chinese men smoke, said one of our guides. Beside a fountain, a huge statue of the warrior god, sword in his hand and a fierce look on his face, dwarfed a

Chinese businessman who sat just below. The businessman, impeccable in an expensive suit, French cuffs spilling out of his sleeves, held out his cell phone, unintentionally mimicking the god holding the sword. The drip coffee was excellent, but the air was too smoky. We wandered up to the health club, which we had to ourselves. The world's largest bowling alley was also empty.

Later that afternoon, we heard huge, bone-rattling explosions. Rocked in our hotel room, we asked what was happening and were told it was "just" the dynamite being used at a neighboring construction site. We were amazed, thinking about our San Francisco neighborhood, where neighbors had been complaining loudly that the new Italian streetcars had a shrill whine to them, and where yet another faction was fighting a small Korean restaurant because it smelled of barbecue smoke.

Guangzhou, however, went about its business amid a constant uproar of banging, blasting, hissing, and haze. And that was apparently true of much of China: booming, rushing, one big building site. American writer Annie Dillard, traveling in China with a group of writers in 1982, had observed that the country was trying "to make it all work with bicycles and bamboo."[4] Now it was 1997, and the Chinese were trying to make it all work with two-cycle engines and huge cranes, it seemed. Plus the odd blast of dynamite now and then.

While we were in China, a marine biologist working up north announced that the famed white dolphin—the *baiji*—that had leapt for centuries in the waters of the Yangtze was on the brink of extinction. In the Han dynasty, the river was filled with the playful and legendary creatures, known as the goddesses of the river. Although the *baiji* was declared a "rare and precious aquatic animal" by Chinese authorities in 1979, its numbers have continued to diminish. In recent years observers had seen only a handful, and feared these last survivors were not long for the river. The Yangtze, once clear, is now filthy with pollution and churning with diesel-powered boat traffic. There's bridge building and dredging, accompanied by blasting. This is threat enough even without the specter yet to come: the world's biggest hydroelectric project, the Three Gorges Dam, which was soon to have a devastating effect on the river.

Ironically, the white dolphin was known in China as a harbinger, warning fishermen of dangerous conditions. "Ah, thank you, Goddess Baiji," said a Song dynasty poem, "you've saved us from a disaster, and we'll always remember your favors."[5]

In old Chinese scrolls, man loomed very small in the universe, the landscape very large. The man-made dam across the Yangtze was about to be the largest undertaking since the Great Wall. Nature vastly diminished by man. And not just in China, of course; China was just playing a desperate game of catch-up. The Chinese had doubled their per capita income in the last decade. The whole country seemed to be remaking itself at a frantic pace. Scanning the news for just one day brought reports of one international conglomerate after another building plants there: Kodak planned to build a factory in China to produce sensitive photo products. Chevron was coming to town. The list went on and on. In Shanghai alone, there were twenty thousand building sites.

People from the countryside were rushing to the cities for work, crowding into the Shenzhen special economic zone north of Hong Kong, and into the bustling corridor around Guangzhou and Jiangmen City. According to the World Bank, the agricultural share of the workforce had plummeted in two decades from 71 percent to just half.

Rural people were thankful for the most difficult factory jobs, reported China expert Orville Schell. "Even most children and young women laborers working under the worst conditions considered themselves lucky rather than victims. Piecework salaries of 200 yuan ($40) a month may have put them at the bottom of the Pearl River Delta's earning curve, but they were still making far more than they could make farming back home."[6]

The rapid pace of change had produced social disruption—not just environmental hazards, but prostitution, high rates of suicide among displaced rural women, exploitation, and horrendous work conditions. Paul Ehrlich, whose landmark book *The Population Bomb* sounded a global alarm about the perils to the environment posed by too many people and too little attention paid to the consequences of industrialization, said that China was repeating the mistakes of the West, charging heedlessly into the future. In the frenzy, much has been lost—including dolphins, including babies.

At twilight a young Chinese woman slipped from the shadows of a small park and planted herself squarely in my path. It was our second night in Guangzhou and Mark and I were walking across the hotel parking lot, a treacherous passage through tour buses and taxis, when the woman emerged from the bushes and blocked my way. In her arms she carried a red-and-white quilted silk bundle. I stepped aside to let her pass, but she moved in front of me, said something very rapidly, a staccato, emphatic rush of Cantonese, and thrust her bundle toward me.

I stopped, said I was sorry, that I didn't understand, and I tried to get by. She began talking more loudly, pointing at whatever she had in her arms and holding out a hand, pleading. She was thin and not more than twenty and her eyes were wild and her voice was shrill.

I stared at the rolled-up comforter, which was beginning to look very much like a baby. Or was it just my imagination? Again, I said I didn't understand and shook my head no to whatever it was she was asking, but she became more insistent, darting in front of me every time I took a step.

She pushed her armload at me and gestured at her mouth. The more I tried to get by, the more desperate and aggressive she became. She began to yell. I was quickly becoming afraid of her and all my internal alarms were going off, warning me to stay out of trouble in China. If the woman wanted money, it didn't seem wise just then to pull up my shirt and dig in my money belt.

Mark, who'd been strolling along ahead of me, looking at the lanterns and the murky reflecting pond beside the hotel, now realized there was some sort of trouble. He stood in front of the woman, said no very firmly and, when she stood her ground, took my arm and pulled me past her. "What was that all about?" he muttered. I looked back to see the woman and her bundle dart off into the bushes. We didn't see her again.

What had she been trying to tell me or attempting to do? Was that a baby she held? Was she saying she needed money to feed her child? Was she trying to give me that bundle? Could she have known that the hotel was full of Americans in search of Chinese babies? Was she a young mother trying to get her child to safety by literally putting her in the hands of a foreigner? Or was she after something else altogether?

Whatever her story, it disappeared with her into the night.

Guangzhou was still gray on day three, but no matter. This was the day of the babies. We woke at the first light of dawn, having slept fitfully among the honking crickets. Hauling our toy rattles and nervous jitters, we were bound for our daughter's orphanage.

Our tour bus crunched down a gravel driveway, passing a few papaya trees and a sign pointing to a social welfare institution. We stopped in front of a tall, boxy orange-and-white building with a pile of gravel and a wheelbarrow in front. We got off, lugging video cameras and baby supplies. We were led into a sitting room and told cordially that we wouldn't be allowed to tour the orphanage, nor to ask how many children lived there. We'd come too far by now to offer any objections, and so we followed the orphanage director, a young, animated woman with a wide smile, dressed in jeans and a blazer. She led us into a sitting room, where tea and bananas awaited us. We were told to wait while the director and Max, our facilitator, ran off on yet another mysterious errand.

We waited.

The banana peels sat limp on the tables and the tea had cooled. Just when we felt we could stand the tension no longer, Max reappeared with the director. She smiled broadly and seemed to bow slightly. The two of them surveyed our nervous faces. "We'll call your names one by one," Max said. "When you're called, come to the front of the room and stand here."

He said our names first. Mark and I shot out of our chairs, hearts pounding. As if walking to a church altar, we approached the front of the room. We faced the door, and in a blur of motion, two women rushed toward us and gently thrust a baby into my arms.

Suddenly we were looking into our daughter's tiny face. Just a year old, Jiang Xiao Yu had soft brown hair, clipped close to her scalp, and she was very sleepy. She was dressed in a pale green jumper and on her small feet were bright yellow, brand-new corduroy shoes. In the fingers of one hand she clutched a green plastic cup. "Hi," we said softly. She opened her brown eyes wide, stared at us for a moment with a look of mild alarm, and then put her head against my chest. Her eyelashes fluttered and she fell asleep.

I gazed at her in wonder and disbelief. More names were called in the next few minutes, and ten more babies were carried in and put in waiting arms, until the small room rang with laughing and crying and the high hum of profound emotional release.

It was like some otherworldly mass birth. Within twenty minutes, there were eleven babies being rocked, cradled, cried over, carried around, and stared at in awe by their new parents. The babies were all girls, all beguilingly beautiful, all under a year old.

Here we all were, a bunch of Chinese babies and a band of parents from half a world away and all our lives had changed at once. That morning these children had been orphans waking up in a high-rise in south China, and soon we were about to carry them aboard a tour bus heading out of town. One minute Mark and I didn't have a baby, and the next moment we did. The same, I realize, can be said of any woman in labor, by any father in the delivery room—and no wonder the moment of birth is so awesome. Those of us who stood in that orphanage waiting room didn't have quite the same physical buildup, the expanding womb, birth pains. Instead we carried around a load of anxieties for a couple of years and met our new babies with butterflies in our stomachs. We were in China. We were sipping tea. We were standing up on shaky legs. We were holding someone very soft with short hair who felt warm and smelled sweet. We were breathless—as if we'd been plunged into a cold ocean or hauled up into thin air. We were scared to death. We were floating on some unfamiliar joyful current. We were, after all these long years, parents.

It was an event so much bigger than we were that we could barely stay in our senses. Later, it would occur to us both—despite eighteen pounds of wiggling affirmation: Were we really in that room in south China? Did this really happen? Just as that story of eggs and semen and gestation hardly gets at the miracle of birth, an account of babies being handed to new parents in an orphanage waiting room does not capture the essence of the adoption experience, either. Something unfathomable is at work—quite impossible to describe, but at around eleven-thirty one fall morning in China, my husband, my daughter, and I became a family. Mark ran his hand softly over the tufts of her hair. We stared at her sleeping face.

In a split second, our lives flowed together like the rivulets of water crisscrossing my daughter's native landscape. What had drawn us to this moment in China now seemed as perfectly timed and inevitable as the ebb and flow of the tides, as if we, too, had been pulled to this place by some invisible force of the earth-moon system. The universe shifted. And not just for us, but for all the other parents with us in that room that day and for all the others in different orphanages and hotel rooms at different times in provinces all over China. In that moment, the lost daughters of China were transformed into miracles.

Several of the orphanage caretakers began mingling with us, talking and playing with the little girls. They had stories about each one—what she liked, what she didn't, how she slept, what she ate. Some of the babies, they told us, had been crib mates; they might miss each other. Our daughter, being a bit older than some of the others, had slept alone.

There were questions from the new parents to the orphanage staff, halting translations of English into Cantonese and back again. What does she eat? Has she been healthy? When does she sleep? And from us, Does she sleep all the time? Two smiling Chinese women immediately tried to wake our little girl, enthusiastically smacking her chubby legs and singing, "Hoya, hoya, hoya."

They pointed to me and said, "Mama, Mama." The child in my arms opened her eyes and closed them again. I began to worry that she had slipped into some kind of trance, perhaps an avoidance mechanism brought on by being handed to strangers. No, a caretaker said, "she just plays hard and sleeps hard." Still, they seemed worried that I was worried, and again tried to rouse her, talking loudly, encouraging her to clap her hands, blow a kiss. She finally woke, mustered a smile, and put her little hands together, which caused the caretakers to exclaim and redouble their efforts. "She can crawl and walk," they told me through the translator. "She eats rice cereal and likes little pieces of apple and banana. And sometimes she's a little mischievous."

And then we all carried our new daughters onto the bus, held them up to the windows, and waved good-bye to the caretakers. I can still picture one of the women, smiling widely, a gold front tooth showing, waving bye-bye over and over to little Xiao Yu. In my lap, the baby responded by blowing a kiss and waving, palm turned up, fingers moving toward her palm, as is the Chinese way. I wondered later which of the women waving good-bye had dressed my baby that day, who had picked out her yellow shoes.

It was wrenching to say good-bye and yet we were eager to go. We left the social welfare home in an altered state. Beautiful, warm, perfect Xiao Yu—now Kelly Xiao Yu—had the brightest brown eyes, eight perfect teeth, strong little legs, and an impish smile.

Who might have been left behind in our daughter's orphanage, how many other babies or children of any age, we couldn't guess. Aside from the eleven babies our group carried out the door, we saw no other children, heard no other laughter, no other cries. I looked up at the nine-story building, but I didn't see any little faces pressed against the windows. One building on the grounds housed elderly people, and a few had come out to see us off. In today's China, baby girls were not the only casualties. Older people, too, wound up rootless and uncared for.

Our bus pulled out and the babies bounced along on new laps. From this moment on, we knew, everything in our child's world—smells, sights, sounds, touch, what she ate and drank, what and who she heard and saw, where she slept—was about to change. We rode through the dusty streets and then turned onto the freeway. With the droning of the ride, some of the babies fell asleep. But little Xiao Yu was wide awake now, looking around, seemingly content. With one hand, she kept a firm grip on her green cup.

Her hometown—presumably—was fast disappearing behind

us, its government bureaus, its factories, its seven hundred thousand men, women, and children; its bustle and troubles; its secrets, floating away into the general haze that blankets south China. We were leaving our daughter's homeland behind. I longed for a chance to stop for a while, wander through town, talk to someone, get a sense of the place. But there was no getting off the bus. We traveled the rest of the way insulated, looking out through dust-flecked windows.

We were brief visitors who swooped in and left with one of the greatest blessings one person could offer another, but the gifts were anonymous. Peering out at the edges of town and the outlying fields, I struggled for clues, trying to imagine the lives lived there. Was a mother secretly watching somewhere when we stepped out of the orphanage and onto the bus, hoping for a last glimpse of her daughter? A father?

Our last stop before the orphanage that day had been a provincial government bureau where we went to get the final notarization of the papers that would allow us to adopt. While we sat in a small plain waiting room, decorated with a map of Guangdong province on the wall, we were told, one by one, where our daughters had been found. "Under a bridge," the facilitator told one couple. "Beside a freeway," he said to another. "In a market," he told us.

The lost parents remained nameless—unmentioned and apparently unknown. Did any walk by the orphanage, see the foreigners come and go, know that their daughters had been picked up and were on their way to the United States? Did anyone harbor a secret hope that someday a daughter would return, looking for a lost family?

On the ride back to Guangzhou, I tried to memorize my daughter's landscape so someday I could tell her how green the countryside was, how carefully tended; how the ridges of the rice terraces curved against the hills, how the old villages were laid out, how the oxen stood so still in the fields. Xiao Yu was holding my finger now, dimples on her smooth, sweet hands. She drank her bottle as we looked out at the blur of the countryside. I tucked away what sights and facts I had gathered about Jiangmen, whose name translates as "River Gate."

The urban bustle had spilled into the surrounding countryside. In a small village that had been a simple farming community ten years earlier, a lamp factory had bloomed, manufacturing high-quality brass fixtures for the European decorator trade. Aside from prosperous factories that made blankets, washing machines, chemical products, and electronics, Jiangmen City had its own stock exchange, where people could stand around and watch their paper fortunes ebb and flow. Yet piecemeal workers in the factories, turning out electronic goods or chemicals, could earn less in a month than I had paid for my "Made in China" walking shoes.

In an earlier time, the young women of this area were frequently exiled from their families at an early age and sent to live in the households of their future husbands. But some of them rebelled. Early-twentieth-century scholars noted reports of a "startling phenomenon: wives who refused to live with their husbands and young women who refused to marry at all." Instead, these women ran off and took vows of spinsterhood. In traditional Chinese society—a society shaped and constrained by a strong patriarchy and Confucian values—this was very unorthodox behavior.[7]

This Guangdong area of China has always been a restless place, peopled by widely disparate minority tribes (some fifty of them, including Zhang, Yao, Hui), peppered with a spirit of independence. The Cantonese historically have been scrappers, the upstarts holding out against the people of the north. "The mountains are high and the emperor is far away," went an old saying. The region's history was filled with insurrection and revolt. People born here were quick to look outward, and when hard-pressed, to go looking elsewhere for fortune—or for sheer survival. In the nineteenth century, streams of people from this area of southern China left their homeland, many of them heading for America and the Gold Rush, working on the railroads, and eventually settling in the United States and elsewhere in huge tight-knit communities.

One group found its way to Mexico. My brother's wife, who is one-quarter Chinese, is the granddaughter of a man who left Guangdong province and settled in Mexico in the 1920s. Today, more than twenty million Chinese, scattered all over the world, trace their roots to this region. In San Francisco, three-quarters of the Chinese Americans are Cantonese, with roots in Guangdong province. The California agricultural industry owes a huge debt to these immigrant farmers from the Pearl River Delta, who built networks of irrigation canals by hand, drained marshes to reclaim the land, and taught local landowners how to grow fruit trees. Many of the first Chinese women who came to America arrived as virtual slaves, forced into prostitution to pay off their travel debts.

In Guangdong today, there are enough people to make up roughly one-third the entire population of the United States—all tucked into an area slightly smaller than North Dakota. The province is one of the fastest-growing economic areas in the world, a hotbed of entrepreneurship and capitalism, fully exercising the economic freedom that has come with the "To get rich is glorious" rationale of modern China. "One country, two systems," the pragmatic philosophy is sometimes called, a handy accommodation between Chinese communism and Western capitalism. Yet there are still small villages where minority dialects are spoken and no one has heard of the stock market.

Jiangmen City had gotten its first American fast-food outlet a few years earlier. Tucked away in this territory, I had heard, were lavish houses with swimming pools, used by wealthy businessmen as weekend getaways. Elsewhere, drab, hastily built factories spit out tired workers and streams of pollutants. Yet the age-old cultivation of mulberry trees for silk was still a big industry. Silkworms, fried, were also a delicacy. "Like peanuts, very good," a local woman told me.

During the Ming dynasty, one of China's most famous Confucian scholars, poets, and calligraphers, Chen Baisha, was born in this area. Today, there's a regional university, Wuyi University, with four thousand pupils, where students are warned that "falling in love" is not part of the curriculum. When a delegation from Jiangmen's American sister city, Riverside, California, came to visit this area, they were taken to a model village. It had been selected, they noted, based upon seven criteria: a quality water supply, a sanitary system, having a concrete village square, having a sign and gate leading to the village, keeping animals in pens, no crimes in the village, and having shown exemplary attention to family planning, payment of taxes, military service, and "villagers caring for one another."

Yet for rural women, who constitute 70 percent of China's populace, life is desperately hard, even in boom times and model villages. The suicide rate among women in the countryside is the highest in the world. China is, in fact, the only nation where the suicide rates for women top those for men. Most victims are young. The means of self-destruction, most often, is a lethal gulp of the poison closest at hand, agricultural pesticide.[8]

There were other indications that life could be a struggle for women in rural China. An American professor traveling in the area where my daughter was born visited a kindergarten in Jiangmen City and watched the girls and boys, roughly an equal number of each, at play. Not long afterward, he went to a kindergarten in the countryside. "There were twenty-eight kids—but just three girls," he says. Just as the social pressure to produce sons has endured, so, too, has the preference to educate sons over daughters.

As we motored along on the bus back toward Guangzhou, we could see the movement of the river's glassy water, but peering beneath its dark surface was just as hard as grasping the reality of life here in this part of southern China, where people went about their business, hopeful or scared, connected or lost. Aside from whatever general explanations we'd heard, I wondered about the other currents that had swept those little girls to that orphanage. I kept thinking about my baby's birth mother—where she might have fit, or not fit, into this landscape.

By the time we reached the hotel, the finest moment of Max's mission as a transcontinental midwife for our group was complete. Our entourage now included eighteen baby girls—eleven from Kelly's orphanage and seven babies from two other institutions. Two little girls previously adopted from China had been given little sisters, and all the adults who'd come to China with us hoping to be parents had fulfilled their dream. The youngest child was probably three or four months, the oldest around eighteen months.

When we got back to our room and began changing our new daughter's clothes, Mark and I peeled off several layers.

Though the weather was mild, the children were well bundled, as is the Chinese tendency. (Had it been cooler, the babies would have been dressed in layer after layer until their little arms stood straight out at the sides and they looked like small versions of the Michelin man.) While Kelly Xiao Yu giggled, we removed her green jumper and a sweatshirt with a little red schoolhouse on the front (made in the United Arab Emirates), and a lighter undershirt printed with elephants (made in the USA). When we reached the last layer, our new baby was wearing a bright red T-shirt imprinted with yellow lettering and a picture of a building with turrets. "Trump's Castle Casino Resort," it read.

"Oh lord, sweet baby," I said, laughing back at her, "where on earth did you come from?"

3

Down the River

Raindrops fall upon my eyelashes
Like a child's tears at parting.
I carefully tap them off
Into the quiet tiny mouths of the spring
    blossoms.
Child, Mama is leaving
For lovelier blooming.

—Luo Xiaoge, "Drizzling Rain"[1]

Each daughter adopted from China is a gift beyond measure, and each comes with her own little mystery. "Just think, here are all these beautiful children, and they are just waiting there, waiting for someone to come and pick them up and say, 'You're mine,'" said one adoptive father. "How could this be?" That question is one that absorbs—and sometimes haunts—the mothers and fathers who have come home with Chinese children.

What most adoptive families know of their daughters' lives before the orphanage is written on the thin pages of official paperwork from the People's Republic of China. The documents are signed and dated and bound into booklets with official seals and red stars stamped on the covers. The papers are beautiful: pale ivory in color, crinkly in texture, and covered with elegant

Chinese writing in rich dark ink. The characters strut boldly across the pages, but they reveal very little.

Translated, one document says simply that this little girl was "found forsaken" on a winter day in a local market when she was about three months old. The local police delivered her to the social welfare institute. Her birth parents and her place of birth were unknown.

Found forsaken. The daughters of China come away with those two words, summing up their short lives. Our daughter, like so many other baby girls in China, was found with no note that we know of, no name, and no family clues. Once these children arrived at the orphanage, the people there guessed at their ages and someone assigned them a birth date and a name. All the little girls in this particular institution were given the surname Jiang, meaning "river," because of the location of the orphanage. "The name Jiang is the same as the Chinese president's," our adoption facilitator told us one day, with a sly smile, "but it doesn't mean these are all his children." All the girls in the group had first names that began with Xiao, meaning "little."

There are several reasons that the backgrounds of little girls from China remain sketchy. First, there's usually very little information to begin with, so the recordkeeping that does go on begins with guesswork and remains relatively casual. Then, in a sort of catch-22, particular to the rules of international adoption, children must be certified as "orphaned" in order to be eligible to immigrate to the United States. Under U.S. immigration law, the definition of "orphan" is liberal enough to include children whose parents have disappeared as well as those whose parents have died.[2] To be given orphan status, a child must be officially on her own in the world. Thus, the parents of abandoned children need to have unconditionally abandoned the child and given up all control over the child or the child's future. The intent of the law, according to U.S. immigration, is to guard against "the splitting of intact, functioning foreign families."

A Chinese parent who wants to give a child a chance at being adopted, then, must conveniently disappear, and so must the rest of the family, if anybody else is around. It's the Chinese equivalent to what's known in this country as "making an adoption plan." Thus, a birth parent who disappears is often intentionally creating a chance for her child to find a new home.

Abandoning a child is against the law in China, another reason why parents are usually careful to leave no traces. A specific provision of the 1992 Law on the Protection of Women's Rights and Interests forbids "forsaking" baby girls,[3] although no one has reported any substantial pattern of prosecution.

Overall, a mix of good intentions, legal hazards, fear, and shame has made birth parents elusive and difficult to identify. One American couple did see a man carry an infant into a park and set her down, while a weeping woman followed, but most parents come and go unseen, leaving no traces at all. Once a child is found in China, the orphanages hold her for a couple of months, until it can be established that no parents or relatives have stepped forward or otherwise been identified. To spread the word, "finding" ads, photos of the babies and details on when and where they were discovered, are published in local papers.

The only time a birth date is really certain for these children is when a woman delivers in a hospital, giving a false name usually, and then disappears, leaving the baby behind, or when birth parents leave a note with the child containing basic information. Otherwise the birthday is an estimate, picked at random or assigned for convenience. It's not at all unusual for pediatricians in this country to disagree substantially with the reported age of an adopted child from China. Occasionally, adopted Chinese girls come away with paperwork that belongs to other children altogether.

When the child and the age don't match up, some adoptive parents change the birth date to one that more closely reflects a child's age, which they are allowed to do when they go through a follow-up adoption procedure in the United States. Others cling to the pieces of the story they are given. "We'll be celebrating our daughter's first birthday this month, even though she is probably younger than the given date," said one mother. "I figure that birthday is about the only tangible past she has, and we better hold on to it." Another friend with a daughter from China told me she felt the same way. "I've chosen to believe the information we had," said southern California mother Carole Sopp. "That's the main reason I didn't change my daughter's birth date. She deserves the validity. If I start to disbelieve what they told me, I'm just perpetuating the myth that she doesn't have a past that we can rely on, and that's even more disconnective for the future."

In a realm of such uncertainty even the barest information becomes precious—a description of the place a child was found, the name given by the orphanage, connection with anyone who might know something, the child's photo from the "finding" ad in the local paper. At one orphanage where the doorkeeper had been the first to pick up a dozen children who'd been left on the doorstep, parents who came to adopt took photographs of the doorkeeper.

Some agencies make a practice of taking adopting parents to the spot where their baby was discovered so that they have some sense of their child's brief history. But those hospital steps, office doorways, and police stations are as far back as most short histories go—and even those stories remain sketchy and open to question. Adopting parents are left trying to put together a life story from the sparest of details. An East Coast mother was told by an orphanage worker that her little daughter's parents had perished in a flood, but a second caretaker said the child had been discovered in a post office. The mother of another child, said to have been found in a restaurant in a midsized southern Chinese city, went back looking for the restaurant. "But there was no such restaurant as far as anyone knew," she says, "so we went to the police station where she was taken. It still brings tears to my eyes that we weren't able to see her place."

Some parents have found the hospital or street where their daughter was discovered and have videotaped the scene to show her one day. Susan August-Brown, who adopted a fifteen-month-old child from southern China, did this and explains, "She'll hear the words from us, but have the chance to see the place with her own eyes. What struck me most as I retraced the steps some thirteen months after the day our daughter had been found in this place was how much I believe her mother had wanted her to be discovered right away. The baby was left in the doorway of a storefront. It was a spot where a small crying baby would be instantly discovered."

Mark and I rolled out of town without getting to see the market where Kelly was said to have been found. Later, when I talked with people in the area, I was led to a young woman at the local university who offered to go to the market and describe it for us. It was a generous gesture. She knew nothing about us, really, just the fact that we had been introduced through an e-mail connection. But she seemed genuinely touched to hear that we wanted to see where our baby had been discovered. Like many other parents, we were trying to piece together a collection of memories.

By the time Mark and I met our baby, she had smiled her first smile, cut her first tooth (and seven more), and taken her first step. According to her birth date, she would have had her first birthday just nine days before we met her, but I doubt there had been any fanfare. We don't know what she was called before she became Xiao Yu. A Chinese woman from the area told us later that the English translation we were first given for our daughter's name—Little Education—was perplexing. "No one is called 'Education,'" she said. "We don't use that word for a name." The word *yu*, depending on the tone used and how it's written, could also mean "jade," she said. "Little Jade—now, that's a beautiful name for a girl." According to Bette Bao Lord, author of *Legacies*, Xiao Yu—pronounced and written yet another way—has yet another meaning: "Slight Change." That's what a relative of Lord's was called, after a magistrate made a mistake about her birth date.

Like most other parents who've adopted children from China, we know nothing about the circumstances of our daughter's birth or about her birth parents. Once we were home, I asked a pediatrician whether our child's belly button would offer a clue as to whether she'd been born in a hospital or not. It didn't. Not that that particular information would have told us much, but I was straining to picture all the events in her life that I'd missed. I also wanted to gather all the information I could to answer all the questions I knew she would have as she grew up.

Whoever had first cared for our child had given her a good start at life. She was in robust health ("Strong baby!" exclaimed the doctor at the government clinic we were required to visit). She'd been well nourished. She had a predilection for crawling on top of me and laying her cheek on my breast, so I think she had been nursed. She sought out that warm spot as if she'd known it well, nestled, nudged me like a kitten. And by all indications—her trust of people, her displays of affection, her rather gleeful outlook on life—she seems to have been treated with love and kindness. From someone she had inherited her long, delicate fingers, her easy, beautiful smile—perhaps a "risk gene" that might explain the enthusiasm she seemed to have for motorcycles. But from whom?

This baby's mother and possibly her father had held her, fed her, carried her, for at least three months before she was found and taken to the orphanage. Babies have persuasive powers to make us love them and three months is a long time. How unspeakably hard it must have been to walk away. And yet someone had. While I was at home in San Francisco, fretting about bureaucratic logjams, someone in south China was bundling up that beautiful three-month-old girl for a last trip to the marketplace.

It was an act so momentous that I'd often find myself trying to conjure such a story from the few details I knew.

It was midwinter, a season of mild weather, I'd been told, but likely to be wet and the market would have been crawling— filled with buckets of squirming local shrimp, live frogs in bamboo cages, and thin shiny eels swimming in tubs. There would have been rice for sale, of course, and just about everything else from turtles to water beetles. Bok choy and long beans tied in neat bunches. Piles of oranges. And somewhere in that large, bustling place, tucked among the rice barrels, maybe, or near the winter melons, was a baby.

Who discovered the child, or just how or when she was noticed we don't know. Perhaps it was a farmer, reaching for a melon. He would have been startled at first, but after the cry went up—"Wait! There's a baby here!"—probably no one was surprised. The baby was a girl. Enough said. Someone called the police and they came, as they'd done any number of times in any number of places before, and took the child off to one of the nearby orphanages, where there was food and warmth, care and lots of company. If this baby girl was crying, it would have been a loud, full-out, heartbreaking wail, mouth wide open, chest trembling, huge tears soaking both cheeks. (I know this child well by now, and this is how she cries.)

Someone fed her, dressed her, and put her in a crowded nursery. And so the second part of her life began, the nine months in an institution, surrounded by an unknown number of other little girls, sleeping two (or sometimes more) to a crib, covered with padded quilts in winter, playing on straw mats in the summer. Eventually she tried her first bite of banana, and learned to clap her hands and blow kisses.

But how had this little child wound up lying alone in a marketplace? She had obviously come into this world with everything a parent could want, and more. She was sweet and strong, bright and beautiful, with an irresistible smile and a laugh that shook her little body. Despite this little girl's exquisite nature, something had gone terribly wrong—and not only to her, but to all the little girls found forsaken in China.

I thought about our daughter's short, mysterious life and tried to imagine all the possible identities for her elusive mother. Motoring through southern China we'd passed farm-workers in the fields and factory workers in the towns. Else-where, I knew, were university students bent over their books, teenagers on the run, mothers on the nightshift coming home at dawn. Each life in all its complexity and difficulty flowing along, hitting obstacles. What circumstances could make any of these women leave a three-month-old baby? Did a girl from the local university deviate from the curriculum, fall in love, and get pregnant? I had heard a story of a single woman student there who had conceived a child, and who was then subjected to immense pressures to leave the school, hounded by the offi-cials, the water in her living quarters turned off, her life made miserable. To say that single mothers did not fare well in China at the time is a massive understatement.

When whole villages fall to the wrecker's ball, when floods turn river deltas into inland seas, families can come untied. Daughters who might have been cared for in tough times may be let go to fend for themselves when circumstances get even harder. If southern China's boomtowns offered jobs to rural women, they also offered new dangers.

Had a poor rural woman come to the city looking for work and found herself instead with an unexpected child? Was my daughter's mother what Chinese officials called a "birth guerrilla"—a woman who fled the hometown authorities to have her child? Did she hope to save this daughter and then re-alize the only way to save her was to give her up? Did she run for a while and then quit running? Did something happen sud-denly to turn her life upside down? Was she a rootless factory worker who had lost her job? Did a woman from one of the out-lying farms have a second or third daughter and become squeezed between the family pressures to try again for a son and the government's edict to have no more children? Was she sixteen? Or twenty-two? Or forty?

Just as the rivers in my daughter's homeland defined the physical landscape—how marked the channels were where the water had cut deep or wandered shallow, what currents and crosscurrents might be at play, what rivulets had dried to mud, what swells had pushed and gushed, flooding, over the fields— there was an invisible human current at work. A rippling flow of people, poor and prosperous, riding to and from the city on motorbikes, bicycles, in trucks and cars. Somewhere back in the Pearl River Delta, I knew, I had a counterpart.

Children who are older when they are discovered or older when they are adopted and have therefore stayed in the orphanage longer, may come away from China with information of their own, of course—the recollection, perhaps, of a mother's face, or some words spoken long ago in Mandarin or Cantonese. But the majority of children adopted from China are aged one year or less, with no easily understood memories of life before the institution in which they ended up. They come away with just their sheets of elegant but iffy paperwork—and whatever tokens or good wishes their caretakers might pass along.

A little girl from near Hangzhou was handed to her new mother wearing thin string bracelets on her wrists and ankles, tied on by the orphanage staff to bring her luck. Other babies in other places have been sent away with red dots on their foreheads for good fortune, stuffed panda bears, or small bags of Chinese soil to remind them of their homeland. The babies from an orphanage north of Guangzhou were given tiny pieces of jade as they left with their new parents, and "lucky money" in red envelopes. On the other hand, a child adopted by a friend from a city in the north of China lacked even a shirt on her back. In the hotel where my friend was handed her child, she had to undress the baby, redress her in the clothes she had brought, and return the original clothes to the orphanage caretakers. It's understandable, given that some of the orphanages are in dire straits.

Occasionally, a handmade bit of clothing or a small trinket left with an infant and passed along to the adoptive parents bespeaks some attempt at a going-away present by the birth parent or parents. A baby in Hefei, the provincial capital of Anhui province in the north, was found with a yam tucked under her arm. "The parents wanted to show some love for the baby and they were very poor, and they left it with the poorest food of China, a dry yam," said a woman who grew up in Hefei. "And once," she says, "a friend of mine found a baby and instead of money the parents had left a bunch of used bus tickets with the baby. The tickets weren't worth anything. The parents didn't even have a penny to leave. It was very sad."

When notes do appear, they are apt to be heartwrenching. They come scrawled on scraps of paper, often written in obvious haste—jotted in crayon on a restaurant bill, for instance. Some birth parents in rural areas can't write at all, but others have tried to spell out the reasons for what happened, accounts that can amount to a kind of impromptu social commentary. One scrap of paper indicated a little girl's name and time of birth, and then said, "I am heartbroken to give her up. But in China women have no power, and I have no choice. I hope someone will care for her." Another was addressed to the child herself: "In this life, in this world, I am not able to provide for you," it said. "I am giving you up so you can have a life. Good luck and be well."

A Catholic priest quoted this note, found with a baby girl lying in an empty field: "Kindhearted people, we are abandoning our child not because we cannot care for her, but because of the official one-child policy. 'Dear daughter, we do not have bad hearts. We couldn't keep you.' Friendly people who take her up, we cannot repay the debt in this life. But perhaps in the next life."[4]

A day-old baby, found in Beijing in front of the Chinese government office that handles international adoptions, was accompanied by a note that said: "This little girl was born and we can't take care of her." The parents begged the people in the orphanage to care for their baby and asked their daughter herself for forgiveness.

A note found pinned to a tiny abandoned girl in Hunan read: "This baby girl is now 100 days old. She is in good health and has never suffered any illness. Due to the current political situation and heavy pressures that are difficult to explain, we, who were her parents for these first days, cannot continue taking care of her. We can only hope that in this world there is a kindhearted person who will care for her. Thank you. In regret and shame, your father and mother."[5]

Heavy pressures that are difficult to explain. If there's a core phrase that gets at the heart of the matter for the birth parents of China's lost daughters, that may be it. What led to that fateful moment for our daughter and for thousands and thousands of other tiny girls discovered in parks and doorways all over that vast country lay buried in centuries of Chinese history—part of a long, hard, complex past and a very difficult present.

The newborn boy
Deserves a bed,
Fine clothes, and
Jade for playthings.
His cries announce his standing.
Grown, he'll wear red
And be honored as the family head.

For a daughter
Bare ground is bed enough
And plain clothes will suit her
As will broken tiles for toys.
Let her live without distinction
And serve her family well
Without disgracing them.
    —*From* The Book of Odes[6]

The troubles for females in China, it seemed, went back at least as far as Confucius. During the Han dynasty, two hundred years before Christ, China's greatest sage laid down a family system built on male lineage. In the Confucian scheme of things, control of the land and all the family fortunes was passed from father to son. A daughter's place began at the bottom of the family hierarchy and stayed there, her lifelong status dictated by her gender. "Women and people of low birth are very hard to deal with," wrote Confucius. "If you are friendly with them, they get out of hand."[7]

The philosopher Mencius, known as China's second sage, followed Confucius and reinforced the system of patriarchy. Of all unfilial behavior, said Mencius, the greatest was to provide no male heirs. Despite changes in government and increasing modernization, the Confucian philosophy has persisted right into the present, particularly in China's countryside.

While a system that so blatantly discriminates in favor of boys may seem completely skewed to the outside observer, within the context of Chinese culture, it had a practical basis. Confucian philosophy defined the relationships within the clan and dictated the fiduciary realities of the family real estate. A son was born into a position not just of respect but of family duty, expected to work his father's land, carry the ancestral name, ensure the worshipping of the ancestral spirits, and care for his parents in their old age. For parents, having a son was simply the age-old Chinese version of a modern social security system.

In some rural areas of old China, the placenta of a girl baby was buried outside the walls of the family home, while a boy's placenta was buried within the house—a symbolic practice that mirrored the girl's standing in the family. That act was just the beginning of a lifelong pattern of discrimination. Boys had first pick of the food and toys and other resources, including whatever medical care was available. Even the gods were assumed to be indifferent to girls: Boys were sometimes given a girl's name when very small, to fool the deities into thinking the child was of no consequence, not worth taking back.

At a month old, a son was given a formal name and carried to the temple by his father, who proudly informed the gods and the ancestral spirits that an heir had been born. The family celebrated with a "full-month" feast, breaking out red-tinted eggs and sliced pickled ginger, symbols of a new—male—birth. Daughters, when they reached a month old (and many did not), did so without celebration.

A daughter was frequently regarded as just an extra mouth to feed until she married and joined her husband's household. Once there, her only hope of respect was to produce a son to carry on the family name for her husband and in-laws. If she failed in this mission, she could simply be cast aside and another woman invited into the family to take her place. Among the numerous reasons that gave a husband the right to take a concubine or to divorce his spouse was a wife's failure to produce a son. (Disrespect to the mother-in-law was also sufficient cause; as was rudeness to a husband's mistress.) "Chinese women put up with this sexual injustice," explained the noted Chinese scholar Lin Yutang, "as naturally as Chinese people put up with political injustice."

Once a daughter married, her name no longer appeared in her own family records, but became part of her husband's lineage. Historically, wives were under great pressure to keep the husband's name and line going, and they couldn't do it with daughters. When a daughter married and moved to her husband's family's turf, she often encountered a whole new set of troubles. Many traditional Chinese stories are devoted to the unhappy lot of the daughter-in-law, who could at worst be treated as a household slave completely under the thumb of the husband's mother, the venerable Chinese mother-in-law.

Out of entrenched tradition grew a pervasive assumption: Having a child was not just a woman's, or even a couple's, private affair, but the intimate and crucial business of the husband's family. The entire clan's self-esteem and their fortunes depended on having a male heir. Producing that much-coveted son was a woman's ticket to family power. The daughter-in-law who failed to produce a son failed the family.

The poem earlier in this chapter, written before the eighth century, is indicative of such thinking. But so is this one, written by Jia Jia in the 1980s:

> *Married for seven days he leaves*
> *Telling*
> *The bride to give him a son*
> *So she gives him a son*
> *But still stiffening his face*
> *As if she had given him a girl*
> *He won't allow her to step into the house.*[8]

Although twelve centuries separate the writers of the two works, the descriptions of family attitudes about girls and boys are nearly identical. Even today, a wife is commonly expected to produce a son, and if she doesn't, her husband can turn a cold shoulder to her, or worse. In the 1990s, a man in northeast China who was accused of suffocating two small daughters so that he could start a new family with a son, explained, "I was unable to continue the family line for my ancestors. What a sin!"[9]

Any number of Chinese folk sayings reflect the bias against females: "Girls are maggots in the rice." "It is more profitable to raise geese than daughters." "When fishing for treasures in the flood, be careful not to pull in girls." Even today, daughters born into families without sons can be given names that translate to such sentiments as "Bring a little brother."

In her book *Bound Feet and Western Dress*, Pang-Mei Natasha

Chang summed up the Chinese woman's age-old destiny when she quoted her great-aunt on the subject: "I want you to remember this: in China a woman is nothing. When she is born she must obey her father. When she is married, she must obey her husband. And when she is widowed, she must obey her son."

"I was clearly taught how cheap a girl's life is at a few years of age," says another woman, who grew up in Hefei in the 1950s and now lives in the American Midwest. "Across the beautiful city moat from our home was the provincial hospital. Now and then when I was wandering around that river park, I would see abandoned babies. I soon learned that they were unwanted girls and handicapped boys.

"As a child, whenever I felt uneasy about my parents giving most of their attention and resources to my younger brother, I was told to feel lucky. My father told me that there were no girls around my age at the villages he visited. The parents had to 'get rid' of them to save the boys during the three years' starvation period. How could it happen? 'Just throw them in the toilet,' he said. Should I not feel lucky to be born in the city?"

Although some women in Chinese history did better than others, it was an uphill struggle. In a prosperous family with a boy or two, there was room for a girl, though she'd traditionally take a backseat to her brothers. In fact, an older daughter and a younger son was often viewed as the perfect combination, with the girl taking on some of the parental responsibility. But when life was hard, which has been the case in Chinese history for most of the people most of the time, it was the daughters who suffered.

And suffer they have. In times of flood and famine and war, when families struggled to stay alive, if there were too many children to care for, it was the girls who were let go. Some young girls couldn't even be sure of waking up in their own beds in the morning. If they survived infancy, they could be sold and raised in other families as domestic servants or given to the family of a future husband, to be groomed in the submissive role of daughter-in-law from a very young age.

"Unwanted daughters were peddled as virtual slaves, sometimes by brokers, to unknown families," writes Adeline Yen Mah in her memoir *Falling Leaves: The True Story of an Unwanted Chinese Daughter*. "Once sold, a child's destiny was at the whim of her buyer. She had no papers and no rights. A few, perhaps more fortunate, ones were legally adopted by their owners. Many more were subjected to beatings and other abuses. Prostitution or even death were the fate of some child slaves."

Girls commonly didn't make it beyond the birthing room. There is evidence throughout Chinese history of the killing of newborns, despite moral and civic injunctions against the practice. Literary accounts of Chinese life offer numerous descriptions of baby girls neglected, left behind, or killed. In the seventeenth century, an observant visitor to China, Italian Jesuit Matteo Ricci, reported the drowning of infants whose parents could not support them. When the character O-Lan in Pearl S. Buck's *The Good Earth* gives birth to a second daughter in the midst of famine, she quietly strangles the newborn. Her husband carries the tiny form out to a graveyard and leaves it, while a ravenous wild dog hovers nearby. According to Buck's biographer, the story was based on an event that Buck had witnessed as a young woman growing up in China.

In *The Woman Warrior: Memoirs of a Girlhood Among Ghosts*, Maxine Hong Kingston recalls hearing tales of midwives who prepared boxes of clean ashes beside the birthing bed in case the baby was a girl. If so, they swiftly pressed her little face into the ashes. "It was very easy," Kingston says her mother told her.

China hardly stands alone in such thinking or family patterns, of course. In many parts of the world, strong patriarchies seem to have replaced female-oriented societies with the coming of literacy, according to one recently advanced theory. Leonard Shlain, in *The Alphabet Versus the Goddess*, points out that in ancient times, the Chinese character for wife also meant "equal," before the Confucians spread their philosophy via the printed word and the patriarchy seized power.

One doesn't have to travel far, of course, or scratch deep beneath the surface of numerous other cultures to find equivalent male dominance or similar suffering among children. Industrialized Europe is not that far removed from such conditions. Witness Charles Dickens's London, filled with tales of cruelly exploited children, or John Boswell's study "The Abandonment of Children in Western Europe from Late Antiquity to the Renaissance," replete with stories concerning the selling and killing of unwanted children of both sexes.[10]

But China's patriarchy nonetheless stands out as a particularly deep-rooted and destructive form. And in China, furthermore, there was a notable difference: The pressures, whether of deeply ingrained belief, poverty, or individual exploitation, fell far more heavily on girls than boys. When children were lost altogether, it was the girls, almost exclusively, who disappeared. When babies were killed at birth, girls were far more likely to die than boys.

China being the complex place that it is, it should be noted, there were also historical exceptions to this broad picture of bias—families, certainly, who loved and cherished their daughters, and throughout Chinese history, women who wielded power, not just within their families but beyond, including women who created pockets of matriarchy.[11]

The legendary heroine Fa Mulan—popularly known as Mulan—is a reflection of the flip side of disenfranchisement, a woman who became a heroine by disguising herself as a man. Numerous ancient Chinese stories include tales of filial daughters who took up a challenge to defend their families and stand up for a cause, and certain Chinese families were known for long lines of female warriors. In a patriarchal culture, women through the ages—from the Empress Dowager Cixi in the last dynasty, right down to rural activists today—have found ways to be strong.

As writer and scholar Hu Shih explained in *Chinese Women Through Chinese Eyes*, "Against all shackles and fetters, the Chinese woman has exerted herself and achieved for herself a place in the family, in society, and in history. She has managed men and governed empires; she has contributed abundantly to literature and the fine arts; and above all she has taught and molded her sons to be what they have been. If she has not contributed more, it was probably because China, which certainly has treated her ill, has not deserved more of her."[12]

An astute observer of his own society, Hu Shih elaborated on this when he addressed an American Association of University Women group in Tientsin in 1931. Sketching in part of the long history of women in China, he concluded, "If there is a moral to this story, it is that it is simply impossible to suppress women—even in China."[13]

Nevertheless, the patriarchy had a long and pervasive force of its own. Even as China has changed, with more people moving to the cities and women gaining education and better jobs, in rural areas where life goes on as it has for centuries, the Confucian values are alive and well. Passed from father to son, mother to daughter, the system that favors boys over girls has permeated Chinese society from one generation to the next. Decades of Communist government haven't altered the reliance of many families, particularly rural families, on sons. "Son preference," it's called simply.

That prejudice reached right into our own living room one evening after we'd returned from China with our daughter. Kelly and I were reading through a modern version of *Chinese Mother Goose Rhymes*, enjoying the illustrations of dragon kites and riddles about ducks and snails, when we came upon this poem:

> *We keep a dog to guard the house;*
> *A pig will make a feast or two;*
> *We keep a cat to catch a mouse;*
> *But what is the use of a girl like you?*[14]

Infanticide, the saddest evidence of ancient prejudice, was on the wane after the Communists came to power in 1949, but severe hardship—first an agricultural disaster of unprecedented proportions, then the government's strict population policies—soon caused a resurgence.

In the Mao Zedong era, there were attempts to improve the lot of China's women, to eradicate infanticide and institute other reforms. The Communists encouraged women to "join the ranks of human beings," get involved in the party, "become officials." "Women hold up half the sky," Mao liked to say. Prostitution, child marriage, the taking of concubines, and the selling of brides were outlawed. Wives were given rights they had never had before. Peasant girls began going to school.

Still, the Great Leap Forward ultimately failed China's women, as it failed the population at large. Mao's reforms were short-lived, and when hard times hit, it was once again the women who disproportionately paid the price. First came famine—the worst in China's history. And then came the government's attempts to curb its population growth. When China put into force the world's most stringent policies dictating family size, the age-old prejudices again rose up and took their toll.

4

The One-Child, Maybe-One-More Policy

One is not too few,
two will perfectly do,
and three are too many for you.

   —*Early population-control slogan*[1]

Sink back into just about any period of China's past and the achievements of an illustrious history—the scholars' insights, the scientists' breakthroughs, the profoundly beautiful art and literature—are shadowed by catastrophes that unsettle the soul. Just as a quick, modern example, China, in a period considerably shorter than the entire history of the United States, has endured five wars of foreign aggression (add to that carnage the infamous Rape of Nanjing) and an equal number of internal upheavals—from the Taiping Rebellion in the mid-1850s, with casualties of twenty million, to the Cultural Revolution one hundred years later. Add to that litany a lion's share of natural disasters—earthquakes, floods, droughts, with enormous numbers of casualties—and the picture darkens further.

So tumultuous has been the experience of this overwhelming

country that it's not surprising that the Chinese people have a long history of losing one another. While working in Hong Kong, I remember, there was talk of jade pieces cut apart like puzzle parts into two distinct and intricate shapes, so no two pieces but these would fit together. A man and a woman, a father and son, a mother and daughter who felt doomed to be separated might each take one piece, hoping to use it one day to identify each other after separations of years, perhaps across thousands of miles. Many old traditional Chinese stories have the theme of families losing one another, going through a long search, and eventually reuniting. Those were the happy endings. More often, people in China periodically scraped by until they could scrape no longer and then dropped in their tracks; children were left along the roadside, husbands disappeared into battle and never returned; whole families, villages, and regions dried into dust or were carried away by floodwaters.

When I first wrote this book, there was flooding along the Yangtze, the worst in half a century. Thousands of people had been killed, millions forced to evacuate. By mid-August 1998, the river's raging waters had destroyed five million houses, according to Chinese news reports. Upward of ten million people, possibly, had been forced from their homes. Buildings still underwater by late summer included at least two orphanages. When winter hit, some observers expected a greater than usual number of children—girls whose parents simply could not care for them—to wind up at orphanage doors. In 2008, the Sichuan earthquake killed more than eighty thousand people, destroyed three million homes, and rendered some twenty million people homeless. It also left thousands of newly orphaned children.

In the long, sad recounting of China's disasters and turmoil, one event in recent history still looms at the top of the list—the famine that happened fifty years ago, following Mao Zedong's bungled attempt to reorganize China's agricultural system as part of the Great Leap Forward. The changes he instilled—forcing peasants out of individual farms and into communal production managed by a central authority, for instance—resulted in massive crop failures and starvation for farmers in the years between 1958 and 1961. Although the immensity of the tragedy escaped serious Western attention until well after the fact, estimates are now that some thirty million people died in a three-year period.

According to Jasper Becker, author of *Hungry Ghosts: Mao's Secret Famine,* the disaster amounted to the least recognized and most severe famine in recorded human history—as if every single man, woman, and child in the entire state of California had perished from hunger and no one outside the California border had taken any notice.[2] Half the casualties were children under ten. Untold numbers of children were left crying beside the bodies of their dead parents. Along roadsides in northwest China, desperate people scooped out holes in the soft yellow clay and left their children, hoping more fortunate travelers would come upon them and have mercy. American parents talking about "the starving children in China" at the dinner table in attempts to get their own children to eat didn't know the half of it.

Even foreign correspondents stationed in China at the time managed to remain unaware of the devastation. Mao himself tried to hide the disaster from the world until it was too late for help. So distanced were some of the later discussions of this tragedy that American academics managed to quibble among themselves about whether it was appropriate for a writer like Becker to use emotionally charged phrases such as "starved to death" as opposed to the more acceptable "excess mortality" when talking about the loss of tens of millions of human beings.[3]

It was against this bleak scenario—though not necessarily because of it—that China's so-called one-child policy came to be. At the end of the Mao era, with the specter of the famine still lingering and with a growing impulse toward economic development, population control became a priority for the People's Republic of China.

Mao, however, had spurned the idea of slowing the nation's birthrate, viewing it as a Western strategy to reduce China's influence. He had, in fact, celebrated the idea of "glorious mothers having more babies," and the voices of those who expressed doubts were brutally stilled.[4] When the Cultural Revolution came along, it managed to postpone any further discussion for at least another five years. It was not until well afterward that the climate changed sufficiently that discussions could resume. By 1972, with China's population swelling toward one billion people, a state council announced that population control was essential to the socialist revolution. When China's new leaders such as Deng Xiaoping looked forward, the emphasis was on chasing the booming "tiger" economies of China's prosperous Asian neighbors.

Although the threat of another famine might seem reason enough to most untutored observers to keep numbers down, the People's Republic viewed population control as a way to boost economic development and growth. The leadership believed that fewer mouths to feed meant a better chance at prosperity for more people. A rising standard of living meant better odds for political stability and a place for China in the world hierarchy of emerging nations. Yet by this point, it was probably already too late. As writer Hong Ying points out, "The disaster would take at least half a century of draconian policy and human tragedy to correct."

In 1980 came the official government announcement that set the ground rules for what came to be known, rather inaccurately, as the one-birth-per-couple, or one-child, policy.[5] With that decree, which became national law, the government wedged a foot into the bedroom door of every household in China. "Use whatever means you must to reduce the population, but do it," came the edict.

The government placed its hopes for prosperity in a mathematical vision of diminishing numbers. "Eight-four-two-one," went one saying, meant to describe the shrinking family—eight great-grandparents, four grandparents, two parents, one child. The target figure worked out to 1.6 children per couple, which built in the government's realistic assumption that a lot of people—some with the government's permission—would have more than one child. At the time a substantial number of Chinese families were routinely having five or six children.

As if the heavy burden of tradition hadn't landed heavily enough on China's females already, the government's population policy ushered in a whole new set of troubles for girls and women both, particularly in the countryside. Had a more moderate course been taken, and taken far, far earlier, there are some arguments that economic development and education might have naturally, over time, reduced the tendency to have large families and might have slowed the booming birthrate. But China put into place the most drastic birth control policies in the world and enforced them, in certain areas, with brutal zeal.

At first, a birth control "high tide" was launched. Early on, the suggestions were relatively gentle. Such slogans as "One is best, don't exceed two" went round, but the state's grip soon tightened, as China forecast an economic crisis and began a huge push toward development and modernization. The general policy called for later marriages (age twenty-two for men, at least twenty for women, though twenty-four for women was considered ideal), fewer children, and a longer space (about four years) between children. In theory, each family would be allowed just one child—sometimes under special circumstances a second, providing that the children were sufficiently spaced, and the officials could be persuaded of a pressing need. Ethnic minorities within China—there are numerous strains, particularly in the borderlands, but they add up to less than 10 percent of the population as a whole—were routinely allowed two children, because their numbers were in some cases diminishing.

A certain piece of paper became immensely important in China. *Shengyu zheng,* it was called—"birth permission paper"— the state's version of blessings for mothers. It gave a woman official sanction to conceive and bear a child, a right she no longer had without it. She was required to have a permit when she became pregnant and to take the paperwork to the hospital with her at the time of delivery.

With marriage came the state's requirement that people sign an agreement to comply with the birth quotas. Those who cooperated could receive a Birth Planning Honor Card and preferential treatment for food, housing, health care, and education. Those who didn't agree could be hounded until they did. If they still held out, they were subject to punishment— fines, loss of benefits and jobs, even jail.

Once the new rules had been set, the very nature of the Communist Party state gave the government the right and the power to interfere in the most personal realm of people's lives. And interfere it did. From the beginning, the government's approach set it at odds with contemporary world guidelines on family planning, which emphasize not forced compliance but the empowerment of women to make informed, responsible choices.

The long arm of the Chinese state had the ability to reach into every household. Women who became pregnant without permission were confronted and, if officials decided it was necessary, marched to abortion clinics. Once a child was born, a woman was required to have an IUD inserted and periodically checked. After the birth of a second child, either husband or wife was to be sterilized. Forced sterilizations, mandatory insertions of metal IUDs—which could be monitored by X-ray to make sure they remained in place—became commonplace assaults on the women of China, as did forced abortions, even at full term.[6]

Party workers and local officials were rewarded or punished, depending on how well they met the quotas set for their areas. Some population control offices had special boxes where anonymous informants could tell officials which women in the community might be attempting to hide a pregnancy. Posters went up, labeling those who opposed the state's birth control policies as class enemies. Officials of the Women's Federation of the Communist Party kept track of women's monthly cycles and their pregnancies, and listed those to be sterilized and those required to have IUDs inserted.[7]

Employers, too, began to supervise their female employees, watching them for signs of pregnancy, sometimes posting their menstrual cycles publicly, pressuring them into abortions if the timing of the pregnancy didn't adhere to the rules or suit the work schedule. Writes Bill McKibben in *Maybe One: A Personal and Environmental Argument for Single-Child Families*: "No parent, for any reason, should ever have to make a choice to abandon a child. But in China, it's hard to avoid. In factories family planning workers monitor women to make sure they do not become pregnant. 'We watch for women who start to eat less or who get morning sickness,' explained one functionary from . . . Changzhou [the home of our second daughter, Franny]. '. . . No one has ever become pregnant without one of us finding out.'"[8]

In 1997, a maid named Sun Lili, employed by a government-owned hotel in Beijing, became pregnant, only to be told by her employer that her condition was "inconvenient." She was ordered to take "remedial measures," meaning an abortion. She refused when a doctor said another abortion (she'd already had two in the past two years when she'd become pregnant without official sanction) would forever end her chances to bear a child. Sun Lili was fined five months' salary, stripped of her medical coverage, and eventually lost her job.

She went on to have her baby, a little girl, and in a rare instance of anyone, much less a woman, fighting the Chinese system, she brought a lawsuit—although the Chinese courts were not known for supporting the rights of individuals against the power of the state.[9] Sun's case was heard at both the district and a higher level of the People's Court. In both cases, the courts ruled against her. With the assistance of the Center for Women's Law Studies and Legal Services at Beijing University, Sun planned to appeal.[10]

China's women, whether they lived in an area where the quotas and enforcement were relatively lax or where the rules were rigidly defined and adhered to, were the focus of enforcement, oversight, and punishment. If sterilization was ordered, it was most often the wife who was sterilized, despite government pronouncements that both men and women shared the responsibility for family planning. In China, as elsewhere in the world, the burden of contraception, state-dictated contraception especially, fell on women.[11]

Birth control workers sometimes referred to women who begged to keep their children, born or unborn, as "pleaders." Since control was exerted over people at the local level, some couples managed to outrun the policies by moving away and having their children elsewhere, going through considerable hardship in the process, and coming to be known as birth guerrillas. They, too, paid a price. The women often gave birth in primitive conditions, with little or no help, and wound up with children ineligible for a residence registration card, or *hukou*, the ticket to state benefits. The relatives left behind were often harassed. And if a woman who fled was caught, she could be forcibly taken in for an abortion, no matter how far her pregnancy had progressed.

Pregnant women would sometimes hide in relatives' homes until they were ready to deliver, hoping to escape the authorities. "But they could be discovered and dragged back to the house. It happened to my sister," said a woman who grew up in the north. "They dragged her to the hospital for an abortion, and it was a late abortion, the kind a baby could have survived.

"And not so long ago," she added, "I heard about a woman who got pregnant without permission, but no one raised a question until she was almost due. Then they said, 'Hey, you violated the policy,' and dragged her to the hospital. The husband panicked and said, 'We're going to lose the baby,' and he called a friend who was a doctor to try to get him to help. But it was too late. They'd already injected the drug and the baby was dead. The couple was very sad."

Another woman, one who fled China, reported that in Fujian, a province known particularly for its harsh enforcement of the government rules, she'd seen pregnant women hiding anywhere they could. "Some of them were nine months pregnant, but were forced to undergo abortion procedures just the same—simply because they had no birth-allowed certificates. The government dismantled the houses of some of them and made them homeless. In my native village, I saw how many women were looking for places to hide at night."

Early reports of excessive force used against women in China were recounted by Steven Mosher in *Broken Earth*, and by John S. Aird in *Slaughter of the Innocents: Coercive Birth Control in China*. In a second book, Mosher told the story of a woman who worked in China as a population control officer and then moved to America, only to have the Chinese authorities attempt to deny her the right to bear a second child—while she was in the United States. Chi An, the narrator of *One Mother's Ordeal*—Mosher disguised her name—now lives in this country and speaks out against the one-child policy, which she blames for the abandonment and killing of baby girls in China.

Other horror stories were documented by various international organizations, including Human Rights in China, which quoted a Beijing gynecologist who told of women seven, eight, nine months pregnant with a second or third baby taken to hospitals by population officials for "induced abortions." Another former population control official who worked in a northwestern province told of noncooperative women pulled out of their homes and forcibly sterilized "in the middle of the night by half-asleep nurses and doctors. The woman usually screams and kicks, and our men hold her down for anesthesia."[12]

Such stories made dramatic headlines in the West whenever they appeared, yet the overall picture of what went on in China was far more complex. From the beginning, the so-called one-child policy wasn't always, in all places, a one-child policy. And over time, it evolved and changed, with different applications in different areas. Since the birth limits were enforced through local districts, procedures varied, with relatively lax rules in some provinces and urban areas, and draconian measures in others. Different rules were applied in different terrains. In some regions, rural peoples who needed more hands to work the land were allowed to have more than one child without penalty. In sparsely populated rural areas the policy was a two-child policy, even a three-child policy, if a family could show sufficient economic need for another child, or if the area wasn't closely monitored. In the most remote areas of China where enforcement was just too difficult, the policies were pretty much ignored by populace and officials alike. In some areas, officials looked the other way or simply imposed fines on people who exceeded the limits. Eventually, in some instances and locales, it became common for people who could afford it to just pay the fine, usually a substantial amount, and have an extra child.

If terror was applied in some areas, gentler inducements succeeded in others. The promise of state benefits persuaded many women to comply with the government's pressures, particularly in the cities where women and families had achieved a greater measure of financial independence, which they could too easily lose. A study at Beijing University found that three-quarters of urban women said they'd like to have two children, but settled for one because they'd otherwise lose valuable subsidies, including housing and medical care.

There were places, too, where the policy experienced breakdowns, particularly in rural areas and among parents on the loose, unattached to any particular jurisdiction. A skit on Chinese television once featured a family who outran the population control officials from city to city, producing a child in each place and naming the youngster after the city of birth.

Nevertheless, by 1987, American anthropologist Susan Greenhalgh, a professor at the University of California Irvine and an expert on Chinese population policy, reported that one out of every eight Chinese women married in the 1970s had suffered the trauma of a second- or third-trimester abortion. In some provinces, such as Fujian in the south, the enforcement was particularly zealous.

"I was a monster in the daytime," said a former birth control official from Fujian, who appeared on U.S. television, on Ted Koppel's *Nightline*.[13] Gao Xiao Duan told American viewers particularly horrifying tales of what she herself had done in the service of the government's policy. But such discussions of conditions in China sometimes made for strange bedfellows. This particular official, for instance, was also invited to appear before a U.S. congressional subcommittee to testify about the terror experienced by Chinese women at the hands of the authorities.[14] The committee was chaired by Republican Christopher Smith, an opponent of birth control anywhere, who used the woman's testimony to bolster his cause—denying China support for voluntary birth control programs because of the purported horrors of the existing policy and the widespread abortions. At the time, Smith noted that these "shocking revelations" had come only a few months after the United Nations Population Fund had resumed cooperation with China's population program.[15]

During this time China was often caught in this sort of double bind—applauded by the outside world for attempting quickly and drastically to reduce its growth rate, then taken to task for its methods, but ultimately denied the assistance for women that might in some ways have helped relax the stringent enforcement.

Although the Chinese government has insisted that it never coerced or used physical force on women (blaming "overzealous fieldworkers" for excesses), the reports of extreme measures, including full-term "abortion," involuntary sterilization, forcible insertion of IUDs, and killing of newborns, persisted. While some physicians, forced to do late-term abortions, resisted, others were pressured to keep up the practice. During campaigns in 1983 and 1991, more than thirty million women were forcibly sterilized.[16] Such surgery, often carried out at inappropriate times, in unsanitary conditions, or without proper rest afterward, took its toll on women's health.

Both the mothers of China and their daughters were caught in an age-old struggle with a contemporary twist. With the efforts of the People's Republic of China to curb population solidly under way, in many families, whether through sheer economic need for a male offspring to provide old-age security or through the timeworn sense of needing a son to hold one's head up in the community, daughters were once again made to suffer.

Whenever the pressures of the government's edict to have just one child (or even two) met the pressures of the husband's family to produce that coveted son, desperate women were forced into desperate acts. With pregnancies so closely scrutinized, the only chance to have a son often depended on hiding—or giving up—a daughter. Untold numbers of Chinese mothers, particularly rural women, who gave birth to girls faced an excruciating decision: Keep the daughter and lose the chance to have a son or sacrifice her and try again.

China's daughters—hundreds of thousands of them, maybe more—struggling already for their place in a biased culture, were forced from their families. Many wound up on the side of the road. Those who were found ended up in state care.

Even a mother or a family who wanted desperately to keep a daughter could be caught in the squeeze. One account involved a couple who had a first baby, a girl, and wanted to have another child.[17] Because they lived in an area where one child was the limit, the only way to gain permission for another pregnancy was to erase the girl from the records. So, they told the government officials that the baby had died. The officials said, "Show us the body." The parents said they couldn't do that; they'd buried the child. The officials said, "Show us the grave." Ultimately, the resourceful parents gathered up some bones that appeared to be human to "prove" their story and satisfy the officials.

But now the daughter's fate was sealed. The parents would have to either hide her forever or find someone else who could take her in, which has happened through the ages in China. They said they'd be willing to find some kindhearted people to adopt their daughter, but at the time the government had made that difficult for Chinese citizens, counting adopted children against the adopting couple's birth quota.

I heard the first part of this family's story, but I never heard the end. The little girl may have been kept hidden, thus slipping into oblivion, listed as deceased and unable to attend school or get medical care. Or the desperate parents eventually may have done what so many others had done—left the little girl where they hoped she'd be found and taken to an orphanage.

While reports of forced abortions circulated widely, one of the least noted results of China's policy was this increase in the abandonment of babies. Although there was a clear correlation between the policy and the tiny human fallout—a new crackdown on family size in a certain district was almost predictably followed by a new flood of abandoned baby girls in that area— the Chinese government tried to avoid political embarrassment by ignoring the subject, even going so far as to direct orphanage officials to keep the numbers under wraps.

There were attempts to reverse the trend and raise the status of girls within China—poster campaigns praising the virtues of girls, for instance, but the old traditions had strong roots. Increasingly, as pressures mounted, more and more healthy baby girls turned up alone—wailing in doorways, tucked under park benches.

The government's coercive measures simply added new weight to the existing bias in favor of boys. While forced abortions affected unborn male and female children alike, the perils for living children fell on the girls. According to Betsy Hartmann, author of *Reproductive Rights and Wrongs,* by the early 1980s, the Chinese press carried a number of reports of parents drowning, suffocating, or abandoning their baby daughters so they would have another chance to try for a boy. The Anhui Women's Federation disclosed that in one village alone forty baby girls had been drowned in 1980 and 1981. And that village was hardly alone.

China Wakes coauthor Sheryl WuDunn observed the effects of the population policy close up among her own distant kin in

China. One relative and his wife hid for several months when she was pregnant with a third child, moving from village to village. She gave birth to the son they had always wanted. But what would have happened, WuDunn wondered, if that third child had been a girl? "Would they have accepted fate and returned to their village with their infant daughter to accept the fines and sterilization?" she wrote. "Or would they, in their torment, have told the midwife to plunge their baby daughter into a bucket of water?"

In the difficult years following the government's edict, untold numbers of desperate parents resorted to the age-old solution: infanticide. Reportedly on the decline after the Communists came to power, infanticide now again played a part in the fate of newborn daughters. So a new enemy, ultrasound technology, which allowed families to learn the sex of an unborn child and choose to abort the females. According to Human Rights in China, both female infanticide and sex-selective abortions—as well as the concealment and abandonment of living daughters—represented a desperate response by peasants to the harsh birth control measures.

China manufactured its first ultrasound machines in 1979, and produced some ten thousand of them in the next decade. Initially pressed into service to check whether women were retaining their government-required metal IUDs, these machines soon found a more popular purpose. According to one report in the 1990s, 97.5 percent of all aborted fetuses in China were female.[18] Although in 1991 it was made illegal for doctors to use ultrasound to reveal the gender of unborn children, according to numerous reports, the practice has continued in China and elsewhere in Asia, with both doctors and hospitals selling the service to those who can afford it.

If wealthy people could pay for an ultrasound test or afford the penalty for an extra child, poorer rural people had neither option and resorted to abandonment and infanticide. There are reports that the Communist Party soon became alarmed at the widespread resurgence of female infanticide in the countryside, and local population control officials were told to try to educate the peasantry out of the ancient prejudices against daughters. But the root cause of the new troubles for girls—the one-child policy—was handily ignored.

Margery Wolf, in her book *Revolution Postponed: Women in Contemporary China,* summed up the suffering of China's rural people: "The decision of young parents to kill their baby cannot be easy. Indeed, it may not even be theirs, but rather made for them by a senior generation for whom it may well be equally hard. The couple, together with their sorrowing parents, see before them a life of increasing poverty, for they have no sons to help them in the fields and no one to provide for them in their old age."

Faced with the resistance of rural people, in particular, to the single-child restriction, the government loosened its grip in 1988, coming up with what's been called the "one-son or two-child" policy. This allowed families in one-child areas whose first child was a daughter to have another child—with the built-in understanding that they were getting a second chance to produce a son. In that way, the revision gave a nod of official approval to the age-old bias: Families with girls deserved another chance to have a son because sons were so important. Oddly, too, the relaxed rules worked against the policy's goals—encouraging some families to keep having children until they produced a son.

The more lenient rules probably meant that more firstborn

daughters got to stay in their families, but the situation soon produced a new group of casualties—second-born girls. After the birth of a second child, parents faced the prospect of sterilization. If they gave birth to two daughters and they still wanted a son, the only way around the rules was to hide the second daughter or get her into someone else's hands. China's orphanages soon found themselves with new mouths to feed.

The Chinese authorities intentionally made it difficult for families to violate the population policies by simply fostering children out to friends or family to avoid fines or punishment for having had extra children. Until the spring of 1999, when that portion of the law was changed, Chinese families who took in abandoned children were penalized the same way they'd be penalized for giving birth to an extra child without permission.[19] Otherwise, the government feared, families would just find a way around the one-child policy by finding temporary or permanent homes for extra children. But that logic resulted in another, perhaps unforeseen, early effect of the one-child policy: In large part, it meant that abandoned children who wound up in orphanages or on someone's doorstep couldn't be adopted by Chinese families. In 1999 those rules were changed, and Chinese adoptions have increased in the years since.

Throughout history in China, there had been informal routes of adoption, even though there might also be some reluctance to adopt children from outside the family lines.[20] Families who lacked sons of their own were often able to adopt the sons of relatives and neighbors who had too many children to care for. Couples unable to have a child might just find one at their door or be handed a baby someone else had found.

A fairly typical account of such an event appears in *Golden Lilies*, written in the early 1900s: "[Kwei-li's] cherished baby boy . . . didn't live long enough for his father to see or hold him. Her faith shattered, Kwei-li fell into despair. Her anxious family found an abandoned baby girl on a nearby towpath, and placed her in Kwei-li's arms. Of this she tells us: '. . . I sat stiff and still, and tried to push away the little body pressing close against me; but at the touch of baby mouth and fingers, springs that were dead seemed stirring in my heart again.'"[21]

But in contemporary China, the officials were watching. Families feared reprisals if they took in a child. Chinese citizens were allowed to adopt "genuine orphans" where it could be documented that the parents had died, but the 1992 Adoption Law officially relegated nondisabled abandoned infants to the status of unadoptable children within China—until the law was changed in 1999. At least one observer has contended that many more Chinese in China adopt girls than is generally believed—though it's not much talked about—and if the Chinese government loosened the law to allow couples with a boy to adopt an abandoned girl, it might relieve some of the pressure on the orphanages.

It's one of the hard facts of contemporary life, then, that the blessed and happy event Mark and I experienced on a fall day in 1997 was shadowed by reports of what had gone on—and was still going on—for the girls and women of China. When we journeyed to Jiangmen, seventeen years had passed since the authorities had announced that the government of China was going to meddle in women's reproductive lives far more than their mothers-in-law had ever thought of doing. The population policy had been in effect for nearly two decades and the nation's orphanages were struggling to care for the casualties.

Worse, the girls who were found and taken to institutions were just the tip of the iceberg. Millions more were simply unaccounted for.

When demographers look at the population of a given area, certain patterns tend to hold true. In a natural ratio, boys at birth outnumber girls by about 105 to 100, an imbalance that ultimately corrects itself because girls have better survival rates than boys. But in China, the natural order of things has been badly skewed. Millions of girls who would be expected to be in the population today are missing—so many lost that China is experiencing a "gender gap." By 1992, a survey sponsored by the Chinese government showed that more than 12 percent of the baby girls who should be growing up in that country were simply not there, a percentage that translated to 1.7 million lost girls each year.[22]

In 1996 there were thirty-six million more males than females in China. The population was already so out of balance that demographers reported in the 1990s that five of China's thirty provinces had 120 boys for every 100 girls. By 1998, according to research by the Chinese Academy of Social Sciences, the overall ratio of boys to girls had climbed to 120 boys per 100 girls.

It is not only the girls of this generation who are missing today. By broad estimates, thirty million females in China—a number equivalent to the entire population of Mexico City, say, or a full 5 percent of China's population—are missing. Gone. (China, by the way, is not alone in this phenomenon. India's statistics also reflect a vast number of missing females, and worldwide, according to Betsy Hartmann, more than one hundred million females who should, by normal expectation, be alive and well on the planet are missing.) By 2008, China's gender gap was wider than ever, with a surplus of some forty million males.

Where are the lost women of China? "Some were killed at birth in the 1930s and '40s and so are not present as elderly women today," writes Sheryl WuDunn. "Some died as girls because they were not given adequate food, clothing, and health care. Some died in the 1958–1961 famine because their parents saved the rice for the brothers."

Others, the victims of ultrasound, and subsequent gender-specific abortion, were conceived but never born. Some were born but didn't make it past infancy, and others may have just eluded official recognition. China has a huge floating population, unconnected to the registries of any particular area, and unknown numbers of girls may be hidden within this group. If this transient population now numbers as many as one hundred million people, as some experts claim, that may mean that millions of unregistered children may have been born to those people in flux.

Whatever the mix of explanations, an enormous number of little girls has disappeared, largely to the world's indifference. As *New York Times* writer Bob Herbert declared: "There has never been the kind of international outcry that there should be over the girls who are missing from the population of China. The world has largely closed its eyes to this immense tragedy."[23]

Strict population measures, according to the Chinese government, have worked—the birth rate has slowed dramatically—but at what price? "In its grave demographic distortion of the Chinese population and in the pain it produces, this policy appears as a monumental form of national self-mutilation," writes University of Washington anthropologist Ann Anagnost.[24] Ironically, of course, many observers from other nations con-

tinue to praise the policy, taking for granted China's need to reduce its rate of population growth, while ignoring the human
suffering involved.

Within China itself, despite individual resistance to the dic-
tates of the policy, or the way it's been enforced, there's actually
been widespread acceptance among the people that the policies
are necessary. Says Anagnost, "At the height of the student
movement in 1989, when students and intellectuals all over
China were demonstrating in support of expanded political
rights, the issue of reproductive rights was never once mentioned." In fact, the demonstrators conceded that the threat
posed by a rising birth rate was something the national government had every right to address.

Says American anthropologist Susan Greenhalgh, who has
conducted research on Chinese population policy since the
mid-1980s, "It's hard to find anybody who openly criticizes the
policy, although these days there is a lot of ferment in the air.
I have not heard anyone, including feminists, criticize the policy on this particular ground. 'The treatment of infant girls is
really regrettable,' they say, 'but we need this policy for national development, we need it to enhance the wealth and
power of the nation.'

"This is very troubling to me as a Western feminist,"
Greenhalgh continues. "It would be bad enough if equal numbers of boys and girls were being abandoned, but the gender
skewing . . ." Her voice trails off. "You have to understand, on
life-and-death matters, this is not a good time to be female
in China."

Others note that the enforcement of China's birth policy has
resulted in a kind of rural-urban schism. Although the problem
of abandoned children and infanticide is widely known in the

cities, urban people tend to blame the problems on "backward" rural people, and few attribute the human cost to the Communist Party's family rules. In fact, says China scholar Eileen Otis, "If it weren't for the broad support of the policy among the urban population, who accept it as the prerequisite for the country's economic development and their own upward mobility, the policy would not be feasible."

By 1991, single-child families had become standard enough in urban China that an American family traveling with two children was a double curiosity. "The moment we stepped off the plane in Shanghai," wrote Ann Anagnost, "we sensed a reaction to the mere plurality of our children that was almost palpable. As we walked the crowded streets, the street vendors, mostly elderly women, would tap out a tattoo with their wooden clappers to the accompaniment of '*You liangge yo-o-o*' (There are two of them!)."

The overall picture to date was a curious, contradictory one, varying from province to province, from city to village. In the broadest sense, it seemed that China's emphasis on economic development combined with the government's surveillance has persuaded urban people that limiting their families was worth it. Peasants, on the other hand, depending on the relative stringency of the enforcement in their area, either had gone about their business much as they always had, or had been forced into a brutal corner if that first (or second or third) child turned out to be female.

On paper, China's females are protected as never before. The Law on Protection of Rights and Interests of Women, which went into effect in 1992, makes clear that "drowning, abandoning or cruel infanticide in any manner of female babies shall be prohibited; discrimination against or maltreatment of women who gave birth to female babies . . . shall be prohibited." Various other laws give men and women equal rights to inherit family property; others forbid domestic abuse and grant women access to divorce and the right to humane treatment in general.

But in practice, China's women, who make up one-quarter of the women in the world, are still caught in age-old restraints. And quite apart from the one-child policy, a woman who makes it through the reproductive minefield, gives birth, and manages to hang on to her child, can encounter other hazards. Working conditions alone can make things difficult for a mother. If she's lucky enough to have a job and keep it after having a child, she can wind up on the night shift or working under horrific conditions with little protection and low pay. In some foreign joint ventures, workplace conditions are among the worst for women, since cheap female labor remains one of China's main attractions for international capital. The work week can be grueling—twelve-hour days, seven-day weeks. Workers' safety is not a high priority in much of China, and accidents—explosions, fires, building collapses—abound.[25] In southern China's boomtowns, most of the victims of such calamities are women in their mid-teens to mid-twenties who have come from the farmland to work in the cities.[26]

When we came home with Kelly, unemployment in China, according to government reports, was running at the highest rate since 1949.[27] Millions of state workers were being phased out at a fraction of their normal salaries. The notion of the "iron ricebowl"—long-term job security—was being dashed, even for men. And overall, China's unemployment woes have hit women hardest of all. This only adds to China's huge population of the dispossessed, the tens of millions of rural people who seek work in the cities. People with nothing cannot care for their children.

So much is changing so quickly in China these days that there are all sorts of new troubles—increasing premarital sex, babies born out of wedlock, babies born to girls who are themselves no more than children. Women on the run may go through pregnancy and birth with no medical care at all.

And then there's what Chinese journalists refer to as the "dark side." In recent years, reports have surfaced of rings of thugs who prey on young women. One well-publicized case involved a twenty-year-old woman abducted and sold to a fifty-year-old peasant man who cut the tendons of her feet so she couldn't escape. Another woman, mentally retarded, was traded to a farmer in exchange for a calf. Under the farmer's brutal treatment, the woman died within a few months.[28]

Most cases involve rural women sold to rural men: women carried off, forced into bondage, repeatedly raped and otherwise abused; women who never recover from the injuries, both mental and physical, suffered at the hands of abductors. Many of the victims have been young women desperate to better their condition, who fall for promises of jobs or money. Even schoolgirls have been abducted and forced into prostitution.

The Chinese government has acknowledged the problem of abduction and sale of women—another old evil undergoing a modern resurgence—uncovering fifty thousand cases involving the sale of women and girls in the early 1990s. But observers say that regulations outlawing the practices haven't been effectively enforced, and the trade in women continues. Paradoxically, one reason mentioned for the trafficking is the shortage of women in China, combined with the family pressures on men to marry and carry on the family line. Some men who have failed to find a wife by traditional means have resorted to buying or abducting one. Imagine, then, if a woman under such conditions were to give birth to a daughter. How many lost infants might lie in the shadow of these kinds of horror stories alone?

I thought of the mysterious woman with the red-and-white bundle that night in Guangzhou. Whether that was a baby she held in her arms or not, whatever had brought her to that point of desperation in a hotel parking lot meant that she, too, was a lost daughter of China.

5

The Taming Power of the Small

A smiling golden buddha
In a golden temple stands,
With a tiny golden baby
In his gentle golden hands.

—*From* Chinese Mother Goose
Rhymes[1]

Kelly Xiao Yu and I spent our first full afternoon together at the hotel, rolling around on the bed, making friends. She climbed me like a mountain, crawling up and over, grabbing handfuls of my clothes to boost herself. Then she'd fall off the other side, giggling, and start over. We laughed and played with each other's fingers and noses. We were getting to know each other on some primal level. She poked a curious finger at my eyes, and rolled hers to the ceiling when she laughed.

When I hugged her, she felt full and warm—and necessary—in my arms, as if she were settling into a dent in my chest that I hadn't realized was so cavernous. Babies are made for this, I know, thanks to some evolutionary scheme that opens mysterious places in us into which only babies can fit. We looked into each other's eyes and I covered her with kisses. It was a transcendent couple of hours, fixed in my memory now, both physical and mental.

She was everything Mark and I could want and more—affectionate and easy-tempered, with a full-out zest for life. For the first few days as we walked around Guangzhou, Kelly riding along in her backpack, she kept pointing at the sights—a bird, a tree, motorcycles by the dozens—gasping, waving high an index finger and shouting, "Da!" She'd lived on the ninth floor of the orphanage, one of the caretakers had said. I had no idea if she'd ever been out of doors. She seemed dazzled and delighted by the world. Yet I wondered where in that small mind and body there might be some sadness, some sense of loss.

We were now an East-West tour group. The babies settled into their armchair cribs, smiled and chortled, broke out in rashes, cried their hearts out, tried out Snuglis and strollers and backpacks, ate with amazing gusto, and seemed generally happy to be along for the ride. There followed another ten days of touring, paperwork, and getting to know one another. We grew close as a group, swapping tips and diaper cream, watching the babies and parents learn each other's ways. We still had to apply for American visas for our children, which involved a visit to the Chinese medical clinic, where the babies would have checkups and inoculations, an interview at the U.S. Consulate, and a wait until the U.S. visas were issued.

Within just a few days, we couldn't recall what life had been like before Kelly, so perfectly did she fit into our hearts and our days. We weren't alone in these feelings. It was amazing how comfortable the new parents and new children looked with one another—as if they had just been waiting to jump into one another's lives and were now at home. Each time we met with the rest of the group for the day's excursion, the babies seemed to open up more, smile more readily, relax. We did, too. The whole group was an amazingly cohesive one. Perhaps something about the hard-fought quest had helped draw us together. We seemed to all share a feeling of immense gratitude, relief, and shocked joy.

We ate nearly every meal together as a group, maneuvering our chopsticks over the bobbing heads of our infants. Dish after dish of tofu, bitter melon, shiny black mushrooms, noodles, and rice spun around on lazy Susans in the middle of huge round tables. We wandered the markets. We visited the memorial to Dr. Sun Yat-Sen and a statue of the "founding goats" of Guangzhou, and played with the schoolchildren in a local park, all in blue-and-white uniforms, the best students wearing red scarves.

People on the street smiled at us with our Chinese babies and many were quick to come up and play with the children—and if the babies' legs were bare, to wave a good-natured finger, scolding us for underdressing them. A woman from Jiangmen later told me, though, that the local people sometimes had suspicions about people like us who took away Chinese babies. "They thought maybe the foreigners were making money from these girls," she said.

Our leader, Max, guided everyone through the next week with uncanny, perfectly orchestrated grace. Speaking softly, carrying a big sheaf of papers, he seemed to be everywhere at once, suddenly disappearing, then reappearing, smoothing the way with Chinese officials, the U.S. Consulate, the hotel, the bus drivers, waiters. When he passed us in the lobby, he stopped and smiled at Kelly and reached out to play with her finger. "How is she?" he asked. "She's wonderful," we chorused. "We love her." "Good, good," said Max, laying a hand on my shoulder, giving Mark a thumbs-up sign.

I don't think any of us had a clue about the behind-the-scenes negotiating that went on, as we were led by the hand through an unknown bureaucratic labyrinth. Max's assistant, Jeffrey, took us shopping and sang Chinese lullabies to us on the bus. A sweet, lilting song called "The Little Swallow" was his favorite. Two extraordinarily capable and sensitive young Chinese women, Mary and Anna, appeared magically at our elbows whenever anyone was struggling with a stroller or otherwise needed a hand. Kelly's small companions all had new Western names now—Lily, Amy, Hannah, Tiffany—although a number of parents had kept the girls' Chinese names as middle names.

For the first few days, we awoke not quite believing there was a baby there beside us, but soon the knowledge gradually sank into our sleeping and our waking. There she was each dawn, lying in her armchair crib. She woke smiling, looking at us in some expectation, it seemed. Now what? She padded around the hotel room, dragging things from suitcases. She howled while we fumbled about with powdered formula and thermoses. We kept saying *Xiao Yu* to her—trying out as many tonal combinations as we could (undoubtedly all of them wrong), but she didn't seem to recognize her name. The one Cantonese word she seemed able to say was *Aii-ya!*—that all-purpose exclamation (for surprise, alarm, or incredulity). Every day we fell more deeply in love. I was amazed at how our baby seemed to take to us, apparently eager for whatever adventures were in store.

Kelly seemed to have no developmental delays we could see. She could walk and hold her bottle by herself and was soon trying to unzip our suitcases. Somewhere along the way, she had apparently learned to bray like a donkey, as had several of the other little girls. As we walked through the streets, she'd periodically begin to hee-haw. It was a long time afterward that a Chinese friend set us straight. She laughed and said it sounded to her as if Kelly were chanting "*Ni hao, ni hao*"—the Chinese greeting.

Trucking around with brand-new babies was a Zen-like challenge. I was living in the present moment as never before, thanks to the steepness of the learning curve. Up and down the hotel elevators we rode, crowding in with visiting businessmen, dropping cookie crumbs while they gave us odd looks and puffed on their cigarettes. At night, while we tried to rock our baby to sleep, the businessmen gathered down the hall, laughing, drinking, and smoking. When Kelly cried, Mark and I lay in the dark, singing "Home on the Range" and "Red River Valley" to her.

By day, as we wandered around Guangzhou, it was hard to get a sense of the undercurrents of terror and turmoil I had read and heard about; stories of the young, hopeful women who came looking for jobs as secretaries or interpreters and wound up working as prostitutes. The people in the adoption bureaucracy, the throngs on the sidewalks, seemed busy, optimistic, and good-humored. Though there were accounts of considerable desperation on these same streets, we remained insulated.

One night we took a river cruise and one member of Max's staff brought his wife and children—a nine-year-old girl and a toddler-aged boy. He told us that, as a member of one of Guangdong's numerous ethnic minorities, he was allowed two children. China has been generally lenient in enforcing population control among its minorities—more than ninety million people altogether, whose birthrate as a result was far higher than that of the majority Han Chinese. While we motored down the Pearl River, neon lighting the buildings on shore, his beautiful little daughter, whom he clearly adored, turned cartwheels on the deck.

The next day we made an unscheduled stop at the local Hard Rock Cafe, and took a group excursion to the popular open area in Guangzhou, the new White Cloud Park, an immaculately kept area on the edge of town with pools and fountains, a huge modern greenhouse, flower gardens, expanses of neatly clipped grass, and some inexplicable touches—rocks incised with pictographs, a stand of Roman columns, and a few Northwest Indian totem poles. This pristine open space was a rare reward for penned-in city workers, a luxury that didn't exist a decade ago.

On weekends, we'd heard, the park was crowded, but we were there on a weekday and it was quiet and empty. A few young couples strolled together, the girls wearing the latest platform shoes, the boys in athletic togs. All of this came with all too familiar background music—an endless stream of American show tunes piped through some invisible speaker system. "America" from *West Side Story*; Engelbert Humperdinck. Kelly fell asleep to the theme from *Cats*. "How many miles have we come," asked Mark, "to be tortured by Andrew Lloyd Webber?"

And then one day, passing through a huge gate on a quiet side street, we entered the Liu Rong Si, the Temple of the Six Banyan Trees, and walked into old-time China. In a quiet courtyard under drooping trees, tourists mingled with brown-robed monks, and visitors tossed coins for luck into a miniature pagoda tower.

We crowded quietly into the old temple with its red doors and glazed-tile roof. Today our babies were to be blessed in a Buddhist ceremony. Holding our daughters, we knelt in front of three immense golden Buddhas. The massive statues weighed ten tons each and reached twenty feet into the air, dwarfing the little Buddhas in our arms. As two monks raised sticks of incense above their heads, smoke swirled in the temple's dusky light, and the monks began to chant. Jeffrey was at the altar, bowing and placing sticks of incense in a bowl.

Afterward I asked him what the blessing meant. "May disaster never touch these children," he said softly. "May they always be happy and no harm come to them." Our daughters received another special prayer for longevity, since banyan trees are believed to impart long life. I hoped the thoughts rubbed off on us, too.

The old temple was rich with history and significance, having survived not just the wear and tear of fourteen centuries, but the Cultural Revolution as well. An early visitor to the temple was Bodhidarma, the Indian monk and founder of the Zen sect, who once stayed overnight, lending such a spiritual presence, it is said, that all the mosquitoes in the temple buzzed away and never came back. Today the old temple is home to the Guangzhou Buddhist Association, part of the resurgence of religious observation in China.

A smaller temple on the grounds contained an altar and a familiar image—a statue of Guan Yin, the Goddess of Mercy. In old China, women were always anxious to touch an image of the goddess, in hopes of giving birth to sons. But the deity known as the Giver of Children is also known as a protector of women. Her name means, literally, "she who looks down and hears the cries of the world." In the classic Chinese book *Golden Lilies*, Kwei-li wrote poignantly of Guan Yin's place in the Chinese woman's heart: "We went from Yuan's palace to the temple of Kwan-yin, which I often visited as a child. It also was a ruin, but it spoke to me of the dead thousands of weary feet that had climbed the steps leading to its shrines; of the buried mothers who touched the floor before its altars with reverent heads and asked blessings on their children's lives; of their children, taught to murmur prayers to the Mother of All Mercies, who held close within her loving heart the sorrows, hopes, and fears of woman's world."[2]

It seemed fitting as I held my Chinese daughter in front of the shrine to the Goddess of Mercy that we devote one stick of incense and a prayer to all the lost girls everywhere—and to all the women in the shadows. If China was full of lost daughters, I knew by now, it was also full of lost mothers.

It was only there in the temple that I got a powerful feel for the old China I'd read about. Cloistered in a garden away from the traffic, with monks walking quietly beneath the trees, it seemed almost possible that the kind of life described by Bada Shanren, a seventeenth-century painter known as "the master of the lotus garden," could have thrived, the China of artists and scholars. This is how he spent his days:

I have a clean table under a bright window. My book closed, I burn some incense. When I feel that I understand something, I am happy and smile to myself. The guest arrives, but we do not stand on for- mality. I brew cups of bitter tea, and together we enjoy some won- derful literature. After a long while, the rays of the setting sun

*light up the room, and I can see the moon rising above the pillars of
my hall. The guest departs, crossing the brook in front of my house.
I then call my boy servant to close the door and put down my rush
cushion. I sit there quietly for a while, feeling carefree and content,
my mind carried away.*[3]

Once we were outside the temple and back in the din and the
bustle, Bada Shanren's vision seemed the rarefied and vanishing
memory that it was.

On Halloween night, we were still in Guangzhou, and as if
things weren't culturally confusing enough, some of the new babies were now sporting costumes. A three-month-old was done
up as a tiny cow, the returning two-and-a-half-year-old was
dressed as an angel, and a troupe of parents and children were
trick-or-treating through the hotel hallways. We passed out
Snickers bars, bought at the hotel sundries shop.

A day later, on Shamian Island, where the intruding foreigners of the last century once staked their claim to commerce, the little girls of China went through some of their last
official business—having their snapshots taken, their little
bodies examined, and their paperwork inspected by U.S. con-
sular officers. Every child adopted from China, whether from
Sichuan in the west, or Fujian in the south, or Shaanxi in the
north, must exit through Guangzhou. In that capacity,
Shamian Island is a kind of way station for underage immigrants. In the month before our visit, 447 little girls were
granted visas—the highest monthly total to date for adoptions
from China.[4]

On visa applications, we filled in what we knew about our
daughters. When we came to the box on the form that asked
about "complexion," we were advised to write "fair." Not so

very long ago, we were told, the United States required Chinese people to write the word "yellow" in that space.

The girls' visa photos were taken in a cramped hole-in-the-wall studio. At a medical clinic, heights and weights were recorded, and the babies examined in production-line fashion, moving from cubicle to cubicle. The point of all this wasn't to check on the baby's health for the baby's sake, but to assure the U.S. government that the children coming to America had no notable, unexpected abnormalities and wouldn't be bringing any contagious diseases into their new country.

The inoculation room, the last stop, echoed with pint-sized pandemonium. Amid piercing screams from the small victims we tried to sort out what shots Kelly was supposed to have and why, and we expressed our concern—our worries duly translated to the Chinese medical staff—about whether three inoculations all at once might not be too much for her. We were told, in translation, that she had to have the shots, period, or else no visa. This, too, was a ruling not by the Chinese medical staff but by our own government (which has since modified the requirements). And so we wrestled a small leg free and held our heaving, screaming child while the shots were given.

After the shots, we fled the clinic and the other babies' screams to stroll outside by the Pearl River, which flows around Shamian Island. The cobblestone riverbank was shady and restful, isolated from the bustle of Guangzhou. Connected only by bridges, Shamian was just a sandbar when the European traders first came. Following the Chinese defeat in the conflict known as the Opium Wars, China conceded the island to the British and the French.

Now, where foreigners once bargained and bullied, we strolled with our daughter in her backpack, her tears drying in the breeze. Under the leafy canopies of tall, stately trees, old colonial buildings had darkened with time. They now housed local offices, as well as residences, restaurants, and small shops. A sign in front of one building said, WELCOME FOREIGNERS TO OUR HOTEL ACCOMMODATION. An old French Catholic church remained, as did an Anglican church, courtesy of the British Empire. Rows of vintage bicycles were parked down the alleyways, and the shouts of schoolchildren filled the air.

The next morning we returned to Shamian Island for our very last bureaucratic stop, the U.S. Consulate, housed in a whitewashed concrete high-rise next to the luxurious five-star White Swan Hotel. We arrived with our baby and our usual clutter of papers, including three years' worth of tax returns, to be interviewed by a U.S. Consulate officer. One of the questions asked was whether the baby we had was the baby we thought we were getting. Kelly—still officially Jiang Xiao Yu—emerged from the proceedings with permission to enter the United States, her stoic-looking mug shot glued to a pink permanent "Resident Alien" card.

Pearl S. Buck, I learned later, had something to do with our successful passage here. Buck, who grew up in an American missionary family in China, was the author of dozens of novels set in China, including *The Good Earth* and *Pavilion of Women*. In 1949, deeply touched by the plight of homeless Asian children, the late author set up Welcome House, the first international interracial adoption agency in the United States, determined to find families for children of mixed race whom other agencies refused to help.

Buck founded the China Emergency Relief Committee, supported twelve orphaned children in China one year, battled the Chinese Exclusion Acts—which drastically curtailed Chinese

immigration into the United States between 1882 and 1943—
and spoke out against racism wherever she found it. When the
nation closed the door to Chinese immigrants, Buck observed,
"We send missionaries to China so the Chinese can get into
heaven, but we won't let them into our country." After China
was closed to foreigners in 1949, Buck's organization went on
to facilitate numerous adoptions from Korea and other parts of
Asia. Just a few years before our adoptive journey had begun,
the agency had started working with adoptions from China.

The fact that American parents now regularly fly to China
and other countries in Asia and return with a child can be
traced in part to Buck's battle against the barriers to transracial
adoption. She argued persuasively that race should not be a factor in finding homes for children. Buck herself was the mother
of eight, all but one adopted.

Buck's views on Chinese women, written nearly half a century ago, foreshadow some of the issues affecting the little girls
who pass through Shamian Island today. The late author's biographer, Peter Conn, writes: "A girl growing up in a relent-
lessly patriarchal household, Pearl was especially attentive to the
Chinese girls and women she met. She found that they, too,
were trapped in a sexual caste system throughout their entire
lives, a system even more punishing than the one she had seen
at home. She was puzzled at the embarrassment that accompanied the birth of girl children, and she grieved when she
learned about the practice of female infanticide. On more than
one occasion, she found an unmarked shallow grave in which the
nude body of a baby girl had been buried."

One of the Korean children adopted through Welcome
House is Conn's own daughter. "Among the success stories in
the Pearl S. Buck Foundation files," Conn writes, is the tale of

a "two-year-old orphan named Kim Kyung Nim—Jennifer Kyung Conn—who entered my life twenty years ago, malnourished and covered with sores. Jennifer came from an orphanage with a 50 percent mortality rate; the children either found a home or they died. Today, she is a graduate of Smith College, an accomplished cook and writer who works for a foundation in New York City that assists the homeless. I would never have known her except for that extraordinary woman, Pearl Buck, who brought us together."[5]

WELCOME, ADOPTION PARENTS, read the sign on a shop just a block away from the U.S. Consulate, the doorway hung with tiny pairs of silk pajamas. With that, any feeling of uniqueness we'd had as Americans carrying a Chinese child through the local streets suddenly vanished. With our new daughter in our arms and our purchases (a small silk jacket, a watercolor of an old Guangzhou neighborhood for her bedroom), we had become part of a crowd. Mark and Kelly and I were used to traveling en masse with our own group, but we now found ourselves bumping into other groups just like ourselves wherever we went— Americans with strollers, diaper bags, sacks of souvenirs, and Chinese baby girls.

After our visa appointments, we retreated with a few fellow travelers to the elegant White Swan Hotel for lunch. Many adopting parents stay at the hotel, a five-star establishment next to the U.S. Consulate that can boast of several heads of state who have slept there, as well as hundreds of newly adopted Chinese baby girls. The hotel sundries shop sells diapers; there's also a fancy children's wear shop. From the dining room, we had a sweeping view of the Pearl River with its dark barges motoring along. A lavish buffet offered foreigners all they could want and then some—from roast beef to Brie to crème caramel to Jell-O. In the ladies' room a Chinese attendant in a silk jacket held Kelly while I went into the stall. I came out to find Kelly bouncing on her hip, happily listening to a rush of Cantonese. "Mama," the woman said as I emerged. She gave Kelly a hug as she handed her back and waved away the tip I offered.

Mark and Kelly and I had other nonverbal moments of communication with local people, but I was hungry for more. In a park, one mother pointed at Kelly, then raised a single finger to ask how old she was, I assumed, and I nodded and held up my own finger. She pointed to her little boy, raised a single finger again, then brought him over to meet Kelly. The two stared at each other and kept their distance. I wanted less distance and wished I had enough grasp of Cantonese to ask this mother what her life was like, what was going on for the women and girls of China. But we just smiled at each other, and I was struck by how apart from it all we were on this trip, partly my own fault, of course, for speaking no more than a few words of Cantonese. We were visitors who peered through bus windows and wandered mutely. I had an uneasy sense of the unknown world we'd soon be leaving behind.

On our last night in China, we had a lavish Chinese dinner to end all previous dinners (spinning on the lazy Susans that night, ostrich meat!), plus karaoke singing, tears, and laughter. Jeffrey gave everybody a tape of Chinese lullabies as a good-bye present, and the beautiful Anna gave each baby girl a little pearl necklace. Could these children have been handed to us with any more love or good intentions? I think not.

Max sat down for just a moment at our table. As usual he seemed to be stopping briefly between tasks, rather than settling down for a meal, but I had time to ask him whether he'd get a break after our group left. "Not really," he said, with a weary smile. He stood up, never far from his briefcase, reached in and pulled out all the children's visas, assuring us that every one of the babies had permission to go home with us. As usual, he said he'd hold on to the paperwork until we were at the airport. He was still taking no chances with us. And then he was off, reminding us to keep track of our passports and to be ready to leave when the bus arrived the next afternoon. Jeffrey stood up with the karaoke microphone to wish us well, and Anna and Mary sang songs with tears in their eyes. The party broke up, and we wandered out into the Guangzhou night, leaving behind our usual wake of spilled tea, sticky rice, and flung chopsticks.

The next day, ten days after first holding our new daughter, having been cleared by all the necessary Chinese bureaus and the U.S. Consulate, Mark, Kelly, and I would be on our way home. In almost every way, we were more than ready, though by now, I realized, we seemed to be in the rhythm of China. We had figured out how to make formula with thermoses of hot water in the bathroom, had settled into a routine of breakfast, lunch, and dinner as a group of sixty, and our child seemed at home in her armchair crib. Another adoptive parent, Susan Lewis, who runs a busy Los Angeles advertising agency, later said she'd never been happier than she was in that hotel room in China with her new baby and nothing else—no job, no phone, no fax—to answer to.

That last evening Mark and I walked one final time past the Chinese Friendship Store—where we'd purchased plenty of souvenirs—and back along the hedge, from which the mysterious woman with the bundle had appeared more than a week earlier. No one popped from the shrubbery this time and everything that had happened in the past twelve days began to seem like a dream, until we looked down into the sleeping face of our daughter and were palpably reminded how our lives had been unalterably changed and blessed.

In the airport our group merged with several other groups, all American parents with Chinese baby girls, people from other agencies who'd been to different orphanages in other provinces. All were heading home with their daughters to cities across the country. As we moved down the line, Max stood at the gate, calm, smiling, standing behind the rail that separated those who were leaving and those who were staying. Anna was misty-eyed, gently saying good-bye to each baby and to each adult. A newly adopted girl of two or three was crying forlornly in her stroller, as if she somehow knew the magnitude of this farewell.

The line snaked along, and behind the barrier, Max waited until every last one of us had gone through a final checkpoint and walked toward the plane. As he raised his sheaf of papers at us to wave a final good-bye, I wanted to run back and hug him, but it was too late. I looked back and thought, I owe as much to this man as I've ever owed to anyone in my life. His achievement over the past few weeks alone would be enough for anyone for a lifetime. To place eighteen little girls in eighteen new homes. To watch the moment, not of birth but of something so close to it, to witness the most heartfelt coming together, each inexplicable moment of love and recognition. It would be enough for me—if I had the political savvy, bilingual skills, persistence, nerve, and grace to do it. I'd call all the little girls my nieces forever, and tack their photos all over my walls, and come to their birthday parties, and watch them grow up. I'd bask forever in this oddly made, extended family I'd helped create.

Now Max was about to go back to the hotel and his phone and his fax machine and prepare to do it all over again. Within a month, he'd have another group of anxious people arriving in China, clutching their passports and their hopes, and he'd walk them through two momentous weeks of baby-gathering. Sometimes, I'd heard, when he walked through the orphanages, he touched the babies on the heads and whispered to them, "Hey, you will have a home very soon."

Nothing is simple in China, but Max had guided us all safely and patiently through the maze. If God is in the details, so was Max. Uncle Max we have called him ever since, or often when we are feeling particularly grateful, Saint Max.

Looking very small in her airline seat, tiny Xiao Yu, born somewhere in the Pearl River Delta in 1996, was now named Kelly Xiao Yu and on her way to California, leaving her homeland far behind. She was traveling on a maroon People's Republic of China passport as a resident alien with a U.S. visa. We held her up to the window to look out at the sights, and as the engines started to roar, we told her to wave good-bye to China. Always eager to raise a hand, she did, waving and pressing her face against the window. She seemed content as the plane, filled with tiny Chinese girls, thrust its nose into the air and took off. This Great Chinese Baby-Gathering Expedition was over.

I felt a tremendous sadness to leave China and all that Kelly had known in her short life, and all that she'd have to leave unknown, possibly forever. A Trump Resorts T-shirt, a pair of yellow shoes, a story about a marketplace—we weren't taking much away that we could someday offer her by way of explanation or history. Yet I knew that somewhere in the landscape that was fast disappearing from sight I had a Chinese soul mate, a mother who had by her own unfathomably sad loss allowed me to realize an almost impossible dream. Where was she, and what was she thinking in that moment that her tiny daughter was being lifted high into the air and out of the land of her birth? My mind was swimming with unanswered questions. I didn't know when, or if, we'd ever be back.

It was only hours later, when we were on the final leg of the journey, heading from Hong Kong to San Francisco, that I allowed myself to breathe easily and let go of the gnawing fear I realized I had been carrying for ten days, the fear that someone could take this baby away.

Twenty hours after leaving Guangzhou, we passed through immigration in San Francisco, presenting Kelly's U.S. visa, while she wriggled around, eager to be unconfined after nearly a whole day of plane travel. Now, for some reason, she chose to entertain the INS official with her loud donkey-like greetings. He stamped her papers and gave us a wry smile. "Boy," he said. "You two are in for it."

Friends had stayed up late to greet our baby when we got to our front door, but we three were too bleary-eyed to say much more than hello. Whatever time zone applied to us at this hour and in this place, the clock had spun way beyond our mental, physical, and emotional limits. When I fell into bed, I saw a vision of a lazy Susan spinning round and round, laden with the ubiquitous dish of huge, shiny black mushrooms, whirring faster and faster, until the dish became airborne, sending flying mushrooms everywhere. In the shower the next morning, my ears still rang with a cacophony of crying babies and honking traffic.

Kelly woke up in San Francisco smiling. She hesitated for just a moment before she reached a hand toward Maddy, the little refugee from the dog pound, who was shivering with excitement and trying to lick her face. Annie the old husky was in her usual spot, lying on the back porch resting her bones, and we carried Kelly out to meet her. Then came a parade of friends. Our families came forth to welcome Kelly. My former mother-in-law called to say she wanted to be an honorary grandmother. Everybody was delighted to have a girl in the family at last; all the grandchildren on both sides—nine so far—were boys.

Wherever we went those first few days, Kelly looked at everything with a wide-eyed expression, pointing a tiny finger and saying, "Ohhh! Ohhhh! OHHHH!" When we first set her down on a patch of green grass, she was afraid to move. She stood stock-still, looking all around her feet at the strange stuff, lifting her arms to be carried out of it. Within a few days, she'd come to terms with lawns and was padding comfortably around the yard and house as if she'd always been here.

To me, for a while, it all seemed surreal. Even after a week, I was still in a state of disbelief when I looked down to see this mite in her OshKosh overalls and her orphanage burr haircut looking up at me. I was surprised, too, to feel an unexpected sense of loneliness, and realized I missed all the other parents and children who'd become our extended family for the past couple of weeks.

Whatever Kelly was going through, she couldn't tell us.

But I knew she was accustoming herself to a huge emotional change and a sensory transformation. Having heard nothing but Cantonese for her first year, she was now hearing English exclusively, and that coming from strange new voices in a strange new world. Some toddlers who'd been speaking words of Cantonese or Mandarin go silent once they are with their new parents. They have to regroup, psychologists say, get their bearings. They need time to listen to new patterns of language and begin speaking all over again. Kelly, though, seemed game to try new words. Some, like "Mama" and "Dada," I knew she'd already been encouraged to practice at the orphanage. Others, like the word "dog," which she mastered very quickly, and "Mah-Mah," an attempt at Maddy's name, came of her own volition.

Within a few weeks, Kelly was becoming adept at making her preferences known (cookies, milk, apple juice), and she was clearly transfixed with what she called "mooms"—motorcycles. She never missed one, whether it was parked or roaring by. She waved to all the drivers and occasionally a helmeted head nodded back. She pulled down a book of Mark's from a low shelf and pored over it. An *Encyclopedia of Motorcycles* had her about as quietly engaged as I had ever seen her. A few nights later, she insisted on taking to bed a booklet of old Harley-Davidson advertisements. Where this enthusiasm had come from, I couldn't say. I wondered whether she was one of the tiny riders on a motorcycle or scooter back in Jiangmen City. Maybe her parents had roared up to their house on one each night while she was still with her family. Maybe she just liked motorcycles because they are noisy.

Sometimes out of the blue now she'd pat my cheeks and say,

"Mama, Mama," and then give me a huge, openmouthed kiss, crinkling her eyes. One day when I was in a coffee shop and a stranger approached and started talking to her, she looked the man in the eye and began patting me and saying very emphatically, "Mama, Mama," as if she were making it clear that we were a pair, as if she were telling the world that she had a mother.

Yet every once in a while she awoke in the middle of the night and was for a time inconsolable. I know this happens commonly to small children, but knowing our daughter's particular history, we couldn't help but wonder if she was having a nightmare of having been left in the market, or if she was missing the routine of the orphanage, or one of her caregivers, or all the other children. When she first awoke in this state, she seemed in another world, bereft, her mouth wide open, her eyes scrunched shut, huge tears bathing her cheeks, wailing so hard her small body trembled. A sound to break your heart. We held her and talked to her, and after a while she calmed and looked around, still shaking, still gasping, but back with us. I wondered just what had happened to her when she was left, and if this is what she felt like before someone found her. It was almost impossible to imagine anyone letting her go. I became more and more sure that they must have held on to her until the very last minute.

At her first doctor's appointment, Kelly was pronounced in good health. When they drew blood for a test, it took two nurses to hold her down. She put every muscle into the battle, screamed more loudly than I would have thought a small child capable of. And the minute it was over, her face still red and wet, she was happily clapping her hands for the nurses.

She took to feeding Maddy, who's been "Mah-Mah" to all of us ever since, cookies under the dining room table. The two were a perfect match. Kelly was bigger, but Maddy was faster. The dog, who'd been so scared of strangers that she hid under the upstairs bed anytime guests came to our house, now mustered a kind of noble courage. When the first visitors walked into the living room to see the baby, Maddy crept down the stairs from her hiding place. Shaking slightly, she crossed the room and sat down beside Kelly on the rug and stayed there, eyes straight ahead, standing firm, as if she had just been waiting to take up her duties. Twelve quaking pounds of guard dog.

Kelly, in turn, was remarkably sweet to the dog, hugging her, softly cooing at her. These small beings seemed meant for each other. Both clearly knew what love was all about, as did our wonderful old husky, who waited just long enough for us to get home from China. Then, sixteen years old and weak as a kitten, Annie slipped out of our lives.

I often looked at my little daughter now and thanked the stars for whatever saved her—most likely the courage of her birth parents; certainly the fortune to land in a good orphanage, the blessings of a sturdy constitution, Max's intercession. I also wondered what survival instincts she might have quickly learned on her own behalf. When we put her to bed one night, she cried to be picked up, and then seemed to swallow her sobs. I thought she'd fallen asleep, but as I peeked into her room, I saw first one little hand come out from between the crib slats, then the other. Silently she pressed her hands together and began playing patty-cake. Did this melt someone else's heart as it melted mine that night? Did she succeed in attracting the attention of the orphanage caretakers when so many other little girls were vying for care? When she was hungry now she would stand beside me in the kitchen, howling and pointing to her open mouth. What happened to more sickly children, to the children who just gave up?

Our concerns soon became the common challenges of any parent of a toddler—how to childproof the house (and childproof it again; she learned so quickly), how to keep her engaged while we cooked dinner or tried to grocery shop. We were figuring things out moment by moment and building a life together. I'd never felt quite so happy or quite so tired or quite so aware of the responsibility I had to another human being. And I knew in my bones that waiting for Kelly Xiao Yu was the best thing I'd ever done in my life.

An old Chinese story describes how lovers are predestined to meet: An invisible red thread leads from one person to another, no matter how far apart the two may be. Maxine Hong Kingston writes of hearing the legend from her mother: "A red string around your ankle ties you to the person you'll marry. He's already been born, and he's on the other end of the string."[6]

Lately, the red thread idea has been taken up by the Chinese American adoption community, to include parents and children who are destined to be together—even though an ocean may lie between them initially. Some adoptive parents attribute the perfect fullness of the match to God or the Buddha or the Great Spirit or Guan Yin. Others give credit to the China Center of Adoption Affairs in Beijing.

"I feel as if the whole connection was there from the beginning," said Carole Sopp, who adopted a little girl in 1997.

"When I first heard about adoption in China, I knew without a doubt that's where I was going and that's where she was, whoever she was going to be and whatever she was going to look like.

"Interestingly enough, I started the process just about the time my daughter was conceived," she said, "and when I first chose to go to China I chose the name May, spelled in the Chinese way, Mei, and I thought that will be her middle name, no matter what her first name was. When the facilitator called me to say I had a child waiting, he said her middle name was Mei. Even he took a deep breath and said, 'Wow,' when I told him the name I had had in mind.

"Everything fit," said Sopp, a single mother who works as a school nurse in southern California. "I look at my daughter and see myself. We have the same hair color, the same eye color. I'm actually amazed with how alike we are in many ways—what things we like and what things we do and what things comfort us. She loves to lie in bed and be covered with a blanket like I do. She shakes her leg to fall asleep and so do I."

For many people who adopt, the reality of a child in their lives is, in and of itself, a miracle, a gift of grace after numerous miscarriages, perhaps, or failed infertility treatments, or, simply, after too much time gone by. But, as so many parents have told me, it's not just a child that's crucial, but *this* child. "I knew she was the one we were waiting for," said a father from Texas. "I pictured her long before I saw her," said a mother from Washington state.

Susan August-Brown, who adopted a little girl fifteen months old from south China and took her home to Maine, said, "She was my daughter from the moment I laid eyes on her. Her caretaker said, 'This baby knows who her mommy is.' It was true. It was magical. We had finally found each other and there was no doubt in either of us. We belonged to each other from this day forward. In my heart I believe from the moment she had been conceived, her little soul was on the journey into my life."

In trying to explain all this, I realize we enter some strange emotional territory, but it's ground shared by any number of adoptive parents I have heard from. Although people certainly exist who view the process with a matter-of-fact, perhaps even a cynical, eye, one after another adoptive parent I have talked with has echoed a consistent conviction: The child they were matched with was the perfect child for them. They knew it the moment they saw the tiny photograph; they knew it the first time they held the baby; they've known it every day of their lives together. "It sounds almost biblical," said a friend, listening to some of the accounts. He was thinking, he said, of baby Moses tucked in the rushes. Bonds were sealed, sometimes in minutes. "It defies reason," said a father in northern California, "but you do feel as if something is at work you don't quite understand."

On a sunny midwinter morning not long after our return from China, I was standing in the kitchen holding Kelly, when I was struck by one of those bolts of clear realization that seem to come out of nowhere. As I pressed her chest against mine, her soft cheek brushing my face, I suddenly, absolutely, knew that I could not love this child any more than I did right then. I loved her without condition, without reservation, forever. There was simply no room left in my heart to love her more.

I can't explain how or why this has happened, but I knew then, just as I have known every moment since, that I am holding nothing back, that there are no other circumstances of birth or fate that could make me love this child any more—not if I'd conceived her myself in some specific and memorable moment (accompanied by fireworks, stardust, or Mozart), not if I'd carried her in my body for nine months, not if I'd held her in my arms any sooner in her young life. No fact of genealogy or physiology or of actual fleshly attachment could add to my certainty that we were fated to be together, that we are completely, whatever the differences in our physical makeup or our ethnic or cultural origins, mother and daughter.

When I mentioned this to Mark, he said he felt the same way: overwhelmed by feelings of love, surprised by how deep the currents were, how quickly he'd been taken over by them. While we were waiting and trying to picture our future child, we wanted to get to China as quickly as possible, pick her up—whoever she was—and bring her home. But the minute we stood in that orphanage and looked into little Xiao Yu's sleepy eyes, I realized that everything had fallen into place perfectly. The memories of the long wait faded away; in fact we were glad for it. Had we traveled to China any sooner, or just a little bit later, we would have missed her. And, had we traveled a month earlier, I would have missed those last days with my father. Had we brought our daughter home earlier, before my father got sick, we might not have named her Kelly. Which of course was the name she was meant to have.

Why such feelings of perfection, emerging from what on the surface seems a rather bureaucratic shuffling of the cosmic deck?

"Who picks these babies, anyway?" asks a woman waiting to go to China. It's a good question. Most people who adopt from China can't walk into an orphanage, look through the cribs, and choose a child. I say "most" because as in everything else in that immense nation, there have been exceptions. Particularly among Americans working in China in the 1980s, there were cases where people visited orphanages and had some say in the selection of a child. And in the case of older children, adoptive parents have on occasion asked for a particular child whose picture may have been posted by an adoption agency.

For a while, a number of adoptive parents alluded to some hypothetical mystical matching room somewhere within the Chinese government adoption bureau in Beijing, the China Center of Adoption Affairs. Early in the process, I myself imagined such a place, where sensitive officials went through dossier after dossier from American parents, looking at the photographs of the applicants, noting certain traits and interests, and then turned to the list of available children, finding one who seemed just right.

In this scenario, I suppose, a professor of music might be matched with a toddler who artfully banged plates, or an athletic couple might be given a child who turned somersaults on the orphanage's straw mats. About the time Mark and I were leaving for China, a rumor went around that sometimes there was even a bit of mischief at work: Parents who'd been pains in the butt to deal with might just be paired up with an equally demanding child; whiny applicants might find themselves with an infant who more than matched their fussing.

According to more reliable accounts at the time, the process by which the Chinese bureaucracy matched a particular child to a foreign applicant was considerably less personal and quite variable—depending on province, orphanage, momentary circumstances, local whim, and the relative clout of various adoption agencies and liaison workers. Parents' hopes and children's futures were negotiated by a variety of people, including provincial officials, orphanage directors, and foreign adoption workers. Though there is a central Chinese government adoption ministry, most pairings were made at the local level, rather than in Beijing. Some foreign agency staff may have sufficient influence to occasionally handpick children, but most referrals were a combination of several factors, including how many children a particular orphanage had available at a particular moment.

That doesn't mean that the matches aren't perfect, or that some unknown hand wasn't at work. I'd seen at least two mothers and adopted daughters, as well as a father-daughter pair, who looked so much alike it was uncanny. Had the facilitator planned this? Had the local officials had a hand in matching the photographs of the parents to the photos of the babies? Was it blind chance?

When Tony Xing Tan, director of the China Adoption Research Program at the University of South Florida, had the opportunity to visit the legendary matching room, long after we'd adopted our daughters, some of the intentional matchmaking was confirmed. "The Chinese Center of Adoption Affairs' matching procedure involves scanning the children and parents' headshots and placing them side-by-side on the computer screen to see if they visually match," Tan reported. "I watched as a staff member tried to find, from a pool of eligible children, a child with curly hair to match the potential adoptive father's curly hair. She was very relieved when she finally found one with a full head of curly hair."

But this being the real world—and not an easy one for small, frail children—there were also times when the red thread seemed to fray. Mixed with all the miracles, there have been sad mix-ups and profound tragedies in the matching process, too. Some babies designated for adoption have died before their intended parents have gotten to China to pick them up. Older children have sobbed uncontrollably when first presented with their foreign parents. Occasionally, after parents have been referred one child, a healthier child has been substituted for an ailing one. Some parents have had to make an agonizing decision on the spot in China of whether to take on the responsibility of a child with health or adjustment problems more serious than they had expected. Some people have said yes and others have said no.

But whatever the bumps on the road, just about every Chinese adoption story I have heard seemed to have its own element of coincidence, sheer magic, or surprise.

Take Amy DeNucci's tale. An insurance agent who works with her father in Atlanta, DeNucci told me how she came to go to China: "I come from a family where my mother had my brother and me and then adopted four children," she said in a soft drawl. "So we pretty much realized that adoption was a natural way of adding members to your family. When I grew up, I always knew I would have an adopted child."

Unfortunately, of her adopted siblings, DeNucci noted, one had been diagnosed with fetal alcohol syndrome, one had suffered the effects of maternal deprivation, and the other two had had their birth mothers attempt to reclaim them. "Of the horror stories you hear about adoption," said DeNucci, "we had one of each in our family."

But eventually, when DeNucci and her husband, Daniel, were living with two young sons in a five-bedroom house, the time seemed ripe for another child, and she particularly wanted a daughter. Through a friend, DeNucci heard about the girls available in China and she sent off her paperwork. At the time DeNucci and her husband didn't fit the parameters, since applicants at the time had to be over thirty-five to adopt a healthy infant. "I was only thirty-one and my husband was thirty-four," she recalled, "but I said, 'I don't care. I want you to do it anyway, because I feel this is what I need to do.'"

DeNucci asked her mother, Jerilyn Burman, to travel to China with her. Burman agreed, and they were waiting for the paperwork to be finished when Valentine's Day brought a surprise. "My parents asked, 'How would you feel if we adopted a baby, too?'" said DeNucci. "They said, 'What a waste it would be to go to China and come back empty-handed.'

"My mother was fifty-four," said DeNucci. "She said the reason she was asking me was that we'd have to take care of the child if anything happened to her and my father." Mother and daughter left for China together in September 1996. DeNucci went to Zhanjiang in Guangdong province in the south of China, her mother went to Hangzhou in the north. DeNucci picked up a seven-month-old daughter whom she named Meredith. Her mother adopted a two-year-old girl who had a severe cleft palate and lip. Sarah, she named her. Meredith had been found on a street corner; Sarah in a shipyard.

Not long after the two women came home with their new children, they were visited by a pair of Chinese officials who were making a tour of adoptive families in the United States. "They wanted to find out why there was so much interest in adopting their children," DeNucci told me, "and they wanted to know how the children were doing.

"They wanted to know how I thought I had the right to apply when I wasn't the right age," DeNucci recalled. "I said I did it because all they could say was no, and if they said no, well then, at least I had asked. Then I asked them, which surprised them, I think, 'Look, you're the ones who gave me the baby. Why did *you* do it?' And they said, 'Well, if you asked, you must have really wanted her.'"

Since coming home to Atlanta, Sarah had undergone three major surgeries to repair her lip and palate, followed by intensive speech therapy, and was doing well. Her "niece" Meredith was also thriving. When I last spoke with DeNucci, she was taking care of both little girls because her mother was off to China again, this time to bring home a sister for Sarah and another "auntie" for Meredith—a two-and-a-half-year-old girl, whom they named Caitlin.

It is out of such desire, persistence, courage, and luck that the subculture of adopted daughters of China has grown, that the red thread has kept winding itself around one family after another.

Sometimes, in strange twists, the thread has tangled itself around a couple of families at once. When two baby girls from one orphanage were put into two waiting sets of arms, the parents, both single mothers, noticed that the two looked remarkably alike, enough alike to be twins. However, the girls had been found separately, each in a different place at a different time, so according to the intricacies of Chinese adoption protocol, they couldn't be classified as siblings—even if they were, in fact, related. So the families just spent time together while they were in China and kept in close touch once they were back in the United States.

Eventually, they decided to have their daughters' DNA tested, which proved the girls to be fraternal twins. Though the two began life in the United States in separate households—

Rachel living in southern California, her twin, Madison, living in the north—the two families soon chose to link destinies, joining each other for trips to Disneyland and family reunions. "The girls have a special relationship," said Madison's mother, Cheri Hutchins. "Madison gets together with other children who were adopted at the same time, but she and Rachel have a different relationship. They are more physical, holding hands, hugging. They stay very close." By the time the girls turned four, the southern California mother had moved north, closer to her daughter's twin. The result was one big, loving extended family, with the grandparents claiming not one granddaughter, but two. In years since, a number of other twins have been discovered, living in two different adoptive households.

In the end, of course, the matter of the red thread is not an issue to be settled one way or another. If you try to unravel the ties with logic, you may succeed. If you believe in the idea, you'll find more than enough evidence for its existence. Maybe the thread is woven partly from strands of destiny, partly from gratitude, partly from love. Maybe it's all a tribute to the openness of the human heart, both young and old. One thing I do believe: These are not ordinary pairings.

I remember a moment in the orphanage waiting room that fateful October day when I looked up from my sleeping child's face to see another new parent, a man in his forties, holding a baby girl, tears running down his cheeks. In that moment, I would have believed absolutely that a very long red thread had wound from that child's tiny Chinese foot in south China to this man's big Caucasian ankle in southern California and had pulled them inextricably together. I'd also wager that the thread would hold for a lifetime.

Kelly and Mark and I trail red threads from our ankles, too,

I am certain of that. The matches are perfect because love is perfect. I couldn't imagine a more wonderful child, a more perfect blessing. The mere fact that Kelly, who'd lost a mother, and I, who'd lost a child, had wound up together one fall day in China was a miracle in itself, and red thread enough for me.

At the farewell dinner in Guangzhou, after the ostrich-eating and the toasting and the karaoke singing, Jeffrey, one of our facilitators, took the microphone and turned serious. "We have a saying in China," he said. "We say that maybe these babies grew in the wrong stomachs, but now they have found the right parents."

6

Matters of Life and Death

To be an orphan,
To be fated to be an orphan,
How bitter is this lot!

> —*Anonymous Chinese poem*
> *from the first century* B.C.

On that last night in China, the families we traveled with lined up the eighteen babies we were about to take home, and attempted a group portrait. The adults quickly propped up the children on a restaurant sofa, then dashed out of the picture. The girls bobbed against one another and squirmed. They chortled, they cried. It was a wild few minutes, and in lots of shots, at least one child, or part of a child, is lost in a blur of motion. Too many babies to deal with at once.

As I look at that photo now, I have tried to imagine the unpictured, the ghost children, the children left behind. Five more full couches would equal another hundred babies or so; one hundred couches, two thousand babies. It's hard enough to stretch the imagination that far, envisioning all the faces. But hundreds of thousands of lost children? One million or more?

Flying home from China with my arms full, I had a bitter-sweet feeling. Mixed with the waves of gratitude about our own good fortune was a kind of undercurrent, a faint cry in the distance. It had to do, I realized, not just with lingering questions about the babies' lost mothers and fathers, but also with the vague knowledge of the other lost children. Numbers too big to grasp circled round our heads.

I have felt that sense of disquiet at other times, too—hearing an American surgeon talk about the children he has seen in Chinese orphanages who desperately need more medical help than the orphanages can provide; or when I have heard recitations of random statistics or vague guesses—about dormitories filled with babies, two and three to a crib; about untold numbers of older girls still waiting, about millions of children who are simply unaccounted for. I think of my daughter's nine-storied former home, and I wonder what sad or hopeful faces were—and are—behind those empty windows.

All it takes to bring the statistics to life is to look into the face of one small child. Then all the numbers come with faces—and they are not easy to look in the eye. Beginning with even the most conservative figures of girls in Chinese orphanages—the 160,000, say, cited by the Chinese government[1]—in a given year, each time a foreigner walks away holding a baby, dozens of others are left. Some, usually the very youngest, are adopted by families within China, others are left waiting, their futures unknown.

According to outside estimates, the number of children in Chinese institutions is undoubtedly far higher—perhaps ten times the official count, or more.[2] Human rights groups say there may be as many as a million children in some kind of institutional care. Moreover, the children who make it into those institutions are probably just a tiny fraction of those who are lost altogether.

Almost every mother or father I talked with on our trip to China and afterward said they would have carried one more child out of the orphanage and home in a minute, had they had the opportunity. Children in China are waiting for homes, willing parents are waiting for children, but a wall of bureaucracy lies between the two and the pipeline is narrow.

An adoptive mother who picked up her daughter in an orphanage outside Guangzhou said the memory of one little girl in that institution stayed with her. There were ten babies in the room, recalled Susan Lakari, and four were adopted by the group she traveled with. "There was a little six- or seven-month-old baby in one of the other cribs and she was the only other baby awake. She was very, very interested in all the commotion. My heart went out to her and I just wanted to scoop her up and take her, too. I even took her picture, which has served no purpose except to make me feel sad when I see it and to tell others looking at our photos, 'She was one not being taken that day.'"

Adoptive mother Jenny Bowen, who heads up a charitable initiative, Half the Sky Foundation, for orphanages, says she remembers best a little girl of three or four in one orphanage, who was wearing a little string bracelet on her wrist, telling everyone, "My mama gave me this. My mama gave me this." Over time, the strings had tightened and pressed into her wrist as the little girl had grown, but, says Bowen, "there was no way she was going to let anyone take that string bracelet off."

On the flight out of China in the seat in front of us was an American man from Philadelphia, with a new six-year-old daughter. She spoke only Mandarin, and he very little of that, but the two were communicating pretty well with a few words, gestures, and smiles. His wife, he told us, had stayed behind in China to go north to another orphanage where they had heard about a fourteen-year-old girl who had no nose. They were hoping to get permission to bring her home, too, for plastic surgery.

At Christmastime, we received a card from our daughter's orphanage. An illustration of Santa decorated the front. "Best wish for you," the card said, and included a handwritten note, signed by the staff, thanking us "for having the kind hearts to take care of a little child." They asked us to send a picture of Kelly in her new home: "How quickly the girls grow." Inside the card were photographs of the orphanage exterior, including several of a new playground with swings, a huge sandbox, and a spring-loaded Mickey Mouse ride. The playground was inviting, but there wasn't a child in sight, not a footprint in the sand. In the windows of the building no little faces were visible.

By any number of accounts, though, the little ones—and not-so-little ones—are there; if not in that orphanage, in another. Innumerable children are waiting and more still are arriving on the doorsteps every day. Some are children with disabilities, cleft palates, for instance, whom orphanage directors wish someone would help. Others suffer from heart problems or other life-threatening conditions, or the more easily correctable effects of malnutrition. There are older children, too, little girls of five, six, or seven, and up, still hoping for a family. Many adopting families, like my acquaintance on the plane trip out of Guangzhou, have sought out the neediest children, but many more children are waiting, including those with serious problems in areas where there is little prospect of help.

While some foreigners ask for older girls, most request infants or toddlers, leaving behind a population of older children. Chinese authorities can be reluctant to place older children, especially those over age ten, fearing that the adjustment to a new country and culture might be too much for them. (If children over age ten are placed, in some cases they themselves must agree to the adoption.) Most children who get to be that old will remain in the institution until they can be trained for jobs.

Some children who remain in orphanages become helpers for the caretakers as soon as they are potty-trained, says China-born writer Anchee Min.

> *They are treated like an eldest child in a family. They know their place and that their efforts are appreciated. They grow up emotionally handicapped and don't know it. They have no idea what affection means, because there are too many children and too few caretakers. It is a crazy household. The little ones will have marks on the tops of their heads—they will lay in the cradles all day without being picked up. They will kick and bounce themselves on the cradle bars screaming for attention. Older girls will learn not to question life and will accept things the way they are. The good part is that this ill-fate is shared by every girl they help carry through the doorway.*

Often the children left behind are mourned by the children who are adopted. One three-year-old spent her first months in the United States looking at the group photographs of all the kids still at the orphanage and trying to feed snacks to the children in the picture. Another adopted little girl of six kept asking about her best friend, adopted by another family in another part of the country. She wondered whether her friend was getting enough to eat.

A couple from New Orleans who adopted a nine-year-old girl in Yunnan province posted on the Internet a poignant story of watching their newly adopted daughter say good-bye to her best friend in the orphanage, a little girl who wasn't going anywhere that day. Both girls tried to hold their emotions in check. "One absolutely filled with sorrow and grief and the other filled with new hope, stealing looks at her new mom." That mother, Martha Osborne, who works with RainbowKids International, a nonprofit e-zine and foundation that works on behalf of children who remain in orphanages,[3] began a campaign to find a family for the little girl who stayed behind. She succeeded.

Whatever the numbers, behind the orphanage walls are many ten-year-olds and toddlers, teenagers and infants, children with disabilities both mild and severe. There are boys, too, many with mental or physical impairment. Overall, far too many children are waiting, all deserving of a home.

Anytime I contemplated such thoughts after we came home from China, I was filled anew with gratitude for my own little daughter of China. She is an exquisitely beautiful, sweet child, and I am still lost in the wonder of how we came to be together. Early on, she displayed a quirky sense of humor that was so like my father's. I know he would have loved her to pieces. As a baby, she quickly seemed completely at home with us, proving herself delirious about ice cream, Chinese shrimp-filled dumplings, baby goats in the petting zoo, and just about any kind of live dance or musical event. At a performance of Chinese folk dancing during a local lantern festival, she sat mesmerized in a folding chair, her small feet dangling in their saddle shoes, as she asked, "More? More?" when the music was over. She paid Joan Baez the same compliment when the singer appeared unannounced at a concert we attended in Berkeley. She casually referred to our carved soapstone statue of Buddha as "Boodie," continued to love motorcycles, and—until she got old enough to know better—assumed that all babies came from China. Whenever we walked outside at night she peered up at the sky, asking, "Where's my moooon?"

When I crept into Kelly's room to check on her before we went to bed, I'd look at her lying there, moonlight on her face, pigtails askew, Pooh bear clutched in her small hands, and I'd say a phrase I learned from my friend the China scholar. *"Yi nu ping an,"* I'd whisper. "One girl peaceful and safe."

If the number of children left behind lingered in people's thoughts, the conditions in Chinese orphanages was another topic of ongoing concern and speculation, especially in the early days of Chinese adoption. If no one had an exact count of the number of orphanages in China, much less a count of the children in them, it was equally difficult to get an overall picture of the facilities themselves.[4] Of the thousand or more state-run institutions, many remained inaccessible to outside observers. Some were tucked away where few foreigners went, although charities and adoption agencies soon began making contact with many needy places. In the early years of Chinese adoption, though, Chinese orphanages kept up their guard when it came to foreigners.

This wariness was thanks in part to the release of a documentary, *The Dying Rooms*—the horrifying coverage I saw while we were first waiting to go to China. First broadcast in London on the BBC, the documentary was seen later by American viewers on CBS during the 1996 Christmas season. In that film, the story of one little girl, Mei Ming, apparently ignored, emaciated, and suffering, shocked television viewers around the world. In the back room of an orphanage in Zhaoqing, just outside Guangzhou—the city through which all adopted Chinese children pass to get their visas to enter the United States—Mei Ming had, the documentary charged, been left to die. "It was the second time in her short life that she'd been abandoned," said one of the filmmakers. First by her parents, then by the orphanage. Four days after they left, according to the filmmakers, the little girl died.

The documentary charged that children who were disabled, too sick to care for, or somehow unappealing to adult caretakers were intentionally starved to death, denied food or water. According to the filmmakers, some of the orphanages in China were "little more than death camps." Watchdog groups and other journalists joined in the accusations.[5]

Although the documentary team also visited a privately run orphanage supported by charitable donations from within China, where the conditions were remarkably good, the weight of the footage focused on the downside. *The Dying Rooms* was awarded a 1995 Peabody prize "for investigating a sensitive issue of human rights with resolve, determination and conviction," but not everyone applauded. Detractors called the film sensationalized, outdated, and poorly researched.

In the years that followed, smarting from the adverse publicity, many Chinese orphanages protected themselves from critical eyes. But others worked to reverse the bad press, turning themselves into showcases and flinging open their doors. When a few American adoptive parents active in fund-raising for Chinese orphanages were invited to tour several of the new model institutions, including one in Wuhan, the images they brought back were not of children suffering behind closed doors, but of children playing in clean, well-lighted rooms, singing and dancing for visitors. Children with special medical needs had ready access to physical therapy and staff physicians. Depending on the particular institution, some adoptive parents could enter the children's dorm rooms and wander among the cribs, taking pictures and videotaping. Other places kept visitors confined to a waiting room, or discouraged visits entirely, instead delivering children to their new parents at hotels, even hotels in a different city.

A 1998 film by Corky Merwin, called *Good Fortune*,[6] also showed interior shots of several orphanages, including the one from which Merwin adopted her own daughter, a captivating little girl of two. There could be no greater contrast to the scenes that had been filmed by the undercover team.[7]

Had things gotten better? Or had China's orphanages never been quite as bad as they were pictured? Perhaps the truth, as is so often the case, lay somewhere in between.

The Chinese government refuted the charges of neglect: "The so-called Dying Rooms do not exist in China," said an official statement.[8] "Our investigations confirm that these reports are vicious fabrications. The contemptible lie . . . cannot but arouse the indignation of the Chinese people." The Chinese also took the opportunity to point out the West's failures with its own children—the harsh impact of poverty in America, widespread violence, crimes against young people. Citing thousands of examples of firsthand evidence to the contrary, some members of the community of adoptive American parents also took issue with the reports.

In a historical context, of course, high mortality rates in orphanages hardly seemed surprising, merely part of a long, tragic reality. Even after foundling homes had been established in China, some as early as the 1700s, few babies from remote regions ever reached such places and those who did didn't necessarily fare well. A Chinese foundling home in the 1850s was known as *shaying tang*, meaning "hospice for killing infants."[9]

In poor countries still, seasoned observers countered at the time, it was a hard fact of life that orphanages—when they exist at all—are likely to have high mortality rates. If poor children in the United States often lacked access to good medical care, in China there were far fewer resources, far more people. If some of China's orphaned children suffered from less than optimal care, their situation was hardly unique. According to the World Health Organization at the time, around the world ten million children under five were dying each year from disease, malnutrition, and violence. If children everywhere had a common enemy, its name was poverty.

Found children in China were often in poor medical condition to begin with. Parents who leave their children wrapped in rags are not likely to have had access to antibiotics, and often lack the knowledge or the resources to get medical care for a seriously ill child. Sometimes children were left because they needed medical attention that the parents couldn't provide. Daughters may have received less than optimum care in the first place, and the act of abandonment itself could cause health problems. The institution into which a child was taken may not be much better equipped to care for a serious medical condition than were the parents. In many places, institutions as well as individuals were barely scraping by; both medicine and expertise were in short supply.

In recent history, whenever birth control measures were tightened in a particular area of China, hard-pressed homes for children faced overcrowding and strained resources as increasing numbers of abandoned children showed up at their doors. Many institutions were unprepared. Some areas in China lacked any welfare centers at all. Early on, there was also bureaucratic buck-passing when it came to the foundling problem. Sometimes children from neighboring regions were brought to areas served by other institutions to be left, taxing the resources of those places. "Traveling abandonment," this was called. If anything, China's drive for economic growth only worsened the situation in some cases, leading to cutbacks in many social service sectors, including orphanages, where orphanage workers were poorly trained and underpaid.

Not long after the initial controversy, writer Amy Tan traveled to Beijing with her eighty-year-old mother. One part of her itinerary included an evening of discussion and support for China's orphanages, an event sponsored by the American Chamber of Commerce to benefit the Wisconsin-based Philip Hayden Foundation. Before his untimely death, Hayden, a young teacher in China, had devoted much time and energy to the cause of Chinese orphanages.

On this festive night, banners—HELP ORPHANS and LOVE CHILDREN—were hung on the walls, and a large contingent of Beijing's expatriate community, plus the directors of two of China's state-run orphanages, had gathered. But before the dinner got under way, a cadre of officials from the public security bureau came on the scene, took down the banners, and announced that certain permits were not in place. No speeches would be allowed. Tan, the intended keynote speaker, was left without a podium.[10]

Conditions in orphanages remained just another piece of the puzzle surrounding China's daughters. If there were institutions like Kelly's former home, with a compassionate director and caretakers who dressed the babies in new shoes, there were by other accounts state institutions that were still dirt poor—struggling to care for children in facilities that lacked heat or running water. It was also true that many, if not most, of the orphanages that dealt with foreigners were in a sense "model" orphanages, receiving additional funds with which to buy medicine, clothing, and toys.

Anyone who sees the numbers of girls remaining, their futures stretching out without hopes of families or homes, naturally wants to do all that's possible to get the children out, or to at least make life in the orphanages a happier prospect. Fortunately, more and more advocates, both inside China and out, were soon working to improve conditions.

All along, too, mixed with even the saddest reports had been individual and heroic acts of kindness—the Chinese foster mother who loves her child as her own and then hands her tearfully to an American mother; the officials who struggle against bureaucratic obstacles to get the children out of the institutions and into families; the adoption agency workers who bargain behind the scenes, negotiating futures for so many little ones.

An adoptive mother and former pediatric nurse said of her daughter's orphanage, "I knew there was a commitment they were putting into the children so that they would be safe enough and healthy enough to have a better life. I have absolutely no disappointment toward the Chinese government, toward Chinese families, or toward her Chinese mom. I'm just incredibly thankful that they made this decision, that they chose to save her."

If one takes into consideration the historic reluctance of the Chinese government to expose itself to criticism, the entire foreign adoption program has been an exemplary move on the part of the People's Republic. In terms of human rights, there is probably no more sensitive issue the nation could allow to be scrutinized than happens each time a Westerner comes to China and flies home with a Chinese child. It's no wonder that in many places the relationship between foreigners—even those intending to be helpful—and the Chinese authorities became temporarily strained after the adverse publicity a few years back.

The fact that any number of orphanages had saved so many children so well was the positive side of a mixed picture.

Add to that picture another factor—foreign adoptive families themselves. Most have asked for healthy babies, as young as possible. It's a natural desire, but it unintentionally fosters a kind of two-tier system, encouraging institutions to place the youngest, strongest, and most appealing children in the adoptable pool. Although many parents over the years have been more than willing to accept children with unexpected and seri-

ous health challenges, others have not, and many welfare directors have come to expect that foreigners want healthy children
only; that those who take children with special needs do so
only because they have been required to. If more adopting parents were willing to accept children with health problems, in
fact asked for children who needed some help, more of those
children might be given the boost they need to survive. What
makes most sense for the children, of course, is to get those
who are most frail out of the institution first.

Sickly children, older children, or disabled children are hard
to place. That's true when it comes to adoption within the
United States and it's true within China. But while few Chinese
families who might want to adopt a child have the resources to
deal with major medical problems, many Americans do.

Most of the children adopted from China have, in fact, been
amazingly healthy, given their time spent in institutional care.
Despite problems here and there—a few of them admittedly
serious—several U.S. pediatricians who've seen a good sampling of the group have pronounced them a pretty healthy
bunch, all in all.[11] "I have heard of some wonderful nutrition in
the orphanages," said our own pediatrician. "At one place, they
cooked rice until it is a gruel (jook, or congee) and they added
lamb bones, which provided valuable minerals, and a touch of soy
for the sodium. It's perfect for the children." Other pediatricians
who've worked with children from Chinese orphanages say,
overall, their condition has been impressive, that they have not
suffered the physical or psychological ill effects seen in some institutionalized children from Eastern Europe, for instance. Although some infants have had developmental delays, most have
quickly made up for lost time. According to one preliminary
survey, even most children described as "special needs" had

tended to have medical problems that varied from minor to nonexistent. But a minority of special-needs children have had additional, undisclosed problems. One thing remained certain: The more resources that flowed into the orphanages, the more children could be offered a good chance at life.

In the decade following our first trip to a Chinese orphanage there has been a transformation in China's social welfare institutions for children. The Chinese government has undertaken national fund drives for the country's homeless children, and various other Chinese entities have stepped in as well, upgrading facilities, increasing efforts to improve the standards of care. In some places, China's building boom extended to the orphanages, with new, showcase institutions going up, new play equipment sparkling on the grounds. With help, institutions began adding programs that emphasized close ties between children and caregivers, and the replication, as much as possible, of a family atmosphere.

For years now, a number of foreign organizations have also been active. As the adoption movement gained momentum, many families in the United States and other countries, blessed by children from China and unable to forget those left behind, began initiating further help. In fact, one of the most profound results of the Chinese adoption movement has been the activism of adoptive families who have raised funds and acted to improve conditions for the children who remain in China. Early on, the Families with Children from China group became active; the Foundation for Chinese orphanages raised money for needed supplies, from antibiotics to clothes dryers to toys, and provided funds for foster parent programs and medical assistance. The Families with Children from China charitable initiatives have generously supported foster-care programs, given tuition for a wide range of students from institutions, helped special-needs children, provided playgrounds, paid for washing machines and other needed equipment, and donated surgical and medical care. (For a list of charities supporting China's orphanages, see the Families with Children from China website, www.fwcc.org.)

"While FCC is primarily an organization that serves American adoptive families, we care deeply about the children who remain in Chinese orphanages," David Youtz told a 2002 Congressional-Executive Commission on the subject of China's institutionalized children. Youtz, then president of Families with Children from China of Greater New York, and an adoptive father, told the committee, "Adoption of children from China into American families is one of the most successful examples of cooperation between our two countries. Despite the ups and downs in the relationship between Washington and Beijing, the adoption process has moved ahead with quiet and life-changing effectiveness. The adoption process and conditions in orphanages are one area where China has made impressive and enduring progress, which should be recognized and applauded."

The Amity Foundation, a Christian social service and relief agency, which had worked in the Nanjing area for a decade or more, continued to assist by supplying medicine, equipment, and toys. The organization also provided stipends for "Amity grandmas," personal caregivers for the babies, and for retired nurses, doctors, and teachers to help the children. The Hayden Foundation funded cleft palate surgeries, and other groups offered medical help as well.

It soon became clear to many of those involved that providing foster care—placing children in temporary homes, or hiring "aunties" or "grandmas," including some who would take the children home with them at night—would be the most compassionate way to help the children left behind, and with help from many sources, a number of orphanages began to have such programs.

Over time, as more and more adoptive children settled into new homes, such efforts continued to expand. Some of the donations to Chinese orphanages soon came with handwritten notes from little adopted girls in America, or Ireland, or Denmark, sending heartfelt good wishes to their sisters in China's institutions.

One woman blessed with a daughter from China had a moment of inspiration that in the next decade was to change the lives of thousands and thousands of children in Chinese welfare institutions. In 1998, Jenny Bowen was in California looking out the window, watching her daughter Maya play in the yard, when she realized how her daughter, who had come home weak and lagging in development, had, with the care of a family, blossomed into a normal, healthy, happy kid.

Couldn't there be a way to get some of that love and care to the rest of the little ones waiting (some waiting forever) in China's institutions, Bowen wondered. She couldn't stop thinking about all the other little girls who hadn't gotten out of the orphanage, and who might not. One was a two-year-old who had had surgery for a benign brain tumor and had lost control of her bladder as a result. All day long this child sat, docilely, on a towel, watching everything that went on around her. "I wanted to find a way to give something back," says Bowen. "I knew in that moment what I was going to do with the rest on my life." She realized that the girls who stayed behind needed schooling. Even those few children who eventually were sent to school outside the institutions tended not to do well because they lacked any kind of preparation. The babies needed someone to hold them, play with them, on a daily basis.

In that moment, the nonprofit foundation called Half the Sky was born. Bowen, who was then a screenwriter and film producer, her cinematographer husband, Richard, and several other adoptive families put together a joint Chinese American venture that combined the talents and concerns of Chinese and American people, including Chinese women involved in the China Population Welfare Foundation (a nongovernmental organization that offered bootstrap help to impoverished women), Chinese and American scholars, Chinese social welfare officials, and early childhood educators and child development specialists.

Half the Sky Foundation began in 1998 by launching Little Sisters preschool programs in two orphanages, plus a Baby Sisters infant nurture program to provide nannies for children younger than eighteen months. The preschool teachers were trained in the Reggio Emilia approach to early childhood development, and the programs also offered preparation for a regular Chinese school curriculum for girls so they could go on to school outside the orphanage. Bowen hoped that the first teachers would go on to train others and that eventually the foundation might provide early education and infant nurture for the children in hundreds of orphanages—reaching as many children as possible.

To get it all started, a group of Half the Sky volunteers traveled to China for an East-West work party. They set up the first two Little Sisters preschool programs in social welfare institutions in Hefei (Anhui province) and Changzhou (Jiangsu province). Small girls who'd been adopted from China returned with their parents and helped prepare the classrooms. When the rooms were freshly painted, furnished, and ready, they were filled with developmental toys, art supplies, books, a puppet theater, and probably the most popular addition, a dress-up corner.

For the Baby Sisters program, a contingent of nannies, local women hired to hold and nurture the tiniest, were trained to provide crucial one-on-one attention. The nannies were older local women; the teachers, recent graduates of teachers' colleges. Thus, as the institutionalized children were being helped, two other generations of women were affected as well. This seemed the second natural phase in the ongoing improvements in China's institutions. Whatever extra money came in was devoted first to the buildings, and once the physical plants were in shape, attention could be turned to other improvements— simple human contact and stimulation.

As Dana Johnson, director of the International Adoption Clinic at the University of Minnesota, and a member of Half the Sky's board of directors, observed, studies on children adopted from Romania in 1990 and 1991 showed that children in orphanages were at a very high risk for permanent cognitive loss. Even a few minutes a day of additional attention could make a profound difference in a child's development.

The American volunteers found this joint venture with Chinese people from many walks of life, as well as local orphanages, an experience almost beyond words. Said Mary Ebejer of Grand Rapids, Michigan, "China has given us so much with our daughter Anna. I had to come and give something back. The experience showed me that kids need the same things every-where, whether at home or in an orphanage—sensory experi-ence, stimulation, attention. It gave me a tremendous sense of accomplishment. The hardest part was seeing that not every child will be adopted. But a program like this gives one a legacy of hope."

David Howard, who with his wife, Vicki McClay, coordi-nated the first work parties, commented about "how simple it really was to make a meaningful change." After the preschools opened, one group of children left the orphanage for the first time ever, on a field trip to a local market. Not one of them knew the name of any of the fruits or vegetables or other foods for sale. But they filled their baskets and went back to the or-phanage to learn all about their purchases and to help cook a meal for the first time. Teachers had each child keep a memory book, helping those who've lost their pasts to create a personal history they can take with them wherever they go. If a child was adopted, she took her memory book with her.

In the Baby Sisters program, one infant's progress report after another showed what a difference personal, loving atten-tion could make: "Her muscles were awfully weak and limp. She did not show interest in toys or people. Now she recognizes toys and actually reaches for them. Whenever she sees her nanny, she smiles. [She] is becoming active and outgoing."

In a Half the Sky playroom early on, I watched one of the foundation's Chinese advisers tenderly wipe one child's nose while holding another girl in his arms. "These are such good chil-dren," he said. "They just don't have homes." The children who had found homes in the United States began to be a subject of growing interest among Chinese officials. Joan Spano, another

Half the Sky volunteer, reported, "Often the officials would make the point that adopted children, rather than being utterly lost to China, are 'little ambassadors,' putting a human face on a political relationship that is sometimes fraught with tension."

Half the Sky's founder is often asked by Chinese orphanage directors and officials why she and others devote so much attention to children still in China. "Because they are our family," Jenny Bowen has answered. "Because they are the sisters of our daughters and sons. That makes them our children too. . . . As much as is within our power, we must treat them as our own." Eventually, Half the Sky expanded its programs to include a Big Sisters program for older girls and a Family Village program to provide permanent foster care for children with special needs.

Today, Half the Sky, supported by more than thirty thousand adoptive families, continues its work across China. In 2008, a decade after the founding of this dream at her kitchen table in California, Bowen and countless others involved with Half the Sky had established more than three dozen centers, each with an infant nurture and preschool program. Through the Big Sisters program, they were helping numerous older girls. They'd created a dozen foster Family Villages, where children whose special needs precluded them from being adopted could have lasting family ties. They'd also established special programs for children orphaned by AIDS. In all, some fifteen thousand children, from a few months to twenty-one years old, had been served by the foundation and its core group of supporters— adoptive families of Chinese children. At any given time, some four thousand children were in Half the Sky programs.

In 2006, when I served on that foundation's board of directors, I walked into a Half the Sky foster village. Several apartments housed retired couples who were each raising several special-needs children. One couple had four children with various disabilities, including cerebral palsy. Another family was celebrating the birthday of a little girl with a disfigured mouth. I watched as the smiling foster mother set the cake down, five candles blazing, on a table in the apartment's kitchen, and the children gathered around to sing. The birthday child rocked on tiptoes until the song was over, then blew out the candles while the rest of the kids waited for the cake.

The foster couple told us how fortunate they felt to be raising this second family. The foster village plan allows children who are not considered adoptable by the Chinese government, because of severe special needs, to grow up cherished in families. They get the support services they need from the welfare institution and can attend Half the Sky preschools before going on to schools in their communities. These children are not lost to China. Foster care linked to orphanages is the trend now, ensuring children the ongoing support and secure love of a family.

In the Big Sisters program, older girls were learning to play the violin, taking painting and English lessons, learning computer science, or going off to vocational school. A substantial number had applied to universities and gained acceptance. One girl who'd grown up in an institution was now working for Half the Sky.

But the biggest news came on Children's Day in 2007 when the Chinese government asked Half the Sky to become a partner in China's Blue Sky Initiative, a program aimed at improving the life of every orphaned child in China. Half the Sky was invited to spread its programs to orphanages in every province. The goals were huge—to touch the lives of more than one hundred thousand children in three hundred institutions over the next five years. The Bowens, who had adopted a second daughter, Anya, in 2000, had by then moved to China to be closer to the work they wanted to do.

In 2008, when Half the Sky celebrated its tenth anniversary of working in China, Amy Tan was the featured speaker, once again lending her support to Chinese homeless children.

Meanwhile, an ocean away from the institutions where they spent most of their first year, it took no time for Kelly's little group of adopted girls to thrive. Gathered together at a birthday party or a Chinese New Year's celebration, kicking through the fall leaves in Maine, going to baseball games in San Diego, they were strikingly beautiful, resilient, and by every indication happy, normal kids. And yet, laughing, running, shouting, in their new homes, they were also reminders of the backdrop of troubles from which they had emerged, reminders of how many other sweet young lives had been lost. Had any one of the babies placed in our arms in that orphanage waiting room been born to a parent less willing—or able—to get her to safety; had any one of these little girls been left farther away, or in weaker health, or for just a little longer; had any one been taken into a poorer institution, handed to a less compassionate caretaker, or not found at all, she too might have faded to a statistic.

7

East-West Lives

*In the beginning
all human nature is the same.
But as people are exposed
to varied educations
and different circumstances,
they grow
ever more different.*

—Confucius[1]

Two little girls with shiny dark bobbed hair sat at a table having whiskers painted on their faces. A toddler toddled around eating an almond cookie, trailing a tiger tail tied around her waist. Amid shrieks of excitement from the children and the heavy drone of shouted conversation from their parents, a troupe of dancers appeared, holding a huge lion's head—jowls shaking, eyes rolling—high over the crowd. To furious drum-beating, the gaudy lion leapt about—one young dancer shaking the huge white head, another wagging the tail. Thus 1998 and the Year of the Tiger on the Chinese calendar were ushered in. Mark, Kelly, and I were at our very first Between the Two New Years event, hosted by the local northern California members of Families with Children from China (FCC). Gathered in a circle, staring at the spectacle, were the little daughters of China, some in Chinese silk outfits, the majority in average American kid clothes, many in shades of red, the traditional color for Chinese New Year.

The event was held at Saint Gregory of Nyssa Episcopal Church in San Francisco's Potrero Hill district—an appropriate venue for such a multicultural spectacle. It's a rather free-form institution as Episcopal groups go, in both body and spirit. The church's impressive shingled exterior is modeled partly on the castle from Kurosawa's epic *Ran*; the interior space on a Jewish synagogue. The sanctuary is decorated with murals of otherwise overlooked saints, including the boy who led a revolt against the exploitation of children in Pakistan's carpet industry. A rubbing from China's ancient city of Xian graces one area, and where an altar would usually stand, there's a carved elephant seat from Thailand.

On this day, Saint Gregory's was overrun by dozens of small girls born in China, most about thigh-high to their parents. According to the children's name tags, almost all had first names that were indistinguishable from any other group of children in an average American city, names like Grace and Kimberly and Maggie and Jessica. There was also one perfect East-West name, Mali McGuire. Kelly was wandering around happily, dragging her striped tail, segments of mandarin orange clutched in each hand. Several other little girls who'd lived in the same orphanage she'd come from were there that day. "Isn't it wonderful," said a grandmother on the sidelines, "a whole generation growing up together."

Ten years later, when the Year of the Pig was celebrated by the girls from China at the Between the Two New Years event, Rosemary Gong was autographing her book *Good Luck Life*, and Kelly was having a great time with Rosemary, helping her make change for the book buyers.

If, on Shamian Island, Mark, Kelly, and I became part of that month's crowd of several hundred immigrating daughters of China and their brand-new parents, upon our return we became part of a larger subculture of tens of thousands of children and their parents. All home now, leading American lives, a good percentage of us continued to be drawn together, for mutual support and in the attempt to keep one foot in the culture of our children's birth.

Families with Children from China, a group that now has ninety-plus chapters including one in every major U.S. city, was started in 1993 by adoptive parents in New York City, who saw it as a way to build a community for their daughters. In the United States, approximately one-fifth of the families who've adopted children from China belong to local chapters. There are also groups in Norway, Canada, Britain, Ireland, the Netherlands, Denmark, Sweden, Spain, and other countries with sizable populations of children from China. The organizations are an important link and resource, bringing together parents and children with a shared history and common issues (see www.fwcc.org for more information).

In the United States, families who have children from China live everywhere from Alaska to Texas, Hawaii to Maine, and points in between, and are astonishingly diverse in just about any other way you could name—professional, political, and religious leanings; family makeup, family history, age, lifestyle, hobbies, or ethnicity. The children have come from areas in China even farther apart than, say, Oregon and Alabama. They come from numerous ethnic strains within China, and their origins may range from a high-rise in Beijing to a hut in Yunnan; from a peasant family in Sichuan province to an unwed teenage mother in Guangdong. In terms of geography alone, the notion of extended family in this group is stretched about as far as it can go.

If, as Hillary Clinton has noted, it takes a village to raise a child, this East-West group of parents and children has become its own global village. Families with Children from China chapters do a conscientious job of trying to provide a sense of enlightened community for the adopted daughters of China. In spirit, it is an unprecedented attempt by thousands of parents to honor their children's origins. Events such as the Between the Two New Years celebration bring families together and encourage appreciation of Chinese culture. Gatherings and regional newsletters offer background on Chinese holidays and traditions, and provide a forum for such relevant issues as transracial adoption, self-esteem among adopted children, the experience of older adoptees, how to talk to children about their birth parents, and ways to handle being a cross-cultural family when confronted with intolerance or ignorance.

In addition to FCC groups, adoptive parents can turn to smaller, informal networks of people whose daughters have all come from the same orphanage, say, or of people who worked with the same agency or traveled to China together or who all now live in the same community. There's a national organization called Our Chinese Daughters Foundation, composed of single mothers as well as a few single fathers (www.ocdf.org). Thousands of American parents, whether merely contemplating adoption from China, slogging through paperwork, or just home with a child, are hooked up to one another via the Internet.

Most of the little girls from China have no enduring ties to their homeland in place, only attempts by their adoptive parents to keep the link to China alive for them, which raises some interesting questions. For adults and older children who can remember the past, the loss of native language, culture, and familiar sights, sounds, smells, and tastes may echo through one's life. But for children adopted as infants, it's hard to know what soaked in, what they might miss, and on what level they might miss it. Eventually, though, these children may long for information about their families of origin and attempt to renew a connection with the country of their birth. Cultivating respect for that culture and imparting as much information as possible during childhood is a way to keep the doors open should the girls someday wish to step through.

When and how to talk to children about the circumstances of their birth and why they came to be growing up an ocean away from where they began is, not surprisingly, one of the perennial topics of conversation among adoptive parents of Chinese children. Most acknowledge that no matter how much love or sensitivity they bring to the parent-daughter relationship, their children will have some crises of identity, or at least some difficult questions to face, as they grow up. One possible solution is to offer these children the companionship of one another, plus the resources to feel as comfortable as possible in both worlds—East and West—by incorporating Chinese art, music, celebrations, fairy tales, and food into their lives and even making sure that they learn to speak some Mandarin or Cantonese.

A good number of parents on the West Coast who've adopted Chinese children are themselves Chinese American, and for those who've grown up with some traditional culture, keeping it alive for their children may come naturally. For other families, people like Mark and me, to impart Chinese culture to our daughters is to impart a culture in translation, with the pitfalls attendant to any translation. In the San Francisco Bay Area or other places with substantial Chinese populations, it's relatively easy to offer children exposure to the Chinese community and the culture into which they were born, even if they have no recollections of it and their parents have to learn from scratch. But introducing children to a dragon dance or Mandarin in a small town in the South or deep in the heart of Amish country, say, may be somewhat challenging.

Nonetheless, there's an effort under way by many adoptive parents to do the best they can, spoon-feeding their daughters bits of the culture left behind. In Boulder, Colorado, parents have formed a cross-cultural Saturday-morning get-together called Little Treasures. "At some point, I know my daughter is going to realize that all these kids she knows who are adopted from China are all little girls and she is going to come to some realization about why that is," says one mother. "This is an attempt to balance out the negative feelings. We're trying to give her some exposure to the positive aspects of the culture." One pair of adoptive mothers in northern California pledged to take their daughter often to Chinatown where she could experience the feeling of being in the majority.

Across the United States, there are also a number of special camps—Chinese heritage camps, Mandarin summer camps—for adopted youngsters and their families. One, an event sponsored by the Seattle-area FCC chapter, had the children painting dragons and playing in wading pools filled with grains of rice while their parents discussed adoptive family life. By 2008, many families and groups were going straight to China for their cultural experiences, and there were a growing number of programs to introduce children to their heritage.

On the Internet, there were numerous links where children adopted from China could learn about their places of origin and hook up with other children from the same area. Pen pal programs were being put in place so adopted children could communicate with one another across the country or with adopted children in other nations. The Ties Program, a Wisconsin-based heritage organization that serves families in the United States who have children from other lands, was soon gearing up for China's daughters, as were other organizations. In the past Ties had organized trips to Korea, Chile, Peru, and Paraguay, taking adoptive families on excursions that include visits with foster homes and orphanages, schools, and private homes—plus explorations of the cultural conditions that influence adoption decisions.

Kelly observed her second Halloween dressed as a pumpkin. When we marked the Autumn Moon Festival the same month, she wore her Chinese jacket from Guangzhou. In December we gathered with our adoption group and the girls drew names for Christmas gifts. By Chinese New Year's, Kelly and her cousins were exchanging traditional Chinese red envelopes. In our small way, we were a living example of what sociologists call bicultural socialization.

Richard Tessler, a University of Massachusetts sociology professor and father of two adopted daughters from China, became interested in how adopted Chinese girls were being exposed to various aspects of their birth culture. The author of *West Meets East: Americans Adopt Chinese Children,* Tessler put together a questionnaire in 1996 for a national survey, the start of what he hoped would be a continuing longitudinal study.[2] Parents, he knew, had choices about whether and how to help their children become comfortable and competent in two worlds, to construct what he termed "a bicultural identity." He also saw an opportunity to gauge how the wider world viewed these East-West families.

Here's what Tessler found, having surveyed more than five hundred people, a voluntary representation he admits was probably skewed in favor of parents already interested in bicultural issues: Parents felt it was most important that their children be proud of their Chinese heritage. Next, they valued exposure to Chinese culture, then a child's awareness of looking like other persons of Chinese descent; learning about the area of China from which their children came; having their child become friends with other Chinese children; and learning about modern Chinese history. Lower on the list of importance were visits to China with their child or being able to communicate in Chinese at home. Interestingly, parents who were very committed to the Chinese socialization of their children often reported prejudice or negative social reactions toward their unusual families.

The parents Tessler interviewed said overwhelmingly they'd had few problems in their own neighborhoods, but two-thirds said they'd had problems with strangers, ranging from nosy inquiries to serious affronts. Some had been asked intrusive questions, even in the presence of the child, queries such as "How much did she cost?" and "Why didn't her mother want her?" Some Caucasian mothers said they'd been asked, "Is her father Chinese?" The most important source of social support for such families turned out to be friendships with other adoptive families in the same boat.

Tessler was planning to return to China, to live for a while in the city where both his daughters began their lives. There, he hoped to learn what Chinese people think about bicultural socialization. Ultimately, he hoped to survey the adopted girls themselves. He was just waiting for most of them to get old enough.

Other, scattered research has looked at the adjustments made by children adopted internationally, and the overall picture seems mixed but generally positive. Such are the shiftings of world affairs that twenty-five hundred Japanese children, left as orphans in China at the end of World War II, were adopted by Chinese families. Two researchers interviewed a sampling of these people and reported that "those who were separated from their Japanese parents before the age of three were less likely to retain characteristic Japanese social or interpersonal behavior. In lifestyle and social-adjustments respects they were indistinguishable from Chinese people."[3]

Chinese officials from the China Center of Adoption Affairs had also come to the United States on several occasions, to visit many of the official entities involved in adoption and to spend some time with adoptive families around the country. It was clear, said Susan Soon-Keum Cox of Holt International Children's Services, that the officials were "reassured by how well the adopted children are thriving in their adopted families and communities."

Potstickers or pizza? Mulan paper dolls or American Girl dolls? Mandarin opera or Hannah Montana? Choices, whether superficial or deep-seated, await. Ultimately, it is the children themselves who will decide. Depending on any number of factors, including family attitudes, the immediate environment, and individual predilection, some children may take up Chinese traditions with great enthusiasm, while others may not want to differentiate themselves from their classmates by learning Cantonese or Mandarin or going to Chinese New Year's events. Nor are all parents equally committed and equally able to explore and honor Chinese culture.

I remember hearing the story about one girl adopted from Korea who turned to her adoptive parents, who'd taken great pains to collect artifacts and decorations from her homeland, and said, "How come we have all this Korean stuff, and what's it doing in my room?" Other adoptees have longed to go back to their country of birth and immerse themselves in the culture there.

These are delicate and complex matters. Children everywhere experience a great desire to fit into the world around them. If parents of children adopted from China push the China connection too hard, some fear they may run the risk of emphasizing differences rather than similarities, of suggesting to their daughters that they somehow stand outside the family and community around them, or that they belong somewhere else. Ignore the links to their homeland, on the other hand, and parents may deny their children the resources they'll need to feel good about themselves and to explore their origins. A level of comfort in both worlds, complete with some facility in Mandarin or Cantonese, may be the best scenario of all—but it takes special resources, opportunities, and parenting.

And whatever a child embraces today, tomorrow she may change her mind. Individual responses will vary, and time will tell. A few summers ago an American mother I talked with returned to Jiangmen with her ten-year-old adopted daughter. The girl studied Cantonese and had a great time, but as much as she enjoyed China, she was eager to get back home to her friends in Ohio. "She feels totally American," said her mother. Maybe the girl will have an urge to return to China at some point in her life, maybe not. As an old Chinese proverb has it, "Human beings are like falling water. Tip them East and they flow East. Tip them West and they flow West."

Probably the majority of China-born children who grow up in America will flow along in the cultural mainstream, tipping—at least initially—far more toward the West than to the East, no matter how much Chinese culture is offered. Even Asian American children who've grown up with Asian American parents in this country say they've largely ignored their roots—until suddenly, in their teens or twenties, perhaps, has come an intense interest in finding out about their background.

There's also a possibility these days that Chinese children raised in America by parents conscientious about including Chinese culture in their upbringing may end up more conversant in some of those traditions than will children growing up today in China's urban areas, children who are at this moment wearing Mickey Mouse watches, watching Da Niao (Big Bird) on television, eating at Pizza Hut, and getting their first introduction to the old Chinese folktale of Fa Mulan by seeing the according-to-Disney, made-in-Hollywood movie.

Our family, plus three other families from this area who traveled with us to China, form a small melting pot all our own, a bit of middle America, with parents of European as well as Japanese and Chinese backgrounds represented. We get together every other month or so, giving the girls a chance to play with one another, while the adults compare notes. Whatever the mix of cultural influences, what seems most important is the fact that the girls are growing up together. At every event, we end the day with our traditional photo—all the kids lined up on the sofa, once again.

Early on, in our own household, Kelly and I read Chinese fairy tales and folk rhymes (skipping that one about the worthless daughter), as well as Dr. Seuss and A. A. Milne. We played CDs of Chinese folk music along with Kelly's favorite children's recording, "Use a Napkin (Not Your Mom!)."[4] When Mark put on the tape of Chinese lullabies that Jeffrey had given us at the farewell dinner in Guangzhou, there was some Chinese instrumental music and songs sung in Cantonese, but then things started to sound vaguely familiar. Soon Kelly was singing along to "Mary Had a Little Lamb," "Happy Birthday," and "London Bridge Is Falling Down."

Whatever our notions of Chinese culture, or just about anything else, I suppose, it's a fact of life that the world often seems to be spinning faster than our ability to catch up with it.

Korean children who were adopted into American homes in a wave that began in the 1950s have blazed an important trail for the current generation of Chinese daughters, as have children adopted earlier from Taiwan. Adoption in general, and transracial adoption in particular, was handled very differently a few decades ago, and the lessons that emerge from those experiences offer a valuable perspective for the current generation of adopted Chinese children.

For almost all adoptive children, not just those adopted internationally, the period from the 1950s well into the 1970s were days of secrecy and sealed files. Caucasian parents who adopted Asian children did so without the benefit of the widespread discussion and group support that families with children from China have today. There were other differences. Adopted children from Korea included a substantial number of boys as well as girls, and few parents traveled to Korea to pick up their children, meeting them instead at an airport in the United States. Parents therefore had less firsthand experience of a child's native culture to pass along, and less inclination, in general, to do so. The emphasis was on assimilation. Joyce Maguire Pavao, a Boston therapist and trainer specializing in adoption issues, comments, "Families with Korean children said, 'What do you mean "Asian" child? This is just our family.'"

Around the time we adopted Kelly, the story of one particular young Chinese American woman was much discussed among the parents of young girls from China. In an article in the *Boston Globe*, reporter Dick Lehr interviewed a college student named Julia Ming Gale, adopted from Taiwan, who'd grown up in a Caucasian family surrounded by a white, upper-middle-class world.[5]

"I think I was always hoping I would become white," the young woman told the reporter. When she looked in the mirror, she said, she didn't see herself, but someone with curly red hair, green eyes, and a few freckles. When she went to college and encountered other Asian young people, she didn't know how to relate to them. Even though her parents had studied Chinese and had Chinese friends, the young girl hadn't experienced the company of children her own age in a similar position. In the year she was adopted (1976), there were fewer than a hundred other adopted Chinese babies brought to America.

Gale told the reporter that she had decided to become a counselor, to help other young people raised in similar circumstances come to terms with their lives.

Although nationwide there are more than a hundred thousand people who were adopted from Korea as children, many now in their forties and older, it has taken decades for the kind of open discussion to evolve for this group that has existed almost from the beginning for adopted children from China. In the past few years, organizations have been formed to bring Korean adoptees together and act as support groups, including the Association of Korean Adoptees/San Francisco, begun in 1997.[6] There are now many organizations and networks to support adult adoptees as they explore their bicultural struggles or try to find their birth parents or come to terms with the fact that they can't or don't want to. Many of these adults are now writing books, producing films, and speaking out about their experiences. Parents of children from China may listen closely to the stories that Korean adoptees have to tell.

Rebecca Hurdis was adopted from Korea when she was six months old. Twenty-six when I first met her, she was working toward a Ph.D. in ethnic studies at the University of California at Berkeley. I met her at a book signing one night, when she asked me a series of pressing questions: How did the adoptive parents of girls from China intend to help their daughters be comfortable with their ethnicity? How were we going to deal with the difficult questions? Did we plan to have mentors? As someone who'd been adopted from Korea as a child, she'd given the subject lots of thought. She also had written an eloquent paper about her own quest for identity.

"One of our first moves for an identity is breaking the silences of our childhood," she wrote. "One of the hardest reasons for us to speak is [that] we fear that we are betraying our [adoptive] parents."

She told me of the pain she'd felt as a child. "I don't know how many times teachers asked me to write a family history. What was the point?" A social studies teacher once asked Hurdis to prepare a Korean meal, even though she'd grown up in an American family and never had any practice. "I was six months old when I was adopted," she told her teacher. "Why would I know how to cook Korean food? Did you know how to flip burgers when you were six months old?"

Hurdis described the sadness she'd carried, and the pain of not being able to see her reflection in a parent's face. She spoke of what it was like as a Korean adoptee growing up in Connecticut, where there were few people of color, and no one she knew who shared her experience. The hardest part was the racism, she said. Even the best-intentioned parents who can talk about racism and be opposed to it may have no idea about how it feels to be on the receiving end.

And that's what the Korean adoptees have to offer our daughters, Hurdis said. "We've had an experience that's as close as you can get. And healing can come."

As an adoptive mother listening to this eloquent young woman, it was difficult to hear the pain. But Hurdis also suggested something hopeful, how sharing the burden can lighten it, and how our daughters and other young people who've had a similar experience may be able to help one another through.

"Ethnicity matters," says Claire S. Chow, author of *Leaving Deep Water: The Lives of Asian American Women at the Crossroads of Two Cultures.* Chow, a northern California family therapist who specializes in cross-cultural issues, has explored in depth the conflicts that can be experienced by women of a minority ethnicity growing up in the wider context of American society. "Parents should realize that they aren't adopting just a child but an ethnically different child," she told me. "Adoption itself carries a primal kind of loss. Add the loss of original country and culture, and you can see the magnitude of the problem."

A person of Chinese descent raised in a predominantly white world, Chow said she spent the first part of her own life trying to become "as white as I could; to disguise myself as a white American," while she has spent the second half trying to reclaim her Chinese heritage. In her book, she summed up the identity struggle this way: "To me it means living in a place where I don't look much like anyone else but in most respects act like them, knowing all the time that halfway across the globe is a densely populated region full of people who look just like me but don't particularly act like me. It means forever holding the contradiction of belonging and not belonging, of feeling 'at home' and wondering where home is."

"Have you noticed that our children don't look Asian anymore?" said one of the women Mark and I traveled to China with. It was a sunny summer day and we were sitting on the grass, three Caucasian mothers and three adopted Chinese daughters. It took me a moment to realize what she meant. "They just look like themselves," said my friend. "They just look like our kids." What she said was true. When I looked into Kelly's face, it was just Kelly's beloved face. Whatever physical distinctions there are between us had blurred with familiarity. Yet other people—including my daughter at some point— would perceive our differences, and therein lay a challenge for us all.

At first, I have to admit, I thought love could bridge all the gaps, but that was the view from my perspective, not my daughter's, nor that of the world surrounding us. My first brush with this reality came in a San Francisco coffee shop when Kelly was just two and a half. I was sipping tea and Kelly was drawing with crayons, when a little girl about five wandered over to our table and started coloring with us. Soon the girl looked intently at Kelly and then at me and said, "Are you her mom?" "I am," I said, and smiled. The girl looked me in the eye. "She doesn't look like you," she said. "I'm her mom," I said, trying to figure out what level of detail was appropriate to this particular age level. The girl shrugged and went on coloring. I was glad I didn't have to get into all this quite yet, but I felt a certain loss of innocence. Almost equally disconcerting, though, was this remark from a maître d' in a Berkeley, California, restaurant. He asked whether Kelly was my daughter, and then said, "I thought so. You two look alike."

I often have been asked, "Is she yours?" To which I have answered simply, "Yes." One man in a post office line put it very gently when he said, "Your daughter is beautiful. What is her ethnicity?" Would that all curious strangers were so sensitive!

Other Caucasian parents of Chinese children have reported more serious challenges. They have been peppered with nosy queries and offended by insensitive observations. How to handle rude questions is an ongoing topic of discussion among adoptive parents.

There's the all-too-common remark, for instance, that these children are "lucky" to have been "rescued" by their American parents, an observation that no parent wants her child to have to hear. It's not the worst thing someone can say, of course, but it's not something I want my daughter to have to contend with. It's easy to assume that life in the United States will offer our daughter a richer life than she had in the orphanage, but who knows what might otherwise have become of her? She's a resilient child, open to the world and all its possibilities, and contrary to all the negative accounts, there is also ample goodwill toward children in China. I'd never want my child to feel she had to consider herself lucky for her adoption or to think of us as her rescuers. Whatever she's gained, she's also left something behind. She needs freedom to feel whatever she feels, which may be a mix of happiness and loss.

If responding to the remarks of strangers takes special skill, we can sometimes be too on edge. As I wheeled Kelly around a store one day in her stroller, the saleswoman sighed and said, "These kids don't know how lucky they are." I was just about to bristle, when she went on. "I'd love someone to push me around in a stroller all day. My feet ache."

The current Chinese American adoptive movement can be seen from any number of perspectives, depending on the experience and points of view of the observer. In transracial adoption as a whole, it's a fact of global reality that most adopting parents are white and most adopted children are children of color. In the past, for some people on the far edges, transracial adoption has been viewed as a kind of cultural genocide.[7] For people on the other end of the spectrum, including the late Pearl S. Buck, finding homes for children, even if it takes crossing racial and cultural lines—as well as the Pacific Ocean—is a good, if sometimes complex, endeavor. There are other thoughtful points of view that lie somewhere in between, including those of enlightened contemporary advocates who ardently support international adoption, but who caution adopting parents to keep their minds and hearts open to any and all questions and conflicts, not just those of adoption in general, but those of cross-cultural adoption in particular.

Writes psychologist Mary Pipher, author of the best-seller *Reviving Ophelia: Saving the Selves of Adolescent Girls*: "In particular, teenagers, who are focused on identity issues, struggle with the meaning of adoption in their lives. When adoption involves mixing races, the issues become even more formidable. Racial issues are difficult for Americans to discuss. We have so few examples of good discussions about ethnic differences that even to acknowledge differences makes most of us feel guilty."

It's also a mistake to confuse ethnicity with cultural leanings of any sort. Just because people have certain identifying features says nothing about the culture from which they have come or about the culture they embrace—or how they themselves might wish the world to see them. Writer Pang-Mei Natasha Chang writes of her own ambivalence and frustration, of being put off when a Chinese waiter automatically speaks Chinese to her, and equally put off when one doesn't. "The dilemma of the person of two cultures," she calls it.[8] In a television documentary about growing up Asian in America, a teenaged girl said plaintively, "I don't want to be ethnic this or that or Chinese-American or hyphenated anything else. I just want to be a person."

Sometimes, I admit, I also wish that all the differences would just go away and that my daughter's childhood could be protected and easy. Yet not addressing the issues directly is the biggest mistake adoptive parents can make, says therapist

Claire Chow. "Parents have to think about what's going to happen when these kids encounter prejudice that the parents haven't had in their own lives."

I often think back to my early, simpler ideas about life with my daughter from China. As has widely been pointed out, it's far easier to be blind to prejudice when one hasn't grown up as a minority in this culture. To cite a rather mild example: The year Kelly was born, Michelle Kwan, the much-admired young figure skater from California, placed second to Tara Lipinski (also of the U.S.) in the Olympics competition held in Nagano, Japan. A television headline announced the results this way: "American beats out Kwan." Chine Hui, a Chinese-American restaurant manager in San Francisco, was disturbed enough by the error to write a thoughtful piece for a local newspaper.[9] "What does it take to be American?" she asked, noting how the TV report casually cast the young Kwan as the "other" when it came to comparisons with a Caucasian skater.

When Abby Scott, adopted from China, watched the TV coverage of that event, and heard the announcer bellow, "The American won!" she was so furious she threw a pillow at the TV. "I guess you don't think *I'm* American, either!" she yelled at the announcer.

Such thoughtless assumptions cause pain, even before they evolve into more damaging statements. And it's that kind of thoughtlessness that ethnic minorities face all the time. Unfortunately, it can get worse. Hate crimes against Asians have, in fact, increased in the United States in the past few years.

"*We heard about you* in China and flew all the way there to get you," Mark was saying to Kelly at bedtime. "We love you, sweetie." Then he looked troubled. "I don't know what else to tell her," he said. "What can we say?"

Kelly's life story begins, by necessity, a bit later than "On the night you were born . . ." But one flaw in its telling—"we went to China to find you"—is that adopted children, hearing how they were "chosen" or "found," may assume they came into this world in a different manner than other children. As Betty Jean Lifton writes in *Lost and Found: The Adoption Experience*: "Where do you connect with the human condition when you are chosen and everyone else is born?"

To point out some minor possibilities for confusion: One of Kelly's playmates, another adopted daughter from China, just past her second birthday, was sitting in the bathtub one day, exploring her body. "What's this?" she asked her mother, and her mother decided it was time for the preliminary facts of life. "That's your vagina," she said. The little girl looked expectant, so her mother went on. "Someday," she said, "a baby may come from there."

The little girl looked down, and then looked up, trying hard to grasp the information. "Va China?" she asked.

Explanations of a child's origins have to come again and again, presented each time in a way that's appropriate to her stage of understanding. Along the way, more "whys" may emerge and there will be thorny issues to tackle.

"Hundreds of ordinary questions that most people take for granted is information I've hungered for," writes Nona Mock Wyman, who lost her mother at the age of two and a half. "Where was I born? What were my mother and father like? How did they meet? Did I look like my mother or did I look like my father?"

I met Wyman, a charming Chinese American woman then in

her sixties, when a friend saw an announcement of a lecture she was giving at the International House at the University of California at Berkeley. Wyman had grown up in a Chinese orphanage, the notice said, and I was eager to hear her perspective.

As it turned out, Wyman had grown up in an orphanage not in China but in America, in an affluent area south of San Francisco. In an old mansion, the Ming Quong ("radiant light") home had been established in the Depression years to care for young Chinese American girls who were casualties of a turbulent time. Women who'd left China searching for a better life found their plight worse, Wyman said. They were exploited, forced into prostitution, enslaved.

Wyman, who had recently written an autobiography called *Chopstick Childhood*, was just old enough to remember when her mother took her to the orphanage, walked out the door, and never came back.[10] It left Wyman with a lifetime hunger for answers. "I'm a second-generation Asian American woman," Wyman said, "the product of a dark side of history."

Each year on Mother's Day, it was the ritual at the Ming Quong home to pin a rose on each girl's Sunday dress—red roses for girls whose mothers were living, white roses for those whose mothers were dead. And each year when Mother's Day came, Wyman was left in limbo. No one could tell her whether her mother was alive or not, but she asked to wear a red rose anyway.

"Miss Hayes paused and scanned my hopeful face," Wyman wrote in her memoir. "Canvassing her large assortment of rose bushes, she strode over to a bush at the corner of the garden and expertly snipped a pink rose. Beaming, she handed it to me."

Most of the daughters of China today, I knew, would also be wearing pink roses.

The adoption literature is full of stories chronicling the life-long task adopted children can have of coming to terms with the loss of a birth parent. Such children often harbor a hope that somewhere, sometime, a birth mother will come looking. "The mother who abandons her daughter leaves a pile of questions behind," wrote Hope Edelman in *Motherless Daughters*. "Who was she? Who is she? Where is she? Why did she leave? There can be an intense feeling of grief at some point in the life of a child who has lost birth parents, for whatever reason."

The prevailing issue for the child is "Why did it happen?" followed closely by "Was there something wrong with me?" Adopted children are profoundly curious about how they came to be relinquished. Each child who asks such questions deserves to hear the truth from her birth mother, of course, but few of the daughters of China will ever get that gift. For this generation of adopted daughters, there will be additional questions. Why, for instance, were almost all the lost children in China girls?

"Abandoned" is a harsh word, and it is tempting to soften the explanation, though the *A* word is long out of the barn, used, for instance, in the official documents each girl takes away from China. It's worth noting, however, that parents in China who take their children to the doorstep of a police station—or even more blatantly, to the front door of the Chinese Center of Adoption Affairs—with every intent of getting them to care and safety, are said to "abandon" their babies. In contrast, American women who bring their infants to the attention of a social service agency are said to "give up" or "relinquish" their children, and even that terminology now has given way to the gentler and more politically correct phrase, "make an adoption plan."

"The word 'abandoned' should be used only when it's absolutely true," says therapist Joyce Maguire Pavao. "When the little prom queen in this country leaves her baby in a trash can, that's truly abandoning a baby. Here, in America," she continues, "you can take your child to the department of social services, take yourself as a pregnant woman to an adoption attorney. In Asian countries it's different. Leaving a child on the hospital steps or on the road en route to the hospital is as close as anyone can get to making an adoption plan."

Whatever words are used, there is no turning back, and eventually our daughters will want to know what happened. "Tell your daughter the truth. Tell her you don't know where she came from," says a young Chinese woman who has studied adoptive families in the United States. "I don't believe we do any harm by saying 'I don't know' to tough questions," observes Jeanette Chu, who has dealt with these issues from the point of view of an adoptee as well as that of an adoptive mother.

"Soft landing" is the phrase Chinese professor Huang Bang-han uses when he talks about his hopes for the adopted daughters of China as they work their way through the questions of ethnicity, identity, cultural leanings, and the difficult explanations about their origins. One of two Chinese professors from Anhui province who has studied American adoptive families, Huang has also studied birth families in China. He talks of "building a bridge" between China and the United States, a bridge that will eventually help the children, their adoptive families, and the Chinese people, as well, understand one another and grow closer.

According to Huang, many Chinese people don't understand the intent of the foreigners who come to China to adopt their homeless children. He has been asked why the Americans don't adopt babies in their own country. Might these adopted children, it is feared, be used for medical experiments or pressed into servitude or prostitution? Do childless foreigners even know how to care for Chinese children?

As part of his research, Huang came to the United States and visited fifty adoptive families on the East Coast, including Amy DeNucci and her extended clan. He came away reassured that the current wave of East-West adoptions was beneficial for both adopted Chinese children and their American parents. He spoke of increased understanding between the two cultures, a "great experiment" in a new kind of family. And he predicted great success for the endeavor.

Huang went on to work on a book for readers in China, attempting to provide birth parents with information about the fate of some of the children. "We want to publish this book and say, 'Some of these girls are in America and they have happy lives and their adoptive parents are very nice to them,'" one of Professor Huang's assistants told me. "We hope to publish many pictures, so the birth parents may know that these girls are happy."

As for the girls themselves, it seems clear from the experience of Korean children adopted in America that life as an Asian child, and particularly as an adopted Asian child, in a predominantly white world can be a struggle and sometimes painful. When that is the case, the best comfort of all seems to come from other young people in the same position. For adopted daughters from China, groups of peers and older children who've paved the way may eventually offer the greatest companionship in an ongoing journey of self-discovery.

Kelly's extended family includes seventeen "sisters" or "cousins"—all the other little girls adopted by the families with whom we traveled to China. This family is growing all the time as we meet other families and welcome one little girl after another into the fold. When our second daughter, Franny, came home, we added a whole new group. Just about everywhere we traveled now, there seemed to be at least one moment of recognition when we saw another family that looked like us. It happened at a restaurant in Ohio's Amish country, it happened on a beach in Hawaii, it happened in my hometown of Boulder, Colorado. Sometimes I think families whose little girls have come from China need a secret handshake. Usually a gentle inquiry, out of the children's earshot, does the trick.

Over time, as is probably natural, Mark and I, and other families I have talked with, have come to think less about the sad and baffling background events in China and more about our astonishingly good fortune, the sheer richness of our lives together. These girls may have once been lost, but now they were clearly found, deeply and completely wanted. We may still have those blank pages in our daughters' baby books and issues to face down the road, but we—and they—have lots of company. Beyond our small circle is the wider community of East-West families, as well as people back in China—not just Professor Huang, but orphanage caretakers, foster mothers, and Buddhist monks chanting in that Guangzhou temple—all wishing China's daughters a soft landing.

Just as Kelly was about to celebrate her third birthday, we received sad news, word that one of her unofficial cousins, four years old, adopted the previous year from the same orphanage, had died of cancer. We had never met this little girl, who lived in the Midwest with her adoptive parents, but Mark and I were profoundly saddened and affected by the news. We could so clearly imagine the events in her short life—the orphanage she lived in, how long her new parents waited for her, how they felt when they first held her. In part at least, this girl's story was Kelly's story. She was a member of our extended family, and her loss was a loss for us all.

8

In the Light of the
Autumn Moon

My loving mother, thread in hand,
Mended the coat I have on now,
Stitch by stitch, just before I left home,
Thinking that I might be gone
  a long time.
How can a blade of young grass
Ever repay the warmth of the
  spring sun?

—*Meng Jia, "Traveler's Song"*[1]

The full moon was high in the October sky, fat and luminous, the light casting a yellow river of reflection across the waters of San Francisco Bay. I took Kelly out to moongaze, part of the observations for the Chinese Autumn Moon Festival. I thought it was a perfect time to honor my daughter's birth parents, since they, too, might have stared at that same moon during the ceremonies in southern China.

The Autumn Moon Festival is traditionally a time for families to reunite and pay homage to departed ancestors. Also known as the Day of Reunion, it falls on the fifteenth day of the eighth lunar month according to the Chinese calendar. That's when the moon is said to be brightest and fullest, the moonlight most beautiful. In the part of the world where Kelly comes from, families, in the light of glowing paper lanterns, would have been eating traditional round mooncakes made of thin dough stuffed with fruit, nuts, meat, and sweet bean paste.

The first year we were home from China, the festival fell in October, which was an auspicious month for us anyway. Kelly's birthday came that month, and it was in October that we first met her in that orphanage waiting room. My father had also passed away in October, and one of the last sights he saw on the night he died was a full autumn moon in the Arizona sky.

Now, as I held Kelly, saying, "See the beautiful moon?" both of us looking up at the luminescence in the vast darkness of the sky, I said a silent prayer for my father and mother, then for my daughter's birth mother and father. It was a little too early to talk about them with Kelly, but I knew the time would come soon. Bathed in moonlight, did they sometimes think about their daughter and wonder about her fate?

A few nights after our first try at moongazing, Kelly pointed to the door. "Moon?" she said. We'd come up with our own version of an ancient Chinese ritual, I realized. In Buddhist culture the moon can represent awakening. I couldn't think of a better setting in which to tell a child about her faraway first family and the love that can tie all people together than to look up in the sky at that astonishing sight. "Okay, Kelly," I said. "Let's go look at the moon." The moon festival, a young woman from the Pearl River Delta area had told me, was a time for families to tell one another the stories of their lives. I thought what a gift it could be if the daughters of China could someday hear a lost mother's story, but I doubted it would happen very soon.

I had so often tried to picture these mothers in the shadows, particularly the woman who gave birth to my daughter, wondering who she was and what her life was like. There were no real clues, just intuitive thoughts about how she must have been with this baby. Loving and desperate, I think. Loving because her daughter is sweet-natured and trusts people. Desperate because I can't imagine any other state of mind that would accommodate the reality of giving birth, caring for a child for three months, and then laying her down in a marketplace and walking away.

In my imagination, this mythical birth mother moves out of the shadows, comes toward me. She is beautiful and, like Kelly, when she says hello, she talks in a whisper. She carries her grief in the hollows of her cheeks, in the slump of her shoulders. She is far younger than I.

"It is strange, but I had always wanted a daughter," I hear her saying. I imagine this partly out of my own projection and wishful thinking, I know. I want my daughter to have been wanted. Of course, like so much else, I will never know this truth or untruth, either. But the likelihood is worth clinging to.

I nudge her to continue. "Shortly before midnight," she says softly, "in the light of the autumn moon, my baby was born. My girlfriend was with me, and a woman who knows about these things. I lay on a narrow cot and tried not to scream. We had to be secret. It was October and still warm outside, and the windows were open. '*Ai,*' said the midwife when she saw I had a girl. 'Bad news.'

"But I took that baby to my breast. They cut the cord and said my child was healthy. 'A Rat Year baby,' said my friend. 'A strong baby.' I felt exhausted but happy. Happy. And I stayed there for a few hours but then it was daybreak and I had to go. So I wrapped up that baby in cloth and I hid her under my clothes and I went out and walked up the street.

"I knew a place I could go to for a month, and so I did, up some long stairs and into the back hall where a friend lived and that's where I stayed. Back in the village I would not be welcomed. I ran away when I knew this baby would be coming, and I hope no one knows where I am.

"And the father? He might have come around for a son, but not for this. So I didn't even tell him. I stayed and my friend brought food and I thought about what I was going to do, how I could find work in a factory and still take care of this baby. And for a few weeks we just lay there mostly, the baby and I, and I fed her and told her stories about the village where I'd come from, about the oxen and the chickens and the little boys who kept knocking over the water bowl. I longed to take her home with me, but I could not. And so we stayed until the day my friend came home and said her family was coming to stay with her and I had to leave. I walked for two days with the baby, thinking I would meet someone or see someone who could help, that there would be a little place to stay.

"The second night I slept in an alleyway, and the third night I ran out of money and my food was gone and I knew then I couldn't care for this baby. What chance would she have, with a wandering mother who had no milk or money? I left her near the police station, in the market, in a pile of melons.

"I watched. After I left her, I watched, and soon a farmer settling into the stall saw her. He held up my baby and yelled at everybody around to come and tell him, please, just how this baby came to be in his fruit. There was silence. Everybody knew. The police came, and they took her. She didn't cry yet. I wanted to scream, to run out of my hiding place and take her back. But it was too late, and I bit my knuckle and stayed. I watched as they drove away. And that is the last I saw of her.

"I knew someone would find her and feed her, and after that, I hoped, she'd be strong enough to survive. But I don't know what happened. I have suffered ever since. I see her eyes at night, and I feel her cheek in the morning—until I wake up and find it's just the breeze on my face."

In my imagination, the mother leans forward. Her shoulders tremble.

"I know the orphanage in the city. It's big and they have many babies, and I hope that is where she went. They have food and clothing. And sometimes, foreign parents come and get the babies.

"I have seen the buses come with the Americans," she says. "It is my hope that someday years from now I will see a young girl get off one of those buses, a young girl who looks like me, and she will come looking. But I know it's just a dream."

So was my vision of this mother. But for now, it was all we had.

When Mark and I first began gathering what fragments of Kelly's past that we could, the young woman from Jiangmen I'd been in touch with promised to send us some photographs of the marketplace where our daughter was said to have been found. The pictures showed huge yellow squash hanging from hooks, oranges piled on tables, honeydew melons, apples and pears, bunches of greens. Outside the market were fruit stands; inside, the stalls that sold meat and fish.

"The market is usually the most promising and dirtiest place in China," wrote the young woman, on paper thin as a tissue. "It is surrounded by residential apartment buildings. No one here would guess that the people living in those nice apartments would abandon their newborn baby unless the mother got pressure from the traditional idea that boys are superior to girls."

Very evident in the photographs were several of Kelly's favorite items in life—oranges, grapes, and motorcycles. When I showed her the pictures, she studied them intently, then grinned and pointed at the motorcycles. "Mooms!" she said, with her usual enthusiasm. One of the thriving industries in Jiangmen, it turned out, was the manufacture of motorcycles.

I tucked away the photographs so she could look at them again over the years.

For every daughter lost, somewhere there was once a mother and a father, and grandparents, perhaps an aunt or uncle or two. But who, really, are these families left behind? Though any number of adoptive parents have asked that question, it's a query that remained, until the fall of 1998, largely unanswered. Theories had been advanced, anecdotes and occasional clues passed around, but the Chinese government had not volunteered any information about abandoning families. No research had been released that sharpened the portrait of these people or added to a general understanding of their circumstances or their motives. Nor were abandoning families—faced with their own fears of government reprisal, public shame, or both—likely to come forward on their own.

But beginning in 1995, Kay Johnson, professor of Asian studies at Hampshire College in Massachusetts (also an adoptive mother) and two Chinese professors from Anhui University, Huang Banghan (he of the wish for "soft landings") and Wang Liyao, began studying infant abandonment in China. They managed to persuade 237 families, mostly married couples living in rural areas, to tell their stories. The researchers published their report in the September 1998 issue of *Population and Development Review* and later in Johnson's book *Wanting a Daughter, Needing a Son.*[2]

In about half the cases, they found, the decision to abandon a daughter was made by the father. Another 40 percent of the time, the decision was made jointly by both parents, and in only a small portion of cases did the mother act alone. Most parents at the time were in their mid-twenties to late thirties. Most had an average education, primary school or junior middle school, for people of their age living in that particular region.

"In most cases where the father was the primary decision-maker," reported Johnson, "the birth mother knew about and at least reluctantly concurred in the father's decision, although birth mothers frequently expressed emotional pain and remorse for the act." Of the families studied, sixty-nine had abandoned a second daughter, sixty-two a third daughter, twenty-six a fourth daughter, and three a fifth daughter. The vast majority of children were abandoned within six months of their birth.

Most of the daughters in the sample, admittedly a small one, were abandoned close to home, and about half the parents claimed to know what happened to the child. It was extremely rare for an older sibling, rather than the youngest, to be abandoned. Parents were likely to keep a firstborn daughter, as well as sons who exceeded the birth quota.

Thus, the typical abandoned child was a healthy newborn girl who had one or more older sisters and no brothers as yet. She was let go because her birth parents already had at least one other daughter and wanted a son.

The researchers also looked into the adoption of abandoned girls within China. They found this a common practice, although discouraged at the time of the study by government policies. Whereas adoptive Chinese parents named practical and economic reasons for taking in sons, they took in daughters for more emotional reasons—to "increase the joy of life," for instance.

Johnson and her colleagues had done what no one had done before—given parents like me a peek behind closed doors, a glimpse at the circumstances that surrounded some of the mothers and fathers back in China.

If what Johnson found in her study can be applied broadly, perhaps the most important finding to have emerged from the interviews is the fact that it's likely that a fair portion of adopted daughters have a sister (or two) somewhere back in China, and if the family hopes were realized, a brother. To the equation of lost daughters and lost mothers, we could now add another element: lost siblings.

The revelation that half the parents believed they knew what had happened to their daughters made me wonder anew if someone might have been watching the market that fateful day in Kelly's life, or keeping an eye on the orphanage door when I walked away with a child in my arms.

Just after the great film director Akira Kurosawa's death, there was a screening of *Rashomon* on our local movie channel. The Japanese classic is a reminder, of course, of how many conflicting realities can be spun out of a single event. But I had forgotten the scene at the end where the cries of a small abandoned baby catch the attention of one of the characters, who picks up the child. "What evil people," says a bystander. "They have their fun and then throw the child away."

"Oh, no," says the man rocking the child in his arms. "Don't you see the amulet they left with her, trying to protect her? Who knows how they suffered?"

Of course, that was Japan and a scene from a film. But in China, in real life and real times, similar scenes had occurred in provinces east and west, north and south, in probably every village and city in the country. A powerful combination of events had simply collided to produce untold suffering among young and old alike, though the cries of China's lost girls—millions of them—as well as the cries of all their mothers had been largely drowned out.

I still wanted to know more about how the mothers felt, but I was of course viewing everything through the lens of my own experience. A Chinese friend who grew up in Beijing and had to leave after being involved in the student protest movement there, listened one afternoon while I speculated what Kelly's mother might be thinking. She shook her head. "You know," she said, "I think there is not the looking inward in China that you imagine, especially for those in poverty. People are too busy surviving."

Although parents like myself now know more than we used to about some of the lost parents of China, information about particular mothers or fathers remains hard to come by, perhaps impossible. Maybe someday DNA testing and matching might reunite some families, but it was also likely that the majority of birth mothers in China would keep their secrets.

Uncertainty is where we began, and uncertainty may be where we end.

A day or two after I'd been thinking about all this, I woke in the night, stuck by something in the quilt on my bed. As I fumbled about in the covers, I felt another sharp stab. Digging at the tufts of fabric, I found a thin needle. The quilt is hand-stitched, made in China, yet one more item in my household that fills me with uncomfortable ambivalence. It's a beautiful copy of an old wedding-ring pattern, meant to appeal to American buyers, but like the soapstone Buddha on my altar, too much sacrifice undoubtedly went into it.

When I pulled out the needle—a hair-thin shaft with an almost invisible, impossible-to-thread eye—it was as if the quilt's anonymous seamstress had poked me. Someone threaded that needle, sewed the stitches, lost her place in the cotton batting, and lost the needle. I found it, though it had to prick me in the night to get my attention.

It was easy to see how anyone could let such a tiny needle slip through her tired fingers. But what were my chances of finding that needle on the other side of the planet in the middle of the night, just as I was at work on a book concerning my daughter's life back in China? Just as I was trying to fathom the lives of the lost mothers of adopted Chinese babies—the philosophical equivalent, perhaps, of searching for a needle in a haystack.

The needle in the quilt seemed a rather pointed clue to my inquiry. First, it suggested to me that some things are impossible to trace, but second, that nothing comes completely anonymously. The hand of the maker is always there. The stitches in my quilt have their story to tell: They are precise, likely made by small, deft hands flying like birds across the fabric. Intent—probably weary—eyes followed the pattern. A human being, most likely a woman (or women? Were there quilting bees in China?) worked for hours on this quilt, poking and pulling this thin needle through the fabric.

The Navajo always weave some intentional bit of imperfection into their rugs, a flaw through which the spirits can move. So do Amish women, in their quilts. In Chinese art, an empty spot is known as a fertile void. That's what I seem to have ended up with for now, a gap ripe for imaginings. Through the needle in my quilt came the spirit of the seamstress. Someone with careful hands. Someone with a sense of beauty. Someone working way too hard. And through the poke in the night came a new way of looking at the birth mothers of China.

The daughters of China, set down in public places, found and cared for, had blessed thousands of families thousands of miles away. But by necessity in most cases, the blessings came as secret offerings. The vast majority of the birth mothers of China had for their own reasons faded into the distance, an unfortunate fact of life not only for the lost daughters, but for the women themselves. "I'm sad my daughter's mother will never know her child," said adoptive mother Stephanie Chan, "but I'm happy she was brave enough to give birth to her."

"One thing I know in defense of these women who abandon their babies," said an American adoptive mother who lives and works in China, "is that they must have some special kind of love for these unborn souls because it is very easy, and encouraged, to have an abortion here."

Do these Chinese mothers suffer? How could they not? They may be busy surviving, but there is no way they can forget. Grief, pushed beneath the surface, still bubbles up. Shadowing such questions concerning the feelings of birth parents, there's sometimes a dark undercurrent of prejudice among non-Chinese, a supposition that life in China and other parts of Asia is somehow cheap and that people somehow suffer less, and that mothers are less likely to mourn. It's an opinion that was thrown about casually during the Vietnam War and that hovers below the surface of some conversations today. Robert Shaplen, the eloquent journalist who covered Vietnam for *The New Yorker*, put such odious comparisons down very succinctly. Asian mothers hugged their children as tenderly as did any other mothers, he wrote, and if there is more fatalism among Asians because death is more common and more sudden, there is also ample compassion and love.[3]

Furthermore, any woman who gives birth and then loses that infant, by whatever means, still has all the original physiological attachment. As Natalie Angier observes in *Woman: An Intimate Geography*: "There are the stimuli of attachment that we know of, and those that slip in unsung and unknowable. Years and years after a woman has delivered a child, she continues to carry vestiges of that child in her body." A woman who is separated from her child after just a few days or weeks has very specific physical reminders of that infant. A nursing mother who sets down a child will have strong physical nudges from that child for some time to come.

Where did this wonderful daughter of mine come from? From whose flesh, I can't say. Nor at this point can I tell my daughter any more than a generalized story about her origins. Even the geography is a bit loose, vaguer than I used to think. I like to believe the scene I have conjured up of the winter melons, but she might have been found near the flowers for sale, or even miles away in another place altogether. The harder we poke at such information, the vaguer it can become.

This unknown mother's story could be any number of stories. She could have suffered in countless, unfathomable ways. She could have faced the kind of poverty that took her down to her last dried yam or used bus ticket. She could have found herself carrying a child to the public square, sobbing all the way, and have seen no other way out. But with that gesture, as she set her baby down, she probably wished her daughter a future better than her own.

This baby was found; she was meant to be found—that is the important point here. The story that Kelly's mother had to offer, I realized, was closer than we thought. The best evidence was Kelly herself. Her sweetness and courage, her humor and grace. Her mother left the biggest clue of all in this baby's ready smile. Her mother loved her. If I know nothing else about this woman who gave me the gift of this beautiful child, I believe this: When she cared for this baby, she cared whole-heartedly. When she set her down, she set her down gently.

During an appearance of Thich Nhat Hanh's that I attended in Berkeley, the Vietnamese monk took questions from the audience. One man raised a hand and said that he just could not forgive his father, who had abandoned him at a young age. The serene monk gave the most beautiful answer. All humans, he said, are born to love and cherish their children. When they are unable to do that, some sort of overwhelming cause or condition must have interfered with that ability. It seemed such a compassionate explanation—and so close to that phrase in one of the notes found with a Chinese child—"heavy pressures that are too difficult to explain."

9

The Search for Roots

You've just come from my old hometown.
You must have some news of home.
The day you left, was the plum tree
By my window in bloom yet?

—*Wang Wei, "News of Home"*[1]

"The people all rushed out to meet me," said May Wong. A young woman of Chinese heritage who grew up in northern California, Wong was speaking about a trip she took to southern China when she was twenty-five. She walked into the tiny village her father had left forty years before. I spoke with May Wong one afternoon because I wanted to know what it was like for someone Chinese American who'd grown up in this country to go to China in search of her familial roots. "You start to question why you were brought up the way you were," said Wong, a lively young woman with short dark hair. "There's a feeling that you've missed something. Here in America, everyone is always working for the future and there's not much emphasis on where you've been. In China, the focus is on where the family has been."

Wong described feelings that by now sounded familiar. She said her aim growing up in northern California's wine country, was to assimilate, to blend in. "It wasn't until I went off to college at the University of California at Berkeley that I looked around and saw that the population was one-third Asian." Although she'd grown up speaking the dialect of her father's native village with her family at home, she didn't speak or understand the area's more widely spoken Cantonese dialect, and by her own admission, she hadn't paid much attention to the traditions her family had tried to pass down as she was growing up. "Going to college was a turning point," she said. "I realized how little I knew about being Chinese, and I wanted to change that."

She heard about a program at San Francisco's Chinese Culture Center called *In Search of Roots*, and was drawn to it. "I think it happened the year it did because my parents are getting older," she said. "I knew that anything that hadn't been passed along wouldn't be." The Chinese Culture Center leads thoughtfully planned trips to southern China each year for young people like May Wong. A handful of interns, aged sixteen to twenty-five, spend a year researching their individual family trees, the history of Chinese people in America, and background about Guangdong province and China.

As part of the program, the interns take a ferry trip to Angel Island in San Francisco Bay, a beautiful spot now run by the National Park Service but clouded by a regrettable past. A sort of Ellis Island West, Angel Island was the port of entry (and sometimes the point of non-entry) for thousands of Chinese who came to California between 1910 and 1940. After a boat trip from China, which itself often lasted a month, the new arrivals were interrogated, examined for infectious diseases, and made to wait. Over the years, some 175,000 immigrants were detained here, for weeks, for months. Some were sent back to China.

The old barracks and immigration detention center still stand today, and the children of immigrants come here to get a sense of what their ancestors went through, to confront a time of discrimination and suffering. Young Chinese Americans who grew up in America tour the buildings where many of their relatives whiled away their days and nights, often in despair.

May Wong knew that her grandfather had spent time on Angel Island, but when she actually saw the old buildings, read the reflections of those who'd been held here, she found it more distressing than she expected. She had assumed her grandfather entered America just as immigrants of other ethnicities had and was shocked to learn about the discrimination against the Chinese. In the old barracks, where immigrants slept on triple bunk beds, sad poems penned by Cantonese villagers from the Pearl River Delta still decorate the walls. "Nights are long and the pillow cold; who can pity my loneliness?" reads one. "After experiencing such loneliness and sorrow, why not just return home and learn to plow the fields?"

Her eyes opened, Wong went off to China with the other interns to visit the old villages and cemeteries, to search for ancestral tablets bearing their family names. In a tiny village in southern China, Wong was shown the way to her father's family home. "It felt like a window back in time," she said. "There was the family altar, and there on the wall was a picture of my grandparents and of my three eldest sisters. The village was pretty much preserved as it was. They had electricity; that was a change, but everything else had remained simple.

"Everyone wanted to know how my parents were," said Wong. "The people in the village know they're the keepers of history. They know what's going on with my family. We looked at genealogy that went back thirty-six generations.

"I told them I wanted to do the ancestral worship," Wong said. She lighted three sticks of incense and bowed, to unite the past, the present, and the future. "I reflected on the many generations that had preceded me and realized that my family's experience in the United States was a mere visit compared to our history in China. I could understand why they said to me, 'Oh, you've come back.' We'd only been gone a generation."

Not everyone who traveled with her found such close links. "Some were four generations removed from the village," Wong told me. "In past years, people have gone on the trips and not found anything. But even then, going halfway around the world, some found the answers were at home. One person, having gone to China, found a great-uncle in Oakland, California."

While she was in China, Wong tried to immerse herself as much as possible in the local culture, though it wasn't always easy. "As Americans, we were identifiable," she said. "There's something about the way we carry ourselves, about the backpacks we wear, about our glasses."

The exploration of her roots gave Wong, a math teacher in a San Francisco private school, the urge to return to China, perhaps to live there and teach for a while. "Though I'd never been there before, it felt so familiar and so comfortable," she said. "And it's good just to be surrounded by people who look like you." Another intern from a past year had reported that the trip back made him realize, even though he didn't know the traditions or customs of his culture, and though he might not speak a word of his native tongue, that he was and always would be Chinese.

These observations reminded me of something Bette Bao

Lord wrote in her book *Legacies*. Lord, who left Shanghai at the age of eight, returned to China decades later with her husband, Winston Lord, when he was the U.S. ambassador to that country. Going back to China as an adult, Lord said, she was struck by strong feelings of kinship. She described going to her grandfather's grave, bowing three times, and leaving chrysanthemums. She realized that the gravestone would endure "for my grandfather, for us, for my Chinese roots, so when one day the children of my children and their children, who won't speak Chinese, look Chinese, or know China, visit this lone ancestor, they will feel as Chinese as I did that afternoon at his grave."

Author Amy Tan, born in Oakland, California, once said that as soon as her feet touched China, she became Chinese.

When Kelly and I walk through San Francisco's Chinatown, I find myself looking into the faces we pass—grandmothers bent over with bags of oranges; mothers pushing babies in strollers or carrying them on their backs in fabric slings the old-fashioned way; teenagers sitting in a restaurant window eating noodles. I know that most of the people along Grant Avenue or Stockton Street or in Portsmouth Square are Cantonese, from Guangdong province, where Kelly comes from, and that a considerable number are, in fact, from the Pearl River Delta area, where she was born. One of the travel brochures for Jiangmen City notes that the area is known as a destination for overseas Chinese in search of their ancestral roots.

So many people have immigrated over the years that I know my daughter is as likely to have relatives, however distant, right here in Chinatown as back in China. The sad catch remains:

How can she find them with no name to trace, no known place of birth to refer to? Psychiatrists even have a term for what a child in this position may feel: genealogical bewilderment.

In the community of adopted Korean children there is now a move to find some of the birthplaces and birth parents who were once considered lost forever. Years ago, when American parents were adopting from Korea, they, too, heard stories of how their children had been discovered. Alone, under a tree, in a field. "Very often," said Linda Grillo, who has worked with Korean American families seeking to find their children's birth mothers and fathers, "parents were told that children had been abandoned, that there was no information available about the parents and that there was no way to communicate."

But one family found out otherwise when they helped their adopted Korean daughter search for her birth family. As it turned out, the girl hadn't been left anonymously as her American family had been told, but placed for adoption by her birth parents. "They found out way too late what the truth was," said Grillo. "It took a Korean going there and asking the right questions. The shock was that the family in Korea wondered why they had never heard from the adoptive family."

It wasn't long before similar searches began to be undertaken for children adopted from China. Journeys back to China would be the next trend in this story, predicted Val Free, of Heartsent Adoptions in Orinda, California. How right she was! Free traveled to China frequently with groups of adoptive parents and early on had taken all three of her adopted children (two from China and one from Thailand) back to their countries of origin.

It can be a wonderful experience, she said, yet a return trip required plenty of emotional work, before and after, particularly if looking for further information about birth families is part of the trip. Whether a child reacts with silence or nonstop questions, it is a deeply important passage, and it will be different for every child, depending on age, temperament, and numerous other factors, some predictable, some not. What are the returning family's expectations—particularly about further information on a birth family, or about a return visit to the institution? Some former caretakers may shower a child with enthusiasm; others may not remember, or may pretend to recall details that don't fit. "Some parents romanticize China and the whole experience to the point that children may expect foster parents to remember more than they do, or for birth parents to even appear," cautioned Free. "And other families may paint stories that are so traumatic as to make China seem scary." Some children will be eager to go, some reluctant.

Over time, though, especially for families traveling back to China, some additional information was bound to emerge. "People live very closely together in China," said a woman from Beijing, who works closely with rural women in poverty. "There aren't many secrets." Writer Ha Jin, author of, among others, the acclaimed novel *Waiting*, had made a similar observation, that the Chinese language contains no word for "solitude." "The birth parents know where they left the children," said adoption therapist Joyce Maguire Pavao. "With DNA testing, these girls may be able to find something." By 2008, in fact, a number of birth families and biological siblings had been located.

Not every child will have an urge to search out her roots or return to China for a visit. These impulses are very individual. But as the girls adopted from China grow up, many may want to take a trip like May Wong's, to come as close as they can to the place of their birth.

One of Kelly's "cousins," Miranda (Mandy) Wirt, who came from the same orphanage, and whose family is part of our adoption group, wrote this when she was eleven: *I was born in Jiangmen, China. It makes me feel kind of lucky that I get to have more than one pair of parents in my life, but it makes me sad to not know who my birth parents are. It's also nice to know the girls who you are adopted with, and to have other friends who are adopted, because you can talk about how you feel. When I get older I want to find my birth parents. I might like to visit China.*

"Someday, when these girls are twelve or thirteen, maybe we can all travel back to China together for a reunion," Max told us when Kelly and her cousins were five. He was taking some rare time off, visiting families across the country into whose hands he had placed a daughter. There were by then hundreds and hundreds of them. A group of us had gathered for a potluck in his honor. A dozen daughters of China were talking, playing, and sticking their fingers in cake frosting. They were placed one by one in Max's arms for a photograph. The littlest girl there had just come home from China a few months before, the second adopted daughter in her family. Jeffrey, our guide on the China trip, was along on this visit, too, and late in the evening he was persuaded to sing the "Little Swallow" song that he'd sung on that tour bus long ago in China.

Maybe we'd all sing that song again someday on a bus rolling through the south China countryside. Though our daughters may have no ancestral home to return to, no place that may feel as familiar to them as it did to May Wong or Bette Bao Lord, there were compelling reasons to keep the connection with China alive and to help our daughters make a journey back if and when they feel it's time.

I knew we'd have to prepare ourselves thoughtfully. For one thing, even a few years after Kelly had come home, much had changed in Jiangmen. The director of Kelly's institution was retired now, though some families had still stayed in touch. We saw her on one of our earlier trips back to China and have photos of her hugging Kelly, as well as a little sun hat she gave our daughter that day. Not long ago, she wrote a letter to another family in our group. "We never forget any child's face or their love," she wrote.

Still, for children who do make the trip, to return to some parts of China in ten years or so may be to return to a China that is almost unrecognizable. Even assuming that someone might know which village to look for, the village might be gone. If Mark and I could find our way to Kelly's particular marketplace, the market might be just a memory, the heavy foot of a skyscraper, or a Starbucks coffeeshop, resting where piles of pole beans used to be. In the ten years since our life-altering bus ride to Jiangmen, the population of that city had more than doubled. Both the social welfare institutions our daughters lived in might still be there, although as I write this I find myself hoping, in a way, that eventually they will be gone, or at least used for something else. Not so my daughters couldn't see them, but as affirmation that things by then will have changed enough that orphanages full of little girls will no longer be a fact of life in China.

Mark, Kelly, and I frequently leaf through the memory books of our trips to China, looking through photos of Kelly's orphanage and the Pearl River Delta area and Guangzhou, and

Franny's book with its photos of Changzhou and Nanjing. With each girl, we always come back to that page labeled "questions with no answers." And with each discussion, we seem to take on another little piece of the puzzle. Whatever our plans for handling all this, I've learned that the subject is going to pop up when we least expect it, and that the girls will shed their own special light on whatever we could present.

When she was small, Kelly saw the film version of E. B. White's *Stuart Little*, in which a pair of "real" mouse parents show up to take Stuart away from his adoptive family. The next day, she began asking us, "When are my parents coming? Are they going to take me away?" We spent a long time assuring her that we were her parents (a word she'd not used before), that we'd never let her go, that no one else was going to come for her. "We're your parents, forever and ever," we told her again and again. She listened quietly, and then went to bed. The next morning she came running into our bedroom. "Parents!" she announced in a loud, booming voice. "Wake up! I'm hungry!"

As for the future of our daughters' birthplaces, just two things seem certain: first, that conditions in China will remain fluid and unpredictable; and second, that China will continue to keep some secrets. It's hard enough to take in the reality of present-day China, much less forecast the future. At least one anthropologist has said that it's no longer feasible even to look at China as an entity, so varied are the traditions, economies, people, politics in different regions. Then, on top of an already complex picture is a constant rumbling of tumultuous, galloping change. Says Jeanette Chu, an American who has lived and worked in Guangzhou, speaks several Chinese dialects, and is the adoptive mother of a Chinese daughter, "I live here and see real people and real life on a daily basis. I have been in the homes of the affluent and the very poor, observed everything from centuries-old rural life to high-tech boomtowns. I still know nothing about China."

My father spent his last days working on his family tree, filling in some twigs, adding some branches. This was before he knew, officially at least, that he was dying. It seems as if humans are programmed to do these kinds of things, as birds are driven to build nests. We examine pictures of our forebears and wonder about their lives; we try to understand where they've been as a way of knowing where we are going. The urge seems to accelerate as people get closer to the end. So Dad filled in an actual family tree, with apples for all the members of his family. My little apple dangles from one of the branches as solidly as any of the other apples. No distinction has been made for my adoptive status, and I know that's how he saw it in life as we lived it, too. We'd made our way through the questions and come to a lasting attachment.

When Kelly was first home, a card came from Dad's cousin, a wonderfully sweet man in his late eighties. "Welcome to the clan," he wrote to Kelly. No requirements for admission here. A bunch of Welsh immigrants were ecstatic to have a small Chinese girl in the family. So was Mark's French German Ohio clan, the English and Scottish contingents, and the Japanese American Florida branch. Family members on my sister-in-law's Mexican Chinese twig kept inquiring about "La Chinita." I was, and am, exceedingly grateful for our mixed and loving group. What my daughters will make of all this, I don't know.

More than thirty years after Alex Haley's best-selling book

Roots came out, *Time* magazine ran a cover story on family history in the computer age: "Genealogy is America's latest obsession. And thanks to the computer, it's as easy as one, two, three."[2] Well, not for everybody, at least not yet. For most of the adopted daughters of China at the time, the search links to China stopped at the orphanage. Tomorrow, who knew?

In the meantime, Kelly was continuing to bless and amaze us. Early on, she seemed to evince a Zen-like approach to life. Sitting back in her car seat when she was four, she said, "Mom? Some things come and some things go."

"That sounds right to me," I told her.

"Mom? Some people have homes and some people don't, and that's not okay.

"Mom? Sometimes kids are sad."

And one day, she said, "My grandfather with the three broken teeth told me some things."

Kelly occasionally talked about things that seem to have no links to our life together in northern California. Where the image of this grandfather with three broken teeth comes from, I haven't a clue, but she had been telling me stories about the old gentleman for some time now.

"Who is this grandfather with three broken teeth?" I asked her after she'd quoted him again on some subject. "He lived in China," she answered. "He was my Baba. When I got him he was new, but then he died." She shook her head sadly. "He wanted to have more life with me."

Memory? Imagination? Pieces of something she has seen or overheard? I don't know, and probably never will. But living with mysteries and vaguely understood pieces of the past is part of our work together.

When one of Kelly's four-year-old cousins adopted from

China, Amy Komatsu, heard that her preschool teacher was about to have a baby, she confronted her teacher with what, for her, was the obvious question: "When are you going to China?" It's no wonder our children think this way.

In my daughter's small preschool there were five girls from China. They were a spirited group, with their own particular worldview. Two of them were sitting in the playground one day, talking about their origins, when another little girl joined the conversation. Blond and blue-eyed, she told them that she, too, was adopted, and that she came from North Carolina. "No," they chorused, "you're from China."

At a bar mitzvah we attended when Kelly was five, at one point in the ceremony the parents spoke to their son in front of the assembled guests, telling him how proud they were of him and how much they loved him. They told him what a good teacher he was for his younger brother. I got tears in my eyes listening, and Kelly leaned over and said softly, "Mom, why are you crying?"

"They're telling Jeremy how much they love him," I said, "and it's so sweet."

"Oh," she whispered, "they're celebrating becoming a family."

"Yes," was all I could manage at the time, but it struck me later, once again, how much our kids struggle to make sense of their lives, try to understand their own story in the context of what they see and hear around them. The hardest questions were yet to come. It made me appreciate anew one of my favorite quotations from the poet Rainer Maria Rilke: "The point is to live everything. Live the questions now. Perhaps then, someday far in the future, you will gradually, without even noticing it, live your way into the answer."[3]

And with help, I think we can do that.

If families created through transcultural adoption offer particular challenges, they also offer a new way of looking at the world. Evan Eisenberg, the adoptive father of a girl from China named Sara Xing, wrote a thoughtful essay on how adoption seems to fit into the human scheme, in which he made this observation: "Adoption urges us toward a more fluid sense of family, a broader sense of community. . . . We move into a richer environment than the nuclear family can provide. Although modern adoption remains firmly within the nuclear orbit, it is inherently a part of this richer notion of child raising, this soup of relations that may be thicker, even, than blood."[4]

The larger the family, the better. For one thing, there are always those on the road ahead, to help us through. Nona Mock Wyman, an orphan raised in northern California (see chapter 7), for instance, tells the story of how each year on Mother's Day, all the girls in her orphanage were given roses to wear. Red roses for girls whose mothers were alive, white roses for those whose mothers had died. And a pink rose for Nona, who didn't know whether her mother was alive or dead.

Later, Wyman wrote to say that one night when she was doing a book reading, an old friend of hers, Reynold Lum (who had himself grown up in an orphanage for Chinese boys, in El Cerrito, California), appeared to wish her a happy birthday. "He surprised me with two beautiful long-stemmed roses," she wrote, "and yes, one was pink and one was red." And then he presented her with a poem he had written for her:

And a child asked,
"Is my mother still living?"
And someone answered, "Your mother lives in you."[5]

Among the many blessings of adoption is the possibility of healing in the wake of loss, a re-weaving of family and an expansion of the idea of kinship. The family of young Daniel Mauser, killed in the Columbine High School shootings in Colorado, went on to adopt a Chinese baby girl, Madeline HaiXing.[6] When the twenty-fifth anniversary of the airlift of Vietnamese orphans came around, on April 5, 2000, it turned out that one of the children who'd been brought from Vietnam to this country had become a schoolteacher, and now, among her students, was a young girl adopted from China. As the world continues to mix in such amazing and intimate ways, weaving sorrowful events into joyous reunions, I am struck more and more by the extraordinary sense of community and generosity and willingness—on both sides of the globe.

From Spain, I have heard from adoptive father Jaume Josa, who has translated parts of this book into Spanish (*Las Hijas Perdidas de China*) for families in that country. One of those readers wrote recently, "I can assure you that the red thread (*hilo rojo*) really exists. You couldn't go before or after, it can't be in one city or another. It has to be that day and in that place, since your daughter is already waiting for you there."

I have heard from people whose daughters lived in the same orphanage as mine did. "Shayna was one of the first out of the Jiangmen orphanage," Stefani Ellison wrote. Shayna came away not with a green plastic cup, as Kelly did, but with an apple. "We pried it out of her hands at night and she grabbed it first thing in the morning. When we went back the second time, the director, Mrs. Chen, sent us home with a clock for Shayna. She wanted it kept on Chinese time, so that Shayna would always know what time it was in China. Shayna may never know the love of her birth mother, but she was truly loved in China."

After the first edition of this book was published, I heard
from the father of the little girl adopted from China who had
died of cancer, Steve Allen, who lives in Akron, Ohio. He wrote
to say that he'd donated a copy of my book to the University of
Akron library, inscribed in memory of Natalie Xiaoqing Allen,
who'd come from the same orphanage as my first daughter.

Months later, Allen wrote again: "I thought you would be as
excited as anyone to hear this. We got word tonight that an
eight-month-old girl named You Qi is waiting for us in Hunan
Province." He quoted from a "progress report" he'd received
from China, and his recounting of the story echoed so many of
the thousands and thousands of accounts of little girls lost, little girls found: "On December 23, 1999, Mr. Lou Wen found a
[nine-day-old] baby dressed in an old green coat and red cap. He
brought the baby to our orphanage. Six months have passed
since the baby arrived. The baby is healthy, development is
good. She shows a great interest in everything around her." In
late October, Steve and his wife, Shelley, composed a letter to
You Qi (soon to be renamed Joni Qi), pledging their love and
thanking her for coming into their lives. And then they left for
China, carrying Natalie in their hearts.

Cory and Marlene Barron journeyed from St. Louis to
Wuhan, and discovered the deepest possible meaning of that favorite Chinese phrase "double happiness." First, they took into
their arms a beautiful ten-month-old, their new daughter,
whom they named Abbi. They met the foster family who'd
taken care of her for most of the first year of her life, and then
they went off to get to know their child.

Five days later, the Barrons were in their hotel lobby when a

Chinese family walked in and began waving to them. The Barrons recognized Abbi's foster father, and in his arms was another baby. Not just any other baby, but a child who looked identical to Abbi. "She was smaller, not as healthy," recalls Cory Barron, "but all the same features were there."

Marlene Barron will never forget that moment of recognition. "Both of us were thinking, It's her twin. She must be Abbi's sister. We knew in that moment we could not separate them."

The foster family, the Barrons learned, had boarded a bus on their day off, traveled several hours from their home to Wuhan, and gone searching, hoping to find the Americans who had walked away with only one girl. "They probably just felt that we had to know before we flew out of China that a twin would be left behind," says Cory. "They took a risk. They had no way of knowing what our reaction would be." Marlene Barron looked into the second child's face and said, "We'll take her."

Within days, after concerted work by the adoption facilitator and Chinese officials, word came that the adoption of both girls would be approved. A DNA test confirmed what the eye could see. The girls were identical twins. The other adoptive families in the Barrons' group spontaneously showered them with the money they needed to complete the adoption.

As they were handed their second daughter, a Chinese official noted that the child seemed to have "dropped from heaven." And so, a week later than they expected to head home with one daughter, Cory and Marlene Barron flew home with two, Abbi and Grace. Almost three years old now, the twins are inseparable. The Barrons are planning a trip to Wuhan when the girls are ten or eleven. "We want to take them back to visit the foster parents," says Cory.

By 2008, thanks in part to the well-connected community

among adoptive parents, many other families had found that the child they adopted had a twin or close sibling who'd been adopted by another family.

Since that fateful trip in October 1997, the group Mark and I first traveled with to China has stayed in close touch. United by fate, we have grown into a close-knit extended family, and always feel blessed and eager to see one another. In another world and another time, what could possibly have pulled us all together? And yet here we all are.

"My thoughts on the trip to China were initially that we were going to go, get Claire, and come home," said one mother, Sharon Ogomori. "Now I am tied by the hip to all of you. I relish any news of our girls and their parents."

Susan August-Brown was another who'd never imagined becoming part of such a group. "But in a hotel lobby in Hong Kong in October 1997," she said, "I was folded into eighteen families, and I have had a change of heart. We have stayed connected, some individually, some as the larger whole. I wish to watch these little nieces, whom I have come to love, grow. There is also a greater hope: One day my daughter may find within this little band a soul mate with whom to share her feelings for the unknown family left behind."

After Congress passed the Child Citizenship Act, which became effective on February 27, 2001, granted automatic citizenship to children adopted abroad by American parents, spontaneous parties broke out across the country.[7] "We're celebrating today," Richard Caballero told me from Los Angeles. Earlier in the year our family had welcomed in the Chinese New Year with Richard and his wife, Rosalie, their daughter

Roxann Dawson (a.k.a. Lieutenant B'Elanna Torres on the TV series *Star Trek Voyager*), her husband, Eric, and their daughters, Emma and Mia, who was adopted from China. The law was an important milestone; at the very least it represented one less pile of paperwork that adoptive parents had to face, since applications for citizenship earlier took some doing and a wait of a year or more.

If there is one more reflection to be made on our side of this transcultural exchange, it's this: I have never anywhere met a more grateful or happier group of parents.

10

Double Happiness

Here they were again—
Spring's tender buds of hope, rinsed
With rain and eager.

—*Karin Evans*

The small faces haunt everyone who sees them. In China's institutions they peer up at visitors, sometimes only mildly curious, as if they know people will come and go, but their own lives will remain the same. Sometimes, there is a small sea of babies, rolling around the institution floor in wheelie chairs, whiling away their time. Or an older child, sitting alone, who shyly smiles in your direction.

If you are allowed into a crib room when you visit, you wander through the rows, looking at the tiny faces, crib after crib, baby after baby, and it's all you can do to keep from lifting each child up, and then another, and another. . . .

Well, you want to take them all home, and of course you can't. But maybe just one? One more? By the time Kelly was four, several families in our adoption group were heading back to China for a little sister and it wasn't long before we, too, began talking about the possibility. Kelly, now four, liked the idea of a little sister—she said she wanted to name her Pokémon Snow White. We weren't so sure about that, but we thought it would be good for two girls to have each other. So in 2000 we set off down the paper trail all over again.

This time, I was angst-ridden in a different way. I didn't worry so much about all the paperwork and our passing muster. Somehow I knew it would all work out, in its own time and in its own way, and it did. We said we would be willing to take an older child or a child with special medical needs. When a two-year-old showed up, a little girl with a congenital heart defect, we took one look at her photo and, again, fell in love. That's when the hard part began—seeing her face, longing to get to her, worrying about her.

She was in an orphanage in Changzhou, where one of the first Half the Sky programs had been put in place, so we knew she had good care. Still, she had surgery ahead of her and her medical condition wasn't fully known. According to the details we eventually were given, she had been taken to a local hospital at eighteen months and left there, presumably by her birth parents. Given her age and condition, they were probably desperately seeking medical help for her, but couldn't afford to pay for it. Their child had a large ventricle septal defect, a hole between the two chambers of the heart. This is a relatively common congenital malformation that's usually easily corrected in infancy in places where early medical help is available. Lacking surgery to correct the hole in her heart, the child could not thrive.

After the hospital and police tried to find her family, to no avail, this small girl was taken to the local social welfare institution, where she was given the Chinese name of Yi Xuan. Her Chinese nickname was Xuan Xuan, pronounced *shwen shwen*. To English speakers, she was known as "Peanut."

A pair of Chinese American pediatricians who were visiting institutions with an agency, offering what help they could to children who needed medical attention, saw her—standing quietly, not much energy, pale, so tiny—and knew she needed help. They arranged for her to go to a Project Hope hospital, and they offered to pay the bill. Yi Xuan was taken to Shanghai, where she underwent surgery to repair the hole in her heart, and she came through fine. We heard she was soon toddling around the hospital, winning friends, "running the place."

We bought another made-in-China Pooh bear to send to Changzhou, a red silk thread tied around his arm, to keep her company until we could get there. Four months after her surgery, we received permission to travel to China to adopt her. Mark, Kelly, our dear friend "Auntie" Mary Adrian, and I flew to Shanghai, then to Nanjing, and then took a car trip to Changzhou. Kelly carried a white wool lamb into the orphanage to give to her new little sister.

When we met her, our new daughter was not quite three years old. She weighed just nineteen pounds. She was wearing a little turquoise blouse-and-shorts outfit, and shoes with soft silk socks, and she looked very delicate. In the orphanage waiting room with its white lace table cloth and bowls filled with huge red grapes, the *ayis*—the "aunties" who'd cared for her—and the orphanage director explained to her in Chinese that we were her new family, and she burst into tears. We tried to console her and the *ayis* peeled grapes for her, to no avail.

She had already traveled a hard road, we knew. And seeing it from her perspective, it was not just one loss, but a series of upheavals: You are left in a hospital, your birth parents suddenly gone. Then you are taken to an orphanage, and later to another hospital where you undergo heart surgery, then back to the institution. Just a few months later, you are told by your caregivers that you are going to meet your new mother and father, who intend to take you away. Forever.

One day the big strangers arrive. They turn out to be Caucasian people bringing a little girl, older, who looks like the people you are used to, and who seems to have a place in the family already. She seems sweet, and she brings you a present, but really, what is going on here? You will soon be taken away from everyone and everything that has felt familiar, from the moment you woke up in the morning until you closed your eyes at night. You will miss the babies in their cribs that you used to check on each day, walking between the rows, saying good morning. You will miss the bowls of familiar food and your own crib. You have no idea who these new people are or where you are going.

When the staff tried to take the official family portrait for our paperwork, Yi Xuan wailed inconsolably. They decided to wait awhile. She cried and cried and finally they took the picture anyway—a photo that still wrenches my heart: Kelly leaning toward her new sister, looking baffled, Mark and I trying to look cheerful, and Yi Xuan trying to struggle out of our arms, sobbing.

The orphanage director took us all for lunch at a restaurant near the institution, where Yi Xuan briefly cheered up when Mark gave her a lollipop and she found she could threaten to bop him with it and make him flinch. He threw himself into the game, rearing back dramatically, and she finally began to laugh. When lunch was over, she bravely, silently, followed us out into the waiting car and her new, unknown life ahead, as all the orphanage staff stood and waved, and the director brought out a little bag with our new daughter's belongings—a pair of sparkly red shoes, a soft blanket decorated with red hearts, and her Half the Sky memory book.

We were driven back to Nanjing to our hotel, and both girls fell asleep in the backseat. Leaving Changzhou, we saw quiet streets lined in sycamore trees, piles of watermelon on the sidewalks.

Over the next few days, we went about completing the paperwork, which meant Yi Xuan walked away as Frances Yi Xuan, nickname Franny, named for a beloved family friend who was then in her late eighties. While the details were taken care of, we toured around Nanjing—museums, temples, parks. It was summer and it was hotter than hot. "Nanjing is one of the five furnaces of China," our guide said cheerfully. It was also the site of the tragic Rape of Nanjing, and the museum there commemorating that event is one of the most horrific places I've ever seen and no place for children.

As we visited the sights in Nanjing, Franny sang the "Mama Hao" song for us, which every child in every Chinese orphanage seems to learn, with its sad refrain, "Mama is best . . ." Sometimes Franny got so frustrated with our inability to communicate with her that she muttered and mildly swore at us.

One day we visited the Sun Yat-Sen mausoleum. In hundred-degree heat Yi Xuan climbed every one of the 392 steps leading to the top, refusing help, plodding ahead on her own. I stopped her several times, offering to carry her, but she pulled away and said no. I bent down several times to listen to her heart, afraid she'd overdo it, but she seemed okay, and she gallantly marched on, making it very clear to us that she was no frail flower and had a mind of her own.

She was going to fit into our family just fine—and it was going to take some time. Again we felt that sense of the miraculous, how everything had fallen into place so perfectly, how we'd been led to China at just the right time for just the right child.

The red-thread idea, I think, having lived with the concept for a while, could be an adoptive parent's spiritual substitute for the more concrete link of DNA that occurs in other families, a sort of poetic version of the umbilical cord. Mark and I have talked at length about the difference between the profound kinship we feel with our daughters and the actual genetics of attachment. Do we wish, for instance, that they had our genes? Not really. I could go so far as to say there are certain things I'm glad they didn't inherit, at least not from me.

When Kelly and Franny turn out to love music, singing beautifully, taking up instruments, or dancing across the living room, it would be natural, were they our birth daughters, to credit the genetic contribution of Mark's grandfather the accordion player, say, or my mother the dancer. Yet the process of falling so completely in love with these girls has changed whatever thinking I might have had about genetic inheritance. Whatever Kelly blossoms into is completely hers. What Franny enjoys and brings to our family is all hers alone, too. We'll probably never know who their talents and inclinations came from or through, and it doesn't matter.

I know not everyone shares this point of view. As I read Jill

Ker Conway's book *True North*, I came across this passage: "I wasn't interested in adopting children. It wasn't the experience of caring for adorable infants and toddlers I wanted. It was a much more primitive desire to produce the combination of my genetic material and John's." That kind of desire is obviously a natural and strong motivating factor for lots of people who want to have children. According to the Evan B. Donaldson Adoption Institute, "One-half of the American public believes that adoption is 'better than being childless, but not as good as having one's own child.'" But for those of us for whom reproductive biology has broken down, other powerful forces seem to be at work.

I find myself, in fact, circling right back to those first thoughts I wrote to my unknown daughter in my early letters—the belief that any infant, whether the genetic patterns are traceable or not, is a gift and a mystery, a spirit conceived in the vast imagination of the world. As Kahlil Gibran wrote in *The Prophet*: "Your children are not your children, they are not of you, but they come through you. They are the gift of life's longing for itself."

At the least, there's no tracing anything easily. To balance Gibran the old mystic, I turned to scientist Richard Dawkins, author of *Unweaving the Rainbow* and other books. In his own, more intellectual way, Dawkins seems to hold a rather similar opinion. Even if we could identify our child's biological parents, apparently there would be no nailing down which traits came from whom: "A child's chromosomes are an irretrievably scrambled mishmash of its grandparents' chromosomes and so on back to distant ancestors," Dawkins wrote in *River Out of Eden*. "All early living things are certainly descended from a single ancestor. We are much closer cousins of one another than we normally realize."

Search through distant time, and we all wind back to each other. It's that old stuff of exploded stars and dinosaur dust. To put it another way, perhaps the red thread is longer than we can possibly imagine, winding around us all, back to the beginning of time.

11

Through the Chinese Looking Glass

The white sun sinks behind the hills.
The Yellow River rushes to the sea.
Want to see a thousand miles further?
Let's climb a little higher.

—*Wang Zhi-Huan,*
"Climbing Stork Tower"[1]

In the fall, in the light of the autumn moon, my thoughts drift back to China. The memories of our times there still are palpable: The first time I touched the smooth dimples in a soft, small hand, the incense wafting around the Goddess of Mercy in the Buddhist temple, the faint and not-so-faint sound of babies crying. Franny in Nanjing, bravely trudging up 392 steps in the scorching heat.

In Guangzhou at this time of year, the air has lost the heaviness of summer's heat; the Pearl River is flowing along, sparkling on the surface, bearing a burden of sludge underneath. Barges chug on the riverway; oxen plod along the muddy banks. In Changzhou the watermelons are piled high in the shade of the sycamore trees. On Shamian Island, barring any cataclysmic changes in China or unexpected turmoil in

U.S.–China relations, stroller wheels are clattering over the cobblestones. Though the numbers have surged since we were there, then slowed down again, this month, if all goes well, another three to four hundred daughters of China will pass through the hole-in-the-wall passport photo studio, the medical clinic, and the adoption unit of the U.S. Consulate before heading across the Pacific to new lives. Others will fly off to Ireland or Sweden or Canada. Max will put more babies in long-waiting arms. As he wanders through the orphanages, he will occasionally pause, as he always has, put his hand on a small head, and whisper a secret: "Your mama is coming soon."

In Kelly's hometown at this time of year, the market would be busy as usual, the putter of motorbikes echoing through the street; shoppers crowding against one another, carrying their loads of bok choy and fish—or maybe a baby. The lychees would be ripe in Changzhou, and the hospital staff there would undoubtedly have found other infants on the doorstep.

Over time, my sense of my daughters' fateful trips to those places has changed. No longer does it seem fair or accurate to say that they were abandoned or even left there. Rather, I think, they were "delivered" to safety in both those places, so clearly was it their birth family's intention to save them.

When filmmaker Changfu Chang persuaded several birth families to tell their stories on camera (see page 296), he filmed stories that we found very similar to the ones we were given for our girls. One family, harassed by the authorities for having an over-quota child, left her in a market, saying they hoped she could find an adoptive family who would love her and care for her. A second family, desperate to find medical help for a baby boy with a brain tumor, took him to a hospital and left him there, hoping someone with more resources could save him.

Such deliveries will undoubtedly go on. For many baby girls in China, tough times will likely persist, though the patterns of found children have changed over time. Most observers argue that the desperate measures resorted to by women and families will continue until the one-child policy is completely lifted, the soaring economy benefits a wider portion of the population, or some kind of pension is in place for poor rural people. More of the children winding up in China's orphanages now are the result not just of the population policy, but of unwed pregnancies and other woes common to the uprooted rural people who've come to the cities looking for work. A significant number of children in institutions have special medical needs.

In numerous orphanages all over China, in Hubei and Jiangxi and Hunan, more Chinese babies will wait. Those orphanages that deal with foreigners, and others infused with more than average funding or attention, will save more children than they once did. But there will be tragedies as well as happy endings.

Around the time of our first adoption, anytime I had the opportunity to talk with someone whose area of study included China, I asked this question: Has anyone in China spoken out about the missing girls or taken up the cause of all the daughters lost to infanticide and sex-selective abortion and abandonment?

"No, I haven't heard of anyone," an American university professor specializing in Chinese history told me. "There's a limit to what people speak out about."

"The need for sons is just so deeply, culturally ingrained," said another university professor, whose field is early Chinese literature.

"People accept it as a necessary cost of economic development," said an international business consultant active in China. "But they are making a problem for themselves with all the men who won't be able to find wives."

Chinese daughters themselves will one day speak up and search out the truth about their homeland, said dissident author Harry Wu. "When they are twenty-five, they'll join together and they will tell the world what's going on: Why are we here? We love the United States, we love our American parents, but what about the other baby girls? How many were there and why did they disappear? Under what kind of circumstances did we come to the United States? Where are our sisters?"

In the past, it was striking how little was known or acknowledged within China about the high incidence of girls lost and found. Now more and more people were becoming aware. Zhu Chuzhu, a professor of women's studies at Xian Jiaotong University, and a former track star, has fought for an end to the coercion against women, and for education, family planning help, and increased opportunities.[2] She has worked with rural women to foster economic opportunity and improve their status, and has been rewarded by seeing the birth rate for such women drop. Her program has been helped along by both China's Family Planning Office and the U.S.-based Ford Foundation. If women can realize that there are other life goals besides having a son, Zhu believed, they could begin to change the culture.

Not far from the ancient city of Xian, women in Zhu's program were now growing and selling apples and other crops and tending dairy cows. One part of the program is a kind of consciousness-raising session, in which women meet and talk about the pressures to produce sons and reflect on how attitudes might be changed. Government campaigns, trying to convince rural people that girls are as valuable as boys, continue. "Girls are fine descendants, too," is their underlying refrain. One poster shows a girl and a boy both holding a good-luck fish, with the slogan "Having a girl is as good as having a boy."

Among Zhu's research was a look at patterns of the disappearance of girls in one rural area of Shaanxi province. Her findings: Girls in China have been at risk if they were born at home, if they were the second or third child, if the other children in the family were female, and if their parents lived in areas where the bias in favor of sons still prevailed. A primary reason for early deaths among girl babies, Zhu found, was inadequate health care.

China's so-called gender gap, the profound demographic skewing in favor of males, continued to worsen, with some regions reporting two boys for every girl. By 2008, the most dire estimates pointed to an imbalance as many as forty million more men than women in China, a statistical bulge that some demographers referred to as the "boy bubble."[3]

An increasing disparity between poor families and wealthier ones was also a fact of life. That meant that China had growing numbers of very poor children. According to a *New York Times* report in early 2001, "Huge numbers of China's 800 million rural residents are in a medical free-fall, as the once-vaunted system of 'barefoot doctors' and free rural clinics has disintegrated over the last decade."[4] The central government had backed away from providing medical care, and infant mortality rates were up, as were deaths of women in childbirth. Many poor peasants could not afford prenatal care, much less a hospital stay during delivery. In some parts of Yunnan province, one out of every five children would die before age five.

Other social problems loomed. There were fears for the prospects of urban elderly, who must turn to a diminishing pool of grandchildren for their support, and reports of lone children feeling "unbearable pressures" of family expectations.

The sad plight of girls extended beyond China, of course. Reports from India indicated that gender ratios there were skewed even more badly in favor of boys than was the case in China. Although ultrasound testing for the purposes of selective abortion is illegal in India as in China, the law is not enforced. In India's large cities, billboards advertise the availability of testing, and it is commonplace for families who can afford it to take advantage of the screening and then to have female fetuses aborted. The same reasons are stated as are offered in China: Because of the land and family system, boys are simply considered more necessary than girls.

Yet among China's people as well as in its landscape, change was rampant—rapid transformation affecting some of the social welfare institutions as well as the city skylines. The institutions that dealt with foreign adoption, especially, continued to see great improvements, including a building boom. Given an infusion of interest and money—some from groups supported by adoptive parents—improvements in foster care, medical attention, and the nurturing services of extra caretakers had multiplied. At the same time, institutions were seeing more and more children needing their care who suffered from serious disabilities.

In years to come, assuming all goes well on the diplomatic front and in the offices of the Chinese adoption ministry, small miracles will continue to happen, but on their own time schedule. The pipeline between waiting parents and waiting children will probably remain narrow, with both continuing to bide their time while bureaucratic gears roll at their own speed—a pace that was slowed down considerably after new rules went into effect in 2007.

For foreigners seeking to adopt from China, the unforeseen will always loom as an added obstacle, as the United States and China continue to tiptoe their way through diplomatic minefields. After NATO bombed the Chinese embassy in Belgrade, Yugoslavia, in 1999, angry Chinese demonstrators attacked the U.S. Embassy in Beijing and demonstrated in front of the U.S. Consulate in Guangzhou, which briefly closed down. American adoptive families in China at the time bit their nails as they completed their paperwork, some sequestered in the luxurious White Swan Hotel, the noise of protesters at the consulate next door drifting up to their windows.

Throughout the tense times, the Chinese Center of Adoption Affairs continued to process the paperwork for foreign adoptions, but who knows what could happen should there be future problems on the same scale. The incident didn't just harm contemporary relations, already delicate, but opened old wounds for China, the bitter legacy of a historic mistrust of Western intentions. After all, as China scholar Orville Schell has pointed out, "no large nation has been more historically aggrieved by foreigners than China."[5]

In the United States, too, there were discouraging notes as

well as progress. In the wake of the U.S.–China spy plane incident in April 2001, a number of U.S. media reports fell back on extremely insulting stereotypes to describe the Chinese, remarks that made me cringe for my daughter, and for us all. One radio talk-show host called for a boycott of Chinese restaurants. The American Society of Newspaper Editors convention featured a blatantly racist anti-Chinese skit, which Chinese American scholar and author Helen Zia cited as an example of the "knee-jerk racism" that can surface all too easily. As writer William Wong noted afterward, "This isn't going to make life any easier for me and other Chinese-Americans."[6]

Any future strains between China and the U.S. might produce a similar wave of negative commentary. "When racism happens, it rains down on the heads of people like our daughters," said adoptive mother Pam Zumwalt.

By every guess, the winds of change in China will keep blowing, and the world's most populous nation will continue to experience growing pains, as evinced especially while the nation prepared for the 2008 Beijing Olympics.[7] All this growth and westernization has brought mixed blessings. "Cultural pollution" is what the Chinese called some of the instrusions. Ten percent of Beijing's children were now obese, a condition previously unheard of. Medical experts attribute the problem to the arrival of American fast-food outlets—Pizza Hut, Dunkin' Donuts, and other enterprises have now joined the Kentucky Colonel in China—and the increasing reliance on the automobile for transportation, rather than walking or cycling.[8] Ironically, the children feeding on fast food in China's big cities may be less well nourished than some children in the better orphanages eating their congee and slices of banana and apple.

Several decades after the one-child policy went into effect, *Washington Post* foreign correspondent John Pomfret interviewed a farmer in Miaoxia, Henan province, who finally had a son after seven daughters. He named the boy Gaifeng, or "Change in the Weather," and only then did he decide to quit having children. Along the way, the farmer was said to have given away one daughter, whom he could not feed, but he would not say where the girl had gone. Why the quest for a son after so many other births, Pomfret asked. "My girls will belong to someone else," said the farmer. "Only [my son] will feed me rice when I am old."[9]

This rural portrait was part of the reason for the mixed results of the one-child policy by the year 2000. While most urban areas had held the line at a single child, in some of China's poorest regions, families with multiple children were the norm.

Over time there were sporadic adjustments in the population policy, indications that persuasion would replace force, that "service" to women of childbearing age would now be emphasized, rather than rigid enforcement of regulations. Some regions of China had already eased the policy, allowing families to have an additional child if they proved they had the economic means to do so. In other places, it had long been possible, with cash, to persuade officials to bend the rules.

In fact, some prosperous citizens were happily and routinely paying for the privilege of having a second, even a third, child. It had even become a status symbol. There were reports that extra children occasionally were given nicknames based on the amount of the fine their parents paid in order to keep them:

"Little Two Thousand," for instance. A number of these hard-earned extra children were daughters, reflecting the common desire to have a son and a daughter whenever possible. In Beijing and Shanghai, the fines were stiff, as much as three years' wages for an additional child.

Overall, if one looked just at the total numbers—and not the individual lives underscoring them—China's stringent population control policies had worked, at least according to the government. Two decades after Premier Deng Xiaoping's history-altering announcement putting the one-child policy into place, China's average family size had dropped from six children per woman to two, according to Chinese government reports.[10] Although there were questions of serious under-reporting, if that boast were true, China's population growth had declined by more than 50 percent in just one generation, and the projections—for a population kept to a maximum of 1.3 billion by the millennium—had been met.

As always, there were outsiders who questioned China's rosy reports. Traveling through the Chinese countryside, reporter Mark Hertsgaard noted how many families seemed to have two, three, even more children. "Chinese birth rates did not decline substantially during the 1980s and 1990s," he wrote in *Earth Odyssey*. Hertsgaard suspected there was a flaw in the official calculations.

Whatever the true figures, since lowered population growth rates had been achieved by official pressure, some factions have feared that any relaxation of the rules or the enforcement may unleash a new growth spurt—unless, as has been the case in other countries, the status of Chinese women improved sufficiently that they themselves began voluntarily to have fewer children. More and more families, faced with the prospects of raising children in an increasingly expensive environment, were deciding themselves to have just one. Younger women, gaining independence, doing better for themselves, might hasten China's move toward smaller families without the harsh methods of the 1980s.

There was already evidence that young women in China were more likely to want smaller families than their husbands and in-laws want. But they still didn't have equal say. There remained in the most traditional families that ingrained belief that a woman's fertility is somebody else's business, that she had a duty to produce a son. Even if the state lets up, it doesn't mean the relatives will.

Nonetheless, China's women are making considerable gains. As far back as 1995, a Chinese woman journalist noted that the international women's conference in Beijing that year was an eye-opener: For the first time, Chinese women realized that their reproductive health and freedom could be their own business, could be theirs to control. "In the past," wrote Chuan Renyan, "Chinese women either had to consider producing descendants for their husband's family as their sacred duty or first think of sacrificing their needs to the state's population control efforts. Now women are beginning to think about their own rights."[11] That recognition will probably continue to build (though in an atmosphere of caution). Among other changes in China, a sexual revolution is under way. In cities, contraception is increasingly available in drugstores and "adult health" stores, and consumer information is becoming more accessible. Sex education classes, certainly a new feature in China, have become available.

Chinese American scholar and author Helen Zia attended that international women's conference, and says women have come a long way in the thirteen years since. Then, there was just one program, a telephone hotline, for victims of domestic abuse in all of China, she reported. "But feminist activists within China used the conference to create many new initiatives for women and girls, such as programs to end female infanticide and sex-selective abortions, to help rural girls get the same schooling that boys do, and to address the issue of family violence."

In 2007–2008, Zia spent five months in Shanghai. She said she was impressed with the diversity of opinions among China's people, and struck by how outspoken they were. Nearly everyone she talked with told her they believed China was changing for the better.[12]

Rural women working in the cities are gaining a new measure of independence. Girls, stepping out on their own, are sending money home to their aging parents. Increasingly, China's women are making their own choices. A Catholic priest living in southern China noted that "in rural areas where the mothers can't read or write, the daughters are going to college in the U.S. and studying Greek tragedy."

A young woman I spoke with at Wuyi University in Kelly's hometown impressed me as a living reminder of the changing times. Smart, independent, and optimistic, she'd come from the north on her own and was making a living teaching English. She'd done enough traveling to find Jiangmen City a little boring. She said that daughters are valued more these days, and that once she herself decided to start a family, it wouldn't matter to her whether she gave birth to a girl or a boy.

"I think things are changing a lot," said another young Chinese woman studying in this country. "In my family I have an older sister and an older brother. We live in a small city. My mother at first wanted to have a grandson, but then my older sister had a daughter, and then my older brother had a daughter. My mother said, 'It's okay. I love them.' She changed her attitude. Even in the countryside now peasants are changing their attitudes." Couples who have ended up with two daughters are adapting to their fate in ways that may promote more favorable attitudes toward girls in the future. Such families may marry a son-in-law into the family, rather than marrying the daughter out, as has normally been the case.

A 2008 *New York Times* article profiled several single mothers in Shanghai—women who had chosen to keep a baby and raise the child alone, against huge odds. While they described the uphill challenges they faced trying to register their children so they could go to school, or protect them from social stigma, these women were nonetheless indicative of the dramatic changes that were becoming possible, albeit slowly, in the lives of Chinese women.[13]

And so the changes were slipping through in the complex and contradictory world that is China.

Fa Mulan might live on as the historical example of a Chinese heroine, but the country boasts real, contemporary heroines as well—women who aren't just stepping into a man's role and saving the day, but staying in their own lives and looking out for one another. Women like Xie Lihua, for instance, who first brought the high suicide rate for Chinese women to the attention of the world in the magazine she founded, *Rural Women Knowing All*, a publication that includes self-help articles on reproductive health and other empowering information for its female readers. "[Chinese] women have lost something," Xie Lihua told a *Washington Post* reporter, "but now we can choose our own lives."[14]

Interestingly enough, as men have left rural villages looking for work, the women have been left behind to run things—and they run things very well.[15] The China Population Welfare Foundation's Happiness Project was offering support—such as livestock and small loans—to help such women help themselves. In numbers alone, rural women are a force to be reckoned with: More than four hundred million women and girls live in China's countryside.

In a traditionally closemouthed society, a young Beijing journalist named An Dun had encouraged women to speak out about their most intimate problems. Her books *Absolute Privacy* and *Going Home*—filled with poignant details of unwanted pregnancies, agonizing love affairs, and other personal difficulties—are being eagerly read by Chinese women hungry to hear and share one another's experiences. In 1999 the Chinese edition of *Our Bodies, Ourselves* was released—albeit with a few omissions, such as the section on lesbian concerns. In Wuhan province, the former home of thousands of adopted daughters of China, the New Sun Marriage Shelter, the first women's safe house in China, had opened.[16] Women who had grown up in China were currently writing one powerful book after another about conditions in their homeland.[17] And the 2008 Beijing Olympics would bring out the women athletes, numerous Chinese female competitors to make our daughters proud. China's women's soccer team, of course, had years earlier come within a single field goal of winning a world title.

In Hubei province, I read with interest, a woman who made some extra income tending mulberry trees and raising silkworms had used the money to buy her daughter a computer. In a strange way, it made me feel good to know that China's time-honored silkworms and mulberry trees were continuing to weave themselves through the country's fast-changing way of life. The gift of a computer to a daughter also seemed a heartening thing.

There are also unsung heroines all over China today: aunties in orphanages, caring for little girls who have no one else; foster mothers, taking babies into their homes and bidding them emotional good-byes when their adoptive families come for them; birth mothers, who are every day finding a way to give their daughters a future that they themselves, for whatever reason, could not provide.

To the list of unsung women of courage should be added every single lost daughter of China, too—those still in orphanages, some growing older, waiting for families who haven't yet come and may not—and all their sisters and cousins growing up across America and Canada and Europe, who will someday muster the courage to face all the questions that await them.

Girls in China's orphanages by now have an ever-expanding international network of well-wishers—adoptive families, including big and little sisters, who keep in touch. It's my guess that some of the best grassroots diplomacy in years to come will be accomplished by China's lost daughters themselves and by the growing links among orphanages, orphanage officials, and adoptive American parents. It is natural for people to want the best for a country that has allowed them to come home with such beautiful little children.

"I thank my daughter's mother every day," said San Diego adoptive mother Marty Foltyn, echoing the gratitude of thousands of other American women. "You may get no thanks in your village," says another adoptive mother of her child's birth mother in a documentary called *Letter to Maya*, "but we will not forget you."[18]

One of the Americans we traveled with said she was making it a point to stay in touch with her daughter's orphanage. "It's important to send pictures and letters to be placed in my children's files in case their birth mothers ever want to search or have contact with them, or just to know that they're okay," she said. "It's also important to send those pictures to the orphanage, so that international adoption remains a positive experience for all involved."

But there were other, less heartening clues as to the effects of an increasingly fast-paced and material world, not just on China but on China's children, China's only children, in particular. In China's big cities a generation now has grown up without siblings. (Among other ramifications, this fact may soon cause the terms "aunt" and "uncle" to all but fall out of use.) In an *Asia Week* article called "Little Emperors—Is China's One-Child Policy Creating a Society of Brats?"[19] Todd Crowell and David Hsieh observed parents and grandparents in Beijing indulging their sole offspring. One recipient of too many consumer goods was a grand*daughter*, referred to as "our little precious" by her doting grandfather.

Jan Wong, in her book *Red China Blues*, offered some amazing reports on the spoiling of single children in big cities where the one-child policy had been strictly enforced. "Many parents of the nineties," she wrote, "were part of the lost generation of the Cultural Revolution. After suffering so much themselves, they were determined not to deprive their only child. Beijing's biggest toy store was always jammed with parents buying toddler-sized fake fur coats, imported baby shampoo and red Porsche pedal cars."

Yet she saw good things coming out of the situation. "Many people thought that a country populated with Little Emperors was headed for disaster. I disagreed. Granted it might be unpleasant to live in a nation of me-first onlies, yet I saw a social revolution in the making. For generations, Chinese society had emphasized the family, the clan, the collective over the individual. Now, for the first time in four thousand years of history, the relationship was reversed. Where the Mao generation failed, the Me generation just might succeed." She quoted a British friend, Michael Crook: "If you have a population of Little Emperors, you can't have little slaves. Everyone will want to tell everyone else what to do. You'll have democracy."[20]

China-born international business consultant George Koo has pointed out that there has been, even before the Olympics, more movement toward freedom in China than the Western media usually acknowledges, forgoing such reports in favor of more sensational accounts of human rights abuses. In a story in the *Harvard International Review*, Koo noted: "While the China-bashers in the West dwell on and are fixated by the images from Tiananmen on June 4, 1989, China has moved on. Elections have been held in the countryside in recent years; the most recent ones have been observed by representatives of the Carter Center, sent from the United States."[21]

No sooner does one take heart in such statements than China begins another roundup of those clamoring for democracy or doing something else viewed as a threat to the state. China expert Michel Oksenberg of Stanford University has predicted that China will continue to go through a pattern of relaxation and tightening, relaxation and tightening. In its very pragmatic way the Chinese government is counting on economic prosperity as a crucial factor in future political stability. By now the Western model of materialism has both feet in China's door, and the desire for consumer goods and a higher standard of living has been firmly planted.

In the leadup to the 2008 Beijing Olympics, the spotlight cast on China's human rights practices intensified. The Tibet uprisings and brutal crackdowns raised the conflicts and contradictions to another level.

There is reason to hope that increased prosperity and freedom will benefit China's women and girls, particularly if China sees that improvement as a matter of self-interest. But a struggle lies ahead. Working conditions are still dismal and, sadly, foreign companies doing business in China are among the worst offenders.[22] Behind all too many goods made in China, I now knew for certain, were exploited workers, most of them women, any one of whom could be the mother of a child who wound up in an institution or worse.

I long ago put away the notebook in which I wrote those first letters to my little daughter. But before doing so I took the book to a Chinese student so she could translate the Chinese writing on the cover I'd always wondered about. "It is only a fragment of a larger writing, maybe part of a poem," the woman told me. "It says something about the moon and writing, but I can't tell what it means from such a little piece of the whole." Perfect! If there's one lesson to be learned from China, it's to always be aware of how little you know.

In the fall of 2000 in New York City, a number of people whose lives have been touched by adoption, including local families from the Greater New York Families with Children from China group, held a ceremony in the Marble Collegiate

Church, Norman Vincent Peale's old place of worship. "Celebrating the Spirit of Adoption," the gathering was called, and I was honored to be a part of it. Ethereal bamboo flute music and passionate Korean drumming resounded through the sanctuary, as did some Stephen Sondheim and a Hebrew song for peace. The words of May Sarton, Saint Francis of Assisi, and Alice Walker were read. Lynn Franklin, author of *May the Circle Be Unbroken*, read from her account of giving birth to a baby, to whom she said good-bye as an infant, and then meeting her lost son twenty-seven years later.

A young woman named Hollee McGinnis, adopted from Korea as a child, and founder of an organization for adult intercountry adoptees,[23] read these words, the last lines of which have stayed with me ever since:

> *When I was twenty-four, I took the train over from Seoul to Inchon to meet my birth father's family. They had been fishermen in islands in the Yellow Sea before moving back to the mainland. It was five in the afternoon. The train was crowded with commuters. I was gripped by this fear inside and started to cry. I was with a woman, an adoptee, who was half black and half Korean. She said, "You're just making more room."*
>
> *Of course, she was right. In order for me to embrace these people as part of my family, and be the cultural bridge I keep talking about, I had to let go of some things in order to make room. It was terribly frightening. But by crying I began to shift my feelings so I could be open to the experience of being with them and having them become part of my life again.*
>
> *Meeting my birth family opened up a whole new chapter in my life. But I had to decide what to do after the reunion. Should I develop a relationship with them, and if so, what kind of relationship?*

I've always had my family in everything that I do. When I came back, my dad, who's in his sixties, said to me, "We may not be around in twenty years. You should develop this relationship with your Korean family." My mother said, "Hey, I'm planning to be around for a lot longer than that!"

And I realized that because my parents shifted their thinking about what it means to be a family, I truly became their daughter. Similarly, with my birth family, I was given the choice to shift my thinking about family to embrace them into my life again.

I believe that adoption is about the possibility of opening your mind and heart to take in a person because you choose to love {that person}. I was a stranger in a foreign land until my parents chose to love me as their daughter. Imagine if we all walked around looking at strangers and thinking, You could have been my son or daughter.

Imagine.

Epilogue

Floating on its moorings of twilight
  clouds
my small boat drifts along in memories
while I muse on the future. How lovely
this world, how close it is to heaven.
And how unfathomable the water
that embraces the face of the moon.
  —Meng Haojan, "Night-Mooring
    on the Chien-te River"[1]

I knew from the moment I began to write and from the moment I wrote the original epilogue that there was no way to wrap up this tale, no way to make any final pronouncements about this human drama. By its very nature, this story of East and West lives will flow on and on. Soon, in fact, there will be myriad new stories—the most relevant and necessary ones— told by the daughters of China themselves, and perhaps one day we will hear more from some of the birth families.

While newly adopted girls (and boys), most of them in the one-year-old or toddler range, continue to be welcomed into American families every month, the children adopted in the 1990s are now coming of age. Many are teenagers; some are in college. There are nearly seventy thousand stories out there in the United States alone, falling under a huge umbrella, but in the end each story is personal and singular. Already numerous adoption stories have been written—or partly written—by adopting families and by adopted young people. Several are posted on websites.[2] Others are yet to be told. Some might need telling around a campfire with good friends. But no matter how much is written or said, there will always be another chapter. There's so much we don't know, may never know, about the circumstances that surround this story of human upheaval and reconciliation. And who can predict what these girls will think and do as young women—or even tomorrow?

My own daughters were growing up more quickly than I ever could have imagined. Each year, it seemed, they were coming into different questions and new feelings about their lives, including their origins, even as they tackled all the usual transitions that kids go through.

What a journey it has been, and continues to be. What an amazing, blessed, and baffling journey.

The Slowdown

In 2007, however, the adoption community received some unwelcome news from the Chinese ministry in charge of adoption. Already, in years past, the ministry had ruled out single fathers and placed a quota on single mothers, limiting the number presented by any one agency to a small percentage of the total applications. Now the government announced another tightening. Effective May 1, 2007, China would no longer allow adoption by single parents, period. Nor would it allow adoption by applicants over fifty (although people up to the age of fifty-five could adopt a special-needs child). China ruled out would-be parents who have a body mass index of more than forty; those taking medication for major psychiatric illness; those with serious facial deformities, limb deformities, or paralysis; those who are blind, deaf, or mute (although in some cases a person with such a disability might be allowed to adopt a child with the same condition); and those with chronic and debilitating illnesses, AIDS, or other infectious diseases. In addition, China added stipulations concerning divorce and remarriage, and set a minimum figure of $80,000 for a family's net worth.

The Families with Children from China group responded with letters, respectfully and gently making the case that single parents in particular had done very well by China's children. But the Chinese ministry has held firm. Citing the increase in foreign applications, as well as an increase in domestic adoption in China, the government said it could no longer satisfy the needs of all foreign adoptive families.

"The number of applicants is much larger than the number of internationally adoptable children," said the letter from the Chinese Center of Adoption Affairs (CCAA). So, went the thinking, China would have to choose those families they considered best suited, "who have better conditions in all respects." That translated to married heterosexual couples, and priority would be given to couples if at least one of the applicants, or one of the grandparents, had been born in China, Taiwan, or Hong Kong.

The reasons for all this have become a matter of extensive debate. Some experts had all along argued that Chinese domestic adoption was more substantial than was generally thought, and that keeping orphaned children in China was a better solution than letting them be adopted by foreigners and taken abroad. Other observers pointed out that China's orphanages were still full of waiting children, so why not keep the doors open to as wide a pool of applicants as possible? According to those with access to the orphanages, the populations did seem to be shifting—fewer healthy babies, more children with disabilities.

In historic perspective and hindsight, families like ours realize that we adopted during a golden era. Among our extended family of people with children from China are many, many single mothers and some single fathers. There are older parents and two-mom and two-dad families, and adoptive parents with chronic illnesses as well as physical limitations. All the children appear to be thriving, and the parents are most grateful toward China. But China had other ideas. "The purpose of the undertaking of adoption is to find families for children instead of finding children for families," the ministry said in its letter.

Probably never again would the process be so widespread, so liberal, so relatively quick. Our own agency sent out a letter, explaining that the combination of increased adoption applications from all over the world, the liberalization of the one-child policy, and the increase in domestic adoptions in China now meant that adoption in China "has become an impractical choice. Current groups are now waiting two years and more for referrals, and the fear is it may become three years and more. Only 'priority' Chinese families are deciding to adopt in China now."

"Clearly," one adoption facilitator wrote, "China has spoiled all of us in the adoption community, as never before in history were adoptions of healthy infants so easy, so inexpensive, and so fast and fun to do." Now everyone needed to "readjust to a new world of adoption." Agencies at the time began turning their attention toward such countries as Vietnam, Ethiopia, India, Taiwan, Japan, Kyrgyzstan, Kazakhstan, and Nepal. In April 2008, the Vietnam adoption program was halted, following reports of corruption.

In 1996, caught in a reorganization of the CCAA, our own wait for Kelly extended to nearly two years. But in 2007, we knew people who were entering their third year of waiting for a child from China.

Critical Mass

Even with the slowdown, the China movement remains the biggest in U.S. adoptions. It is also probably the most organized, with the networks of Families with Children from China (FCC) groups, as well as the informal communities of people whose children had come from the same orphanage, had been adopted through the same agency, or were in the same Mandarin class or some other Chinese cultural activity. Hanni Beyer Lee, mother of three daughters from different parts of China, compiled a beautiful yearbook for children adopted from Yunnan, the province from which one of her daughters came; other groups from numerous other provinces and institutions kept in touch, creating directories and scrapbooks, sharing stories, bouncing things off one another.

From a broader perspective, adoption, both domestic and international, has been steadily transforming the American family during the past decades. By 2007, the Evan B. Donaldson Adoption Institute estimated that some sixty percent of Americans had a personal connection to adoption. The landmark book *Adoption Nation,* by Donaldson's executive director Adam Pertman, explored the phenomenon from a variety of angles. Each year, more and more people in the adoption triad—adopted children and adults who were adopted as children, birth parents who relinquished children, and adoptive parents—stepped forward to tell their stories in articles, books, poems, and films. For Adoption Month in November 2007, the *New York Times* developed an impressive website devoted to the subject, with stories from all perspectives—those of children and adults adopted domestically and internationally from diverse countries, stories from birth parents, stories from adoptive families.

The largest populations of children adopted from China are concentrated in New York and California; it follows that the largest FCC chapters are also located in these areas. Roughly 20 percent of the U.S. families who have adopted from China are FCC members. Though some children, particularly in smaller out-of-the-way areas, may be growing up without any consistent connection to other children adopted from China, it is possible to find other families and plenty of information on the Internet.

An industry has, in fact, developed around these families. At gatherings of the Families with Children from China groups, tables are laden with Chinese-language tapes, CDs, and books. Catalogs are available with everything from adoption-themed storybooks to cheongsams to Chinese brush painting kits to red lanterns and silk slippers. At the 2008 Year of the Rat Between the Two New Years celebration in San Francisco, there was a brisk trade in outgrown traditional silk outfits, with profits going to orphanage charities. Early on, the Mattel corporation had come up with "Going Home" Barbie, a blond mommy doll holding a dark-haired, dark-eyed baby, a gift presented to adopting families who stayed at the fancy White Swan Hotel on Shamian Island in Guangzhou.

Dozens of books for children as well as parents have been released for this audience, from memoirs to storybooks to poetry to adoptive psychology books to how-to adoption manuals. Websites and magazines are devoted to the adoption experience, including the excellent magazine *Adoptive Families,* run by Susan Caughman, the adoptive mother of a Chinese daughter. There is a magazine, *Mei,* especially for the girls. The Internet continues to hum with group discussions on just about every subject, from skin conditions to attachment issues to suggestions on where to find kid-friendly chopsticks.

For the subculture of children adopted from China, numerous Mandarin tutors are at work, teaching the girls as well as their families. The large cohort has also created a demand for Mandarin-speaking nannies. In areas lucky enough to have large Chinese American populations, and even in places where the numbers are fewer, Chinese dance programs and classes in Chinese music now cater to the adoptive community. Our daughter Kelly tried the *gu zheng*—a beautiful stringed instrument distantly related to the Western zither—and Franny briefly took up the noisy Chinese gourd pipe. Both girls were taught by a young pair of incredibly patient and good-humored Chinese American musicians. Still, there is no pigeonholing this group. There are some dedicated *gu zheng* players, horn blowers, and Chinese dancers in our local community, but not our kids. Eventually Kelly opted for the flute, and was playing Gershwin in her room. Franny turned to the guitar and West African dance.

Many enterprises have sprung up to serve this group of families. One offers to search out the "finding ad"—the newspaper photo and information aimed at locating any birth family before a child was declared an orphan—for an adopted child. By 2008, it was also possible to commission an investigation into what else might be known about a particular child's history—

a search for the person who found the child, perhaps—to seek out any additional papers, such as notes from birth parents or a police report, that hadn't made their way into the adoptive parents' hands. There are now people known as "searchers," who will conduct such investigations and even attempt to track down a birth parent. Groups have formed to explore the possibility of DNA banks for future searches for birth families, including lost siblings. Some of this searching has become controversial. While some birth families might welcome contact, others may not want to be found, fearing repercussions with their families, the neighbors, the government.

A producer of the film *Whale Rider* has been at work on a documentary about older girls adopted from China. The filmmaker, Linda Goldstein Knowlton, mother to a three-year-old from China, said that as her own daughter's adoption group gathered for reunions, she became more and more interested about what these girls were going to be like as they grew up. "I know so many fourteen- and fifteen-year-olds, and I thought, 'What's it like being a transracial adoptee in the United States at fourteen years old? I had all these questions. I couldn't put myself in their shoes, though. I knew the film had to be from the girls' point of view."

The filmmaker began following three teenage adopted girls and interviewing younger girls as well, to fill in some of the formative experiences. "What I am finding," she said, "is that every girl has had a different experience, and has different feelings. When I asked the girls how they identified themselves, one said, 'I'm American,' another said, 'I'm Chinese American,' and another said, 'It depends who I am talking to.' One girl said she hadn't thought much about her birth mother, then wondered if she should feel guilty and asked, 'Am I supposed to?'"

Knowlton says she had been stunned by how thoughtful and articulate this group is. One of the girls was planning to go to China this summer to work in an orphanage. "It's really one amazing kid after another," the filmmaker told me. And yet, she says, she was saddened to hear the extent of the mean-spirited comments some of the girls have had to endure. "I met one girl who lived in Iowa, in the middle of farm country. She was the only person of color at her high school and she was miserable. You'd expect some of the negative comments in a situation like that," said the filmmaker, "but they happened elsewhere, too. I was so disappointed." The documentary by Knowlton will be released sometime in 2009. The working title is *The Sisterhood*.

Other films and books are also in the works. Korean adoptees, too, have continued to make films and publish books about their experiences. *Trail of Crumbs: Hunger, Love, and the Search for Home* by Kim Sunee, is among the newest memoirs. Found in a South Korean marketplace at the age of three, adopted into an American family, and raised in New Orleans, Sunee has written a candid account of her lifelong search for a sense of self. Deann Borshay Liem, whose fine autobiographical film *First Person Plural* told of coming to terms with her adoption and her trip back to visit her birth family in Korea, is following up with a new film about other Korean adoptees.

With the books, films, merchandise, and services have come experts and programs and groups—psychologists specializing in adoption issues for parents, seminars on transracial adoption, programs aimed at helping the children themselves explore their feelings about adoption and race. There are workshops for adoptive parents who want to put together "lifebooks"—artistic photo albums with narrative accounts of what is known about a child's life before and after adoption. In urban areas, there are frequent conferences for parents of adopted children. Among other blessings, I think it's safe to say that this group of adoptive parents has had more information at its disposal than any other such group in history.

Under the Magnifying Glass

This adoption movement, the largest single-gender diaspora in history, is also likely to be the most studied group of international adoptees. At this writing, at least two dozen research projects are under way, completed, or just starting. The children from China were being evaluated for language development, social adjustment, bonding, and health, while their families are being studied for the effects of cross-cultural influences and the ways that transnational adoption might be reshaping the way people in the United States think about family. Various studies are being conducted by graduate students, social scientists, psychologists, research doctors, and interested adoptive parents.

Caucasian adopting parents are the subjects of one piece of research; Asian American of another. The University of Minnesota International Adoption Clinic is looking into the expectations and experiences of the parents of internationally adopted children, while the University of Connecticut is studying the children's behavior, attachment, and well-being. A study of adopted people who are Asian American and Jewish is being conducted. A nurse at the University of California San Francisco School of Medicine, herself an adoptive mother of a Chinese child, launched a study to see how internationally adopted children began developing an attachment to their adoptive mothers in the first six months after adoption. A study funded by the Kellogg Foundation aimed to evaluate the experience of adults who had been internationally adopted and raised in transracial families.

A study by Dr. Tony Xing Tan showed that adopted children from China fared just as well when raised in the United States by a single woman as they did when raised by a married couple, countering claims by Beijing that single parenting was less adequate for Chinese children. Tan's China Adoption Research Program, begun in 2002 at the University of South Florida, is the largest study to date of adopted children's social and emotional adjustment in their U.S. families. Overall, reported Tan, "I've found that these adopted children, especially the preschoolers, are doing better than their U.S. non-adopted peers. Because adopted children have commonly been reported to have more academic, behavioral, social, and emotional problems, these findings came as a surprise."

On the China side, people such as professors Huang Banghan and Wang Liyao, of the Anhui Academy of Social Sciences in Hefei, whose studies of adoptive families in the United States had filled in the picture of international adoption for China's people, continued their good work. Their book has now been published in China. As part of their research, both came to the United States more than once to meet with American adoptive families. At a dinner for Professor Wang, it was touching to see him talking with all the girls from China, conversing with some of the older ones in both English and Mandarin.

Sociologist Richard Tessler, whose research is mentioned earlier in this book, collaborated with a Chinese sociologist, Yu

Ning, to look at attitudes among Chinese people concerning the adoption of Chinese children by Americans. The researchers found mixed reactions. Younger, better educated residents of the larger towns were more accepting, while older and less educated people in small rural villages expressed more negative reactions, partly attributable to China's historic difficulties with the West. Some had not heard of foreign adoption at all. Other respondents worried whether the girls would "feel isolated and alone in America." Tessler and Yu concluded that attitudes in China toward foreign adoption would gradually become more positive as more was learned. "Contact with adoptive parents from America and other western countries will also help to break down cultural stereotypes and allay anxieties about how the children will be treated," they wrote. "International adoption is one venue, among others, for transcending the age-old dichotomy between West and East and fostering mutual understanding and respect."

A woman who has contributed a tremendous amount of research and perspective to this adoptive group is New York City psychologist Amanda Baden. Adopted herself from Hong Kong and raised in a Caucasian adoptive family, Baden has specialized in working with the issues that come with transracial adoption.

The China group of adoptees she's worked with, says Baden, an associate professor at Montclair State University in New Jersey, tend to have access to plenty of other children who share their histories. These are girls, she points out, who have grown up in the New York City area or other places with a high concentration of adoptees and who've also grown up with parents who are involved in Chinese adoption organizations. Other girls in other places may be more isolated. And even within the same city and region of the country, there's a wide range of experience.

Girls in diverse settings still struggle with the challenges many people of color face, says Baden, regardless of adoption status— the internalization of racism and oppression. "The girls are able to observe some of these issues when they are in groups and discuss these issues, but there is much more work to do.

"Another unique aspect of the experiences of adopted Chinese girls is the fairly widespread knowledge that their gender was likely one of the primary reasons for their relinquishment," Baden says. "Although they have the ability to explain the 'one-child policy,' they, like most adoptees, continue to wonder about the degree to which gender, poverty, culture, and life circumstances influenced their birth parents' decisions to relinquish them. Some of the girls have spoken directly about these issues, but none seem to dwell or have excessive concerns."

One thirteen-year-old said, "Throughout my life as an adoptee, I haven't had too many 'issues.' I am not very worried about many things." But one issue that had come up, she said, was having people make fun of her eyes. "For me it isn't an issue that I am adopted. It actually makes me happy to know that people cared enough for me to put me up for adoption, knowing they couldn't raise me, and [to know] there are others who care enough to help children who are and were in orphanages like me. One thing that concerns me a little sometimes is the reaction peopple may have when they figure out that I'm adopted, which I don't mind, sometimes, but pretty rarely, it is a negative effect. I do not feel uncomfortable talking about adoption and my 'story' specifically."

Baden's website offers a teen Q&A section, where adopted children can e-mail questions to a team of other adopted twelve-year-olds (TeenQuestions@transracialadoption.net). The identities of the girls fielding the questions are protected, but their brief bios—"What people should know about me"—provide a spirited micro-sketch of preteens adopted from China:

> "I'm smart, funny, creative, nice. A lot of my friends
> trust me. I've been back to China."
> "I am proud of who I am, not ashamed at all. I have a
> really fun personality and love meeting new people."
> "I am relatively good at solving problems and I try to
> help in any way I can."
> "I love to read. I am small and Chinese."
> "I like pie. I am awesome!"

And yet the surrounding culture still has such huge blind spots. At every stage, every transition, it is clear: Adopted children have more to deal with, and those children growing up with parents of another ethnicity have an added challenge. In the media, in films, in the schoolyard, insensitive remarks and negative assumptions about adoption continue to fly. A supposedly witty remark in the 2008 Oscar-nominated film *Juno* about the easy availability of babies in China caused a great deal of irritation and unhappiness in the adoption community. Though heard by fewer people than was true of *Juno,* the recent David Mamet play *November* contained a viciously offensive bit of dialogue about girls adopted from China.

In schools, the unfortunate practice continues of asking children to write about their ancestors or to make family trees. Adoptive parents have to talk to teachers, help their children come up with alternative assignments, or do something like we did—make a family tree that became a forest, including all our wider human and nonhuman connections—from birth parents and other unknown relatives in China, to all the girls adopted from China, to the extended adoptive family, to family friends and all the family pets. That seemed to paper over the dilemma, but not completely erase its potential for making a child feel different if he or she happens to be the sole adopted child in the classroom. On the bright side, help is available. Among other groups, the Evan B. Donaldson Adoption Institute has pioneered some excellent and useful work aimed at enlightening educators about such issues (www .adoptioninstitute.org). So has Pact, an adoption alliance that offers a variety of services for adoptive families with dual heritages (www.pactadopt.org).

Often, for children adopted from China, the spotlight shines a little too brightly. In *Leave Me Alone, I'm Reading,* National Public Radio's book reviewer Maureen Corrigan told the story of carrying her year-old adopted daughter Molly past the bleachers during a neighborhood softball game. "A man's voice rang out, 'Hey, is she from China?'" Corrigan recounted, "I unthinkingly answered, 'Yes,' and looked up. A bleacher of white faces stared down at us, but no one identified himself as the questioner. I felt as though Molly and I had been turned into curiosities by that bored crowd. I wish I had had the presence of mind to shout back, 'Where are you all from?'"

From time to time there also brewed a kind of psychological backlash for adoptive families who'd gone abroad for their children. In the past decade, the whole international adoption movement has come under increased scrutiny, some of it fueled by reports of child abduction, baby smuggling, and irregular adoption practices in different countries. Even in China, with its exemplary adoption procedures, there were reports in 2005 and

2006 of baby smuggling rings, quickly broken up by authorities. Some of the discussion was spurred by young adults who'd been adopted as children and were not happy about the fact.

I was taken aback the first time I came upon an Internet site called Transracial Abductees, hosted, the site said, by "angry, pissed, ungrateful, little transracially adopted m——f——s from hell." But I had to admit that it did reveal another side of the experience, and that the young people involved were entitled to their feelings, even if those feelings produced a ripple of trepidation among adoptive parents. Would our daughters find their way to the company of the ungrateful and angry? Would they someday refer to themselves as abductees? Had we adoptive parents committed, as charged, an act of global imperialism as we stood in that orphanage waiting room, hearts thudding?

Elizabeth Bartholet, a professor at Harvard Law School, who has written extensively on the political and humanitarian pros and cons of international adoption, ultimately concluded that given the realities of today's world—the number of homeless children, the poor prospects for children growing up in orphanages, the fact that adoption within the sending countries has not managed to empty the orphanages—international adoption is a clear improvement over life in an institution. "In my view," she wrote, "it also pushes us forward on a path to creating a more just world."[3]

No question, though, it takes extra awareness. Hollee McGinnis, whose eloquent words appear on page 268, has gone on to work within the adoption community, offering help to children adopted, as she was, into a mixed world. "At its best, intercountry adoption demonstrates to me the greatness of our human spirits to love across race, nationality, and culture,"

McGinnis wrote in a story published on the *New York Times* adoption website this past fall. "But I also know that it takes a lot more than just love to make a success; it requires courage, honesty, and commitment.

"This means we must be willing to talk about the hard stuff," wrote McGinnis, "the discrimination, inequalities, and prejudices that exist in the world. We must also be willing to change and challenge our societies so the gift we give our children—adopted or not—besides the love and security of a permanent family is a world that values them for who they are and who they will be—regardless of race, nationality, culture, or circumstance."

One thing is certain: The next outpouring of evaluation and commentary should rightly come from the adoptees themselves. As editors Jane Jeong Trenka, Julia Chinyere Oparah, and Sun Yung Shin in the book *Outsiders Within: Writing on Transracial Adoption*, point out, "Over the past fifty years, white adoptive parents, academics, psychiatrists, and social workers have dominated the literature on transracial adoption. These 'experts' have been the ones to tell the public—including adoptees—'what it's like' and 'how we turn out.' Despite our numbers and the radical way we have transformed the color and kinship of white families, the voices of adult transracial adoptees remain largely unheard."

The Bridge to China

From the moment an adoptive family walks into a Chinese orphanage or is handed a bundle in a Chinese hotel, the relationship with China is put in place. What families make of this connection can vary tremendously. For some adoptive parents, China recedes into the distance and stays there. For a few, China becomes a second home and a frequent destination. Some adoptive parents, like Jenny Bowen, founder of Half the Sky Foundation, are called back to China, to live and work on behalf of the children left behind.

In the United States and abroad, girls from China now in their teens were joining teen clubs and doing some serious fund-raising for their sisters back in China. A number of adopted girls growing up in the Jewish faith asked that their bat mitzvah donations be sent to particular charities in China. Still other girls turned their birthday parties into fund-raising events. As one girl put it, "This is my way of giving back to the children and the country of my birth."

Whether the efforts are as large-scale as paying for a foster care program or as humble as one adoptive child's gift of her birthday money to a charity that supports the orphanage she came from, the bridge to China is strengthened, and it's not a one-way proposition. Care and concern flow in both directions across the Pacific.

When one adopted child became severely ill, a U.S.–China miracle unfolded. Having raised three biological children, Linda and Owen Wells, of Albuquerque, New Mexico, had adopted a little girl from an orphanage in Hunan. When Kailee was diagnosed at the age of five with severe aplastic anemia and eventually required a bone marrow transplant, the family literally searched the globe for a match.

At the time, Asian registries of marrow donors were minimal. Kailee, as is true for most adoptees from China, had no known birth family to turn to. But Linda Wells went to China to seek a match and contacted the Red Cross Society. At the time, China had just begun a drive to increase its national bone marrow donor registry, and the government held a press conference to publicize Kailee's plight. Linda Wells did everything else she could, checking with her daughter's institution to see if there was any further information on a birth family. (There wasn't.) She even went in search of the spot in front of a teachers' college where Kailee was said to have been found, tucked in a box, ten days old. The building had since been torn down.

With the help of the Chinese Red Cross and the Chinese donor network, the Wells family widened their search. With the donor drive in China under way, a number of potential matches were tested, but none panned out. Meanwhile, in the United States, adoption groups organized bone marrow donor drives for Kailee. Finally, after a search of two years, a man in China stepped forward. Wang Lin, a young physician from Hangzhou, had seen the publicity about Kailee and the general need for donors. A specialist in blood diseases, he volunteered to be screened because it seemed the right thing to do. To Wang's great surprise, he turned out to be a near-perfect match. He traveled to Beijing to undergo the procedure that would provide his bone marrow to be sent to the United States and to Kailee, and ultimately save her life.

In December 2007, Kailee was well enough to travel with her family to China over the Christmas holidays to meet the doctor. A big celebration was held in Beijing. In a mix of Mandarin and English, Kailee stood at a microphone and thanked everyone in China who had helped. "They had the biggest celebration you could imagine," Linda Wells told me. "When Wang Lin came to the stage, everyone clapped, and he and Kailee hugged each other. My husband, Owen, gave him a hug and both men cried. I was awestruck. Here was this miracle standing in front of us. His DNA was swirling through him and was now swirling through her."

Wang Lin told the Wellses that within a day or two of his donation to Kailee, he and his wife had had their first child, a son. Through the miraculous connection that had saved her life, he said that he now considered Kailee his child as well.

"How can you thank someone enough, give recognition to someone who saved your child?" said Linda Wells. "It was miraculous, and she got to meet him." Given all the publicity about Kailee, there'd been another benefit: the donor registry in China had seen a huge increase. So had the U.S. registry of Asian donors.

Now eleven, Kailee has survived three bone marrow transplants, as well as numerous other medical treatments. At the time of this writing, she was doing well, her mother said, though she still needs to be closely monitored and must stay near her doctors. During her illness, Kailee's family had moved to Wisconsin to be closer to the team of medical specialists who were treating her.

It's been a life filled with miracles, Linda Wells told me. The first miracle was having Kailee come into their lives in the first place. The next miracle was being able to save her. "I wouldn't trade the experience for anything," said Wells. When I last spoke with her, she said that Kailee had been to see *The Lion King*—the first time in six years that the family had been able to take her out to a public gathering without worrying about infection. Linda Wells's efforts to save her daughter had spanned an ocean and touched thousands of hearts in both countries. "I just did what any mother would have done," she said.

Extended, Extended Family

Every adoption leads to new, often surprising, connections. Information and stories flow so freely in the world of Chinese adoption, in fact, that it is as easy to hear how the adopted children living in Ireland are doing as it is to check in with the adopted children in one's own city.

Kelly's adoption group continues to hold reunions for all eighteen families; there are get-togethers for Franny's group, too. In between, our northern California group gathers three or four times a year at least—to celebrate holidays or just catch up. When a little girl adopted with Franny's group fell ill and was diagnosed with leukemia, the adoption group rallied around, providing loving support to the girl and her mother.

In 2005, the little girls from Jiangmen, Foshan, and Sanshui who had all come home together with Kelly that fall day in 1997 had a reunion in Maine, where two of the cousins live. On the Fourth of July, the girls constructed a float on the theme of the Year of the Rooster, put on their Chinese outfits, and marched through the streets of a small seacoast village, throwing candy. They won first place!

Other years, the group has gathered on the West Coast. In 2008, we were all going to meet in Maine again, and in 2009, as Kelly and her cousins turned twelve, we all planned to return together to China for a visit—led by Max, our Chinese American adoption facilitator, the hero who had put all our children in our arms.

In the wide world of Chinese adoption, there are wonderful success stories—adopted children enjoying friends and art and music and sports, excelling in their studies, enjoying their lives. There are uphill battles for those who have experienced developmental delays, learning challenges, or emotional difficulties. And there are tragic tales, too.

A beautiful little toddler, Maiya Novitsky, was struck down with Rett syndrome, a progressive degenerative neurological disorder. Over time, her family saw her lose her ability to stand, to speak, to feed herself. Her father, Scott Novitsky, wrote a poignant memoir of the experience, *My Silent Angel*.

Instead of the ballet and gymnastics lessons he'd envisioned for his daughter, and get-togethers with a Chinese culture group, Novitsky said, his family wound up with medical appointments and the company of other people with disabled kids. "I never wanted to come to this place," he wrote, "and wouldn't ever invite others to come here either, but after being here awhile and taking a deep breath, I have become accustomed to its slower pace and simple joys." He and his family were savoring every day with their beautiful and very challenged little girl.

The Novitsky family heard about two other little girls adopted from China who also had Rett syndrome. They met up with one family and the girls enjoyed a visit to Sea World and Disney World, while the parents got to talk and share support and information. Scott Novitsky was soon deeply involved in raising awareness of the disease—in both the United States and China (www.mysilentangel.com). He says it's estimated that there may be as many as thirty thousand females under the age of thirty with Rett in China, but only about two hundred have been diagnosed and identified. There's been some promising research, he said, and it's important to reach the others, in the event a treatment becomes available. Maiya, who was going on six when we last talked, has touched everyone who has met her, her father said. "She brings out the best in people."

There were many other stories of extraordinary love and commitment and cross-cultural mixing of fates. One of the most haunting was recounted in the book *Saving Levi*, by Lisa Bentley, which tells the story of a tiny baby, covered with third-degree burns over 70 percent of his body, who'd been left to die in a field in China. An old man had picked up the grievously injured child and gotten him to a local government office, and from there the infant was taken to a hospital. And that's where Lisa Bentley entered the picture. Bentley, as chronicled in a *Los Angeles Times* story, was a disaffected American who'd gone to live in China with her husband and four children.[4] The couple had founded a Christian orphanage there for special-needs children, but Bentley was feeling adrift.

When she went to visit that small, severely burned baby in a hospital incubator, Bentley's life changed in an instant. She looked into the child's eyes, his eyes stared into hers, and she knew that he needed an advocate—fast. Using every resource she could think of, Bentley succeeded in getting the child to the Boston Shriners Hospital for Children, and his life was saved. Ultimately she and her husband adopted the boy and named him Levi.

At five, Levi went off to kindergarten, where he cheerfully asked other children for help tying his shoes, since doctors had been unable to save his left arm. By then Levi had gone through twenty surgeries, and faced more. In saving the boy, Bentley said, she also saved herself. Today she continues to live in China with her husband and their six children, two adopted from China. The couple continues to run a foster home and a school for children with hearing loss. On her website (www.lisamisrajebentley.com), Bentley has posted a photo of Levi, wide smile on his face, standing in the field where he was found.

San Diego reporter Elizabeth Fitzsimons wrote another moving account of the blessings and surprises of orphaned children. The *New York Times* published her story of keeping the faith when she got to China and found that the child who had been assigned to her seemed to have some extremely serious medical challenges.[5] Though she was offered a healthier child, Fitzsimons decided that no matter what the health issues, she knew who her daughter was, and she was not about to abandon her now. In the end, the little girl turned out to be fine, but Fitzsimons had no assurance of that when she made that lifelong commitment in China.

Families over the Ocean

When she was four, Franny sat down with paper and paints. On a large sheet of white paper, with unwavering brushstrokes, in colors of black and magenta, she painted a woman, long black hair trailing down her back, her arms reaching ahead of her like a swimmer, and from her hands dangled what looked to be long, looping ribbons, like those used in Chinese ribbon dances. The portrait is of a woman seen from the back and she is floating away, into the sky. "My Chinese mother," said Franny.

Just recently, five years after she painted that picture, Franny awoke from a dream. "I dreamed of my Chinese mother," she told me, lying in her bed, still sleepy. "She had long dark hair, shiny dark hair down to her butt. She held it up for me to play with. I had a new little sister," Franny continued.

"I got to name her. When she cried, I held her. A man came and my mother said, 'This is my husband,' and I said, 'I hope not.'"

"And then what?" I asked. "That's all," said Franny. "We went on a train. I can't remember the rest." The next time I looked at Franny's painting I thought of this dream. Maybe what looked like ribbons was actually her Chinese mother's long, dark hair streaming from her fingers, the hair she let Franny play with.

I remembered, too, Kelly's talk about her "grandfather with three broken teeth."

The elusive birth families of China, how they have lingered in our children's hearts, on the edges of our lives. In the early days of Chinese adoption, it was widely thought that few, if any, birth parents would ever be found by adoptive families, much less come forward on their own. Most children, it was assumed, had forever lost the connection to their families of origin, all of whom—parents, extended family, siblings—had slipped permanently away. Kay Johnson had interviewed a number of people who had let their children go, exploring the whole subject in her book *Wanting a Daughter, Needing a Son,* but few adoptive families envisioned a reunion with their counterparts on the other side of the Pacific.

The next decade would reveal otherwise. By 2008, in fact, the picture had changed dramatically in enough instances that the prospect of locating birth parents—even having birth parents seek out the adoptive family—was no longer an impossible scenario. Filmmaker Changfu Chang could tell you that every July 7 a birth family in Hangzhou made a trip to the famous West Lake bridge, in hopes that the American family who had adopted their lost daughter would show up for a long-wished-for reunion.

All along, there had been a few adoptive families who had learned detailed information about birth families. There were older adopted children who remembered a specific family, children who had, in fact, even reconnected with those families. Then, too, a number of adoptive families had found that their children had siblings, some who remained in China, and others who had been adopted by different families.

Some families had met birth families when they traveled back to China for a trip with their daughters. Jane Liedtke, an adoptive mother who runs the Our Chinese Daughters Foundation in Beijing and puts together tours for adoptive families, says at least eleven families who've traveled with her groups have met birth parents—including families who weren't necessarily looking to have that happen.

Dutch television filmed an account of an intentional search for birth family in a program that was aired in 2006 and made its way through the American adoption community. It told the story of a young girl adopted from China and living in the Netherlands, whose adoptive parents hired an investigator to look for her birth family. They succeeded, and the birth family agreed to appear on camera, talking about the reasons for their decision and its emotional repercussions. A reunion between the birth parents and their daughter was the next step in the story.

Chang, a professor at Millersville College in Pennsylvania, managed to get several birth families to tell their stories on camera for his film *Long Wait for Home*, released in 2008. It wasn't easy to get birth parents to agree to be filmed, said Chang. "Due to mostly cultural reasons, birth parents don't want others to know the experience they have had." Chang persevered, and the stories told through his lens offer rare face-to-face insight into the reasons Chinese birth families might have had to relinquish a child, including poverty, government harassment, and medical needs that went far beyond a family's resources.

Chang, sometimes called "the professor of adoption films," has made a number of documentaries about Chinese adoption. Raised in Fujian province, he came to this country in 1995, got his doctorate from Purdue University, and set out to do documentaries. When he heard from a friend about all the children from China who'd been adopted by Americans, he knew he had a subject. "I started to realize the future of this world of adoption," he told me. "I knew Chinese people were in the dark about it, and that many adoptive parents were left with fundamental questions."

Chang's first idea was to make films that could be shown on Chinese television, but he encountered barriers. The station managers liked the films, but weren't ready to show them. Chang decided to proceed on his own, and has by now made several films that have aired on U.S. PBS stations. *Peer in the Distance* is Professor Chang's film for adopted girls who wonder what their lives might have been like had they grown up in China. The film profiles Wan Wan, a girl being raised in the affluence of the city, and Xing Ping, growing up in the hard-pressed countryside. Another film follows a group of American families as they travel to China to adopt children. Even after a string of films on China adoption, the good professor is not through yet. One current project is to document the experience of older adopted Chinese children as they grow into their own identities.

In *Long Wait for Home*, Chang's film about birth parents, a tearful father tells how he and his wife left their infant son, suffering from a brain tumor, in a hospital elevator because the family had no resources to pay for treatment. Like millions of migrant workers who have come to the city seeking jobs, Tang and his wife could not support themselves farming their small plot in a remote part of Sichuan province. Having moved to Fuzhou, Tang felt he was making pretty good money, less than four dollars a day. But there was no way he could pay for the mounting hospital bills when their ten-month-old child was diagnosed with a malignancy. When they left their baby son at the hospital, it was the couple's hope that some wealthy people could provide treatment and a cure. Sadly, five days after the boy was found, he died.

Another couple, the Xu family from Jiangsu province, recounted how the wife became pregnant with an over-quota child. They decided against abortion, but paid dearly: Their house was demolished and they had to flee their village. Lacking a birth permit, they could not go to a hospital and had to deliver the child themselves. Knowing they could not keep their daughter without further harassment by the government, they took her to a vegetable market, where they hoped she would be found, taken to an orphanage, and cared for. Along with some powdered milk, clothing, and what little money they could muster, they left a note for the hoped-for adoptive parents: They would like to meet in ten years on the West Lake bridge in Hangzhou on July 7, "Double Seventh," the traditional Chinese day of reunion, they said, to see their dear daughter again and to thank the adoptive parents in person. The filmmaker says this meeting hasn't come to pass, but the birth family has returned to that bridge each year. They have also given Professor Chang some gifts, hoping he could pass them on to the adoptive family.

The third family who told their story to Chang described the
dilemma they faced when they delivered a second child and
were under intense pressure from the authorities and community to give her up. They arranged a private local adoption,
only to hear that the Chinese couple to whom they gave their
daughter had changed their minds and taken the child to an orphanage. Before the birth father could get to the orphanage
and reclaim the child, he said, she was adopted by another Chinese family. Nearly twenty years later, the birth parents were
able to search for their daughter and her adoptive family, but
were reluctant to approach the girl, afraid of upsetting her.

The filmmaker says he has never been so shaken as he was
watching the faces of these birth parents and hearing their stories. Their faces showed a "sadness so palpable, and profound
love so indescribable," he says. "Please take good care of these
children," said one birth father on camera. "Don't let them forget their roots." Another says he has thought of his daughter
every day, and added, "Please don't worry about us." Each of the
birth parents Chang filmed turned out to be ordinary parents
caught in a cruel bind of one kind or another, people who have
agonized and grieved, people who hope their lost children have
found happiness. Meanwhile, from time to time, other accounts about birth parents surfaced, presenting a far less caring
picture.

Chang went on to film numerous interviews with people on
the streets of China, asking them how they felt about abandoned children and adoption by foreigners. Though some expressed doubt about the intentions of foreign parents, others
were compassionate. "In speaking with hundreds of ordinary
Chinese, I found that almost all of them had a strong sympathy
for the birth parents," said Chang. "To a certain extent, all of

the Chinese feel as though they are 'birth parents' of these children, whom they care about and hope live a happy life in forever homes."

When I last checked with him, Chang was at work on yet another film—a look at adoption *within* China. He'd already interviewed a custodian in Kunming who had found twenty babies. He'd cared for them all and had also tried to track down their families.

If a number of birth families already have been located, undoubtedly there will be more who will be found or who will step forward, especially if the fears of reprisal ease, especially if the word gets around about other families being willing to identify themselves—although the illegality of abandoning a child still stands, and birth parents may fear getting into some sort of trouble should they come forth, said Chang. And, he added, they may feel such shame about abandoning a child that they continue to keep the secret to themselves.

Another Time, Another Place

My daughters watched in fascination as old men in thickly quilted jackets wielded three-foot-long brushes that looked like giant Q-tips. The men dipped the padded ends in water, and then swished beautiful calligraphy onto the dark slabs of sidewalk stone. The characters shone brightly for a few moments, then began to evaporate and fade away.

We were in Beijing at the Summer Palace. It was our first trip back to China with both girls. When I had a conference to attend in China that fall, Mark and I decided to make it a family trip. It was a chance to reacquaint our daughters—Kelly was then seven and Franny was five—with the land of their birth. Yet such pilgrimages, I knew, could be uncertain journeys at best. Our children had no known relatives to look up, no family homes to return to, and we weren't sure what their reaction would be if we visited an orphanage. With children this age, I knew from brief experience that it was hard to predict what they would find meaningful or fun. When we asked Kelly what she had liked best on our previous visit to China when we adopted Franny, she said her favorite thing had been the yogurt that came in tiny containers with Chinese cartoons on them.

On this trip, we tried to keep our expectations low. We knew the desire for a genuine feeling of connection might be overly optimistic. Still, there was plenty to do and see, and we hoped the trip would help our daughters begin to gain a feeling of ease and familiarity with China, a connection they could build on throughout their lives.

On the promenade along the lake, we found the old calligraphers. "They're writing poems," our Chinese companion told us, as we stepped gingerly through the disappearing messages. "See this character? It means 'mountain,' and this one means 'cloud.'" Our daughters were rapt. The calligraphers smiled at them and went on writing. As one poem faded, another came to life. "Could we do that when we get home, Mom?" Franny wanted to know. "*Ni hao*," said the old calligrapher, looking up. "*Ni hao*," the girls repeated, suddenly shy.

While the girls were tentative at first about saying the few words of Chinese they knew, they were soon tossing their limited vocabulary about with élan, *ni hao*-ing everyone they saw and thanking people right and left. "*Xie xie*," they chorused to the waiters in dumpling houses, the staff in the hotels, the ticket takers at the monuments. People on the street stared at us, a pair of Westerners with two small Chinese girls. "Are they Chinese?" they would ask, pointing to the girls, perplexed. "Do they speak Chinese?"

"We were born in China, but we don't know Chinese," Kelly said to one curious onlooker. "Except maybe a little."

"I was born in China, but I got adopted," announced Franny with her usual exuberance.

We saw the sights in Shanghai and Beijing, the modern sky-scrapers, the restaurants and stores. The girls tried Peking duck and dozens of kinds of dumplings. We visited a number of temples, where the girls lighted incense and bowed to the Buddhas and Guan Yin, smoke curling up into the air. They spent time with an old man in a park, watching his small trained bird peck for seeds. They tried all the athletic equipment in the park that had been set up for elders, and they quietly watched the tai chi practitioners. We found the tiny yogurt containers with the cartoon characters on them.

Eventually, we tired of playing tourist, and not quite sure where we were headed, we accepted a friend's invitation to take a drive in the country. We looked out at the small roadside businesses—old-fashioned brooms and plastic tubs lined up in front of storefronts, simple outdoor noodle stands, men repair-ing bicycles.

We stopped on a tiny dirt road and walked into an old vil-lage. It was just a cluster of dwellings off the road, surrounded by a checkerboard of small family vegetable plots. In the pale winter light, the fields were tinted in strips of russet, feathery yellow, and muted green.

As we walked down the dirt path, a woman came along, dragging a load of dried cotton stalks. She smiled broadly, plucked a few remaining cotton balls off the stalks and gave them to the girls. Then we walked past the rows of bok choy, past mounds of hay, to find a water buffalo and her baby standing tethered and placid.

It was like stepping back a century. The houses plastered with mud, the fields watered by hand. Our daughters were enchanted.

A row of plucked and gutted ducks, rubbed with red chili, had been hung to dry on a fence in the sun. "I see ducks, but they aren't flapping their wings," said Franny. Dogs sat on the stoops, and people strolled out to greet us with curiosity. In the inner courtyards of the houses, chickens were kept in coops, and a pig snorted and came up to rub its nose on the bars of a small enclosure. Through the open doors, we could see that inside the homes the furnishings were minimal—a stove, a table. On one wall were family photos, flanked by a picture of a young Mao Zedong, cigarette dangling from his lips.

People in the area, we were told, get by on $1,000 or less a year. And children who grow up here aren't likely to stay. They head for the cities where there is work. One family was raising a daughter who had been found as an infant.

As we passed one doorway, an older woman motioned for us to come inside. Her face was deeply etched, lines following the contours of her smile. She was small and agile. I could not have guessed her age—she could have been sixty, or eighty.

Taking Kelly by the hand, she led us into a bare room with a concrete floor. She pulled out small wooden stools for us, and we all sat beaming at one another, wondering what was next. She held a hand at the level of Kelly's head and then held up fingers. Seven? Eight? We worked out the children's ages with our fingers. She gestured at me, and then at the girls, talking all the while, a sweet quizzical look on her face. I think she was wondering how we'd gotten ourselves together into a family. But when I tried to tell her, my night-school Mandarin fell apart. It didn't seem to matter.

"Where do you sleep?" Kelly asked the woman, trying to make herself understood by folding her hands and laying her cheek on them. The woman smiled and motioned with her hand to a place over her shoulder.

Then the woman leaned forward and put her hands on my knee and made the gesture of taking chopsticks from bowl to mouth. "Have you eaten," she asked, and she made it clear she wanted to feed us. "Yes, yes, eat," she said in Chinese, and rose as if to bustle off to the kitchen.

I wanted to stay, but outside the door I could see our friends waiting by the minivan. So we got up, saying we were sorry, that we had already eaten, and that we had to get back to the city. We thanked her as profusely as we could. As we reluctantly walked away, my daughters said their good-byes over and over, in two languages, to the woman and the water buffalo.

"That woman was so nice," my older daughter said, bouncing along in the car. "She was really nice, but her hands were rough. She didn't seem like she had much money."

"She was like a grandma," Franny said. "She liked us."

Whatever memories might eventually fade like the calligraphy on the sidewalk, I knew then that this visit had touched some deeper place. As we drove away, Kelly clutched her cotton ball, staring back at the village. "*Zai jian, zai jian,*" yelled Franny, waving good-bye.

Later on this trip, Franny got to visit with her orphanage director. She was shy at first, but soon was sitting in the woman's lap, happily listening to a rush of Mandarin. Afterward, Franny started singing her old songs in Chinese again.

Not Quite Home

By 2008, as predicted, homeland trips were the latest movement. Various groups, including adoption agencies and commercial travel ventures, had begun offering excursions back home to China for adoptive families. Peggy Scott, who traveled with her thirteen-year-old daughter, Abby, on one of the Our Chinese Daughters Foundation's Panda Tours, said the kids had a blast. "They got to love this fantastic land where they look like everyone. They got to fall in love with China before they had to deal with it psychologically."

Along with such trips, more news and speculation about birth parents began to emerge. A trip back to an institution often produced more information than had been offered the first time around. Sometimes a clue led someplace specific, and by now, a number of adoptive families had been in contact with their Chinese counterparts. Birth families had been interviewed in print and film and a few, hearing that Americans with adopted daughters had come to town, had emerged from the shadows to say hello. The assumptions about the impossibilities of finding Chinese families had begun to shift—not for every adopted child, certainly, but for some.

As I was thinking about such things—in the kind of uncanny coincidence I've almost come to expect—my nine-year-old came into my office to tell me she'd written a letter to her birth mother. She had it all folded up, tucked in her T-shirt. She said she did not want me to read it, but wanted me to come out in the backyard and help her burn it, so that the smoke would carry her message to China. I hit "Save" on the computer and we went outside. Franny picked up a small blue and white Chinese pot and placed her letter in it. She set the pot in front of our stone

Guan Yin. I helped her light the letter and she closed her eyes and made a wish as the paper burned to ash. She waved her hand at the trail of smoke. "Go to China," Franny said.

I entertained the thought, far more than I used to, that someday we might have a more specific address. Maybe not. But surprising things seemed to be happening all the time.

Sisters, Sisters

After we came home with Kelly and met the twins who'd been adopted by two different single women and then reunited (see page 157), we began to hear other, similar stories. Over time, stories emerged about a number of siblings who'd been separated and then subsequently found each other, even though it had been the Chinese ministry's stated position that known sets of twins be kept together and the same family assigned both.

Sometimes the discovery of separated siblings unfolds when an adoptive parent happens to see pictures online of another child who looks remarkably like his or her child. Or perhaps two children who are related wind up in a room together and someone notices the resemblance. Eventually, the parents order a DNA test. In at least two curious cases, a set of twins was separated, adopted by two different families, and each of the twins given the same new first name by their adoptive families, who later found each other. Two Merediths, two Meis.

There have been other surprises. In one case in China, a set of triplets was kept together and taken to the same orphanage, and one American family was allowed to adopt all three. The tiny trio had been discovered with a note explaining that they were the eighth, ninth, and tenth daughters of one Chinese clan, and that the birth parents were unable to care for them. They hoped "an honorable person" could raise the girls to adulthood and someday bring them back to China for a visit.[6]

Bonnie Ward of New Hampshire asked for twins when she filed her papers to adopt from China. She wound up with just one referral, though, and soon set out to meet a fourteen-month-old in Changde, Hunan province. A single mother, Ward named her little daughter Creighton. Life was good, she said. "But I could never get it out of my heart that I wanted another baby," she said. "In large part because I am a single mom, I felt it was really important for my child to have a sibling." Plus Ward herself had grown up with a beloved sister, who had died, and Ward still missed her a great deal.

"It was always in the back of my mind that there was another child waiting. So, I started the paperwork to adopt again," said Ward. The day she signed and dated the final papers turned out to be the birthday of her late sister. "I took that as a sign," she told me. Ward asked for a child from her first daughter's orphanage, but the agency told her there were no such guarantees, that she had to be open. "I know," replied Ward. "I'm open, but I just have a feeling my daughter is waiting there in Changde."

Ward got the news of a referral in August 2001. "'You're a mom again,' the agency told me, and I said, 'Where is she?' and when the woman said, 'Changde,' I started jumping up and down!"

Ward and her daughter traveled to China to bring home the little sister Creighton had been waiting for. They named her Reilly. After they got home, they went to Tennessee for a family reunion. By then several people, including Ward's mother, had observed a more than strong resemblance between Creighton and Reilly. Ward was also getting the "grocery store

questions" all adoptive parents know too well. "Are they siblings? Are they *biological* siblings?" After Ward went to a spir-
itualist who told her there was an "extraordinary" connection
between her two daughters, and that Ward's late sister had had
a hand in the relationship, Ward decided to get the girls' DNA
tested. When the news came back, she learned that her daughters were full siblings.

Later, at a reunion for adoptive families, the agency director
said to Ward, "I don't know how this happened." Ward
replied, "I don't think we're supposed to understand."

When Ward took her two girls back to China for a trip,
among their stops was a visit to the China Center of Adoption
Affairs. "I asked to see the matching room," said Ward. "It was
nothing like I expected. It could have been any insurance office
anywhere in America. There were a bunch of women sitting in
cubicles. They had all these file folders, and they took a stack
from here and put it there. But then, miracles are extraordinary
things that happen in ordinary places." During the visit, she
added, a group of young workers gathered around her daughters and began talking animatedly in Chinese. "What are they
saying?" Ward asked. "The interpreter said, 'They're saying
you should have saved the money you spent on a DNA test.
Anyone can see these two are sisters.'"

Of course the obvious question is, how many other lost siblings are as yet undiscovered, growing up in separate adoptive
homes? Or one child living abroad and the other back in
China? Kay Johnson's research, showing that daughters relinquished by Chinese families were often the second born, had already pointed to the widespread possibility that many adopted
children had siblings in China.

Jim and Susan Rittenhouse, whose own daughter turned out

to have a twin living in another state, have formed a website, Sister Far, for families who have found similar, surprising connections (www.sisterfar.com). Such events, as well as the medical needs of a child like Kailee Wells, have heightened the discussions and attempts to form DNA registries for adopted children.[7]

Many children from China, more as time goes on, live with Chinese foster families before they are adopted. The partings for these families are often not easy. There are so many accounts of foster mothers crying inconsolably as a child leaves her care. Newly adopted babies have come with notes tucked in their diapers or pockets, put there by the foster families, containing good wishes—plus their addresses and phone numbers. A number of adoptive families have stayed in touch, sending notes and photos to the foster families and telling them of the child's progress in the United States. For many families with young children, the links to China—for now—are often with the staff at orphanages or the foster families who cared for their children.

Many families who make a return trip to China seek out those foster families. Nancy Simmons (her name has been changed to protect the foster family) has three girls adopted from China. Her third daughter was four when Simmons went to meet her in southern China. Simmons wasn't allowed to travel to the orphanage, and so her new daughter came to the Civil Affairs Office by car, carrying a little backpack, on Christmas Day. In the backpack was a red good-luck envelope. Inside the envelope, said Simmons, was lucky money—twenty yuan—but also a note from the foster mother, including her street and e-mail addresses. Simmons also found that her new daughter, whom she named Carolina, had memorized the foster family's phone number.

Since then, Simmons and her daughter have spoken with the foster mother by phone and exchanged letters. The foster mother sent a package of fancy dresses for Carolina's birthday; Simmons sent the foster mother a video of the birthday party and of other family activities. The foster father sent a heart-wrenching letter describing how it felt to say good-bye. The foster father's sister had also fostered two children, twin boys; Simmons's daughter had played with the boys and called them her *didi*s—little brothers. The boys subsequently were adopted by a family in South Carolina and Simmons and that family are in touch. The old red thread, winding along.

Simmons, a child development professor at a southern university, said she planned to take her three daughters back to China for a visit with the foster family when Carolina turns six and her older sisters are nine and eight. When she brought her middle daughter home, says Simmons, at bedtime the girl kept calling *Mama, mama, mama*. "I knew that she didn't mean me. And then it dawned on me that I was actually her *sixth* mother. She'd had a birth mother, then been in the orphanage, then been put in foster care, then taken back to the orphanage, then cared for by a second foster family, and now I came along. I realized how hard the transition was."

Unfortunately, Simmons says, her oldest daughter didn't have foster care at all, and contact information about her middle daughter's foster family isn't known. For some children, though, such ties—when they are known—may be the next best thing to a birth family. For many adopted children it offers a chance to know that at least one specific person, or a family, in

China did indeed care for them. Ongoing contacts with caretakers in the institutions can offer similar comfort.

When adoptive families return to China, some travel on their own, some travel in groups with other kids for company. *Found in China,* a film made by Carolyn Stanek, follows a group of families from the United States as they return to China with their daughters, who were preteens at the time. With thoughtful background commentary provided by Canadian sociologist, author, and adoptive mother Sara Dorow, the film is a quiet, clear, insightful look at the emotional content of such journeys. Several of the girls are filmed as they visit the places where they were found. One is able to talk to the man who found her. The girls themselves and their adoptive parents offer reflections on the journey back to China, the hopes, the fears, the realities. (See www.foundinchinathedocumentary.com.)

In 2006, when their daughter Phoebe Zhilan was five years old, Lura Dolas and Darryl Brock took her back to China on an Our Chinese Daughters Foundation Homeland Tour. "We traveled with friends in our local adoptive community and others with whom we quickly bonded," said Dolas, who is on the faculty at the University of California at Berkeley. "Phoebe Zhilan was the youngest girl among us and was immediately taken under the wings of the eleven- and twelve-year-olds. She returned to China with us, but saw most of the sights holding hands with one or two of her older Chinese sisters. Her father and I followed at a cautious but respectful distance.

"Perhaps especially because Phoebe is an only child, her 'China sisters' are extremely important to her," Dolas said. "They are role models and constant reminders to her that she is not alone in her journey toward understanding all that it is to be adopted from China." Jane Liedtke, who arranges such tours, says that traveling together on a tour bus is a great experience for the girls. "They gather in the back of the bus, and they are their own therapy group!"

With such trips come new challenges, and the trips can assume a different significance, depending on the age and inclinations of the children traveling back. Though such trips can be healing and enriching, they can also awaken fears, anger, and sorrow—or end in confusion.

One American family on a trip back to China visited their child's orphanage and were given the name and village of the man who'd found their daughter. With the help of the orphanage director, they went looking for this man, which resulted in a warm meeting. The finder, a middle-aged man, was delighted to see their daughter, the baby he'd found ten years earlier. He took her by the hand and led her to the exact spot where he'd discovered her, lying near the village bulletin board.

During the visit, the family's Chinese guide talked to the man at length, and on the ride back from the village he told the family that the finder also knew the birth parents. Apparently the family had had two daughters, and when the third was born, they could not care for her. The adopted child visiting from the United States was quite pleased to learn that she had two sisters in China.

After the adoptive family returned home, they wrote letters to the birth parents, sent in care of the orphanage, but never received a reply. Eventually they planned a visit back and let the orphanage director know they were coming, only to be told that it had been a big misunderstanding. The birth parents weren't known, after all; the finder had in fact found *two* baby girls over time, the director explained, and the birth parents he knew about were connected to the *other* child he'd found, not the young girl who had come to visit.

"It's hard to know what's what," said the American adoptive mother. She said the family planned to return to China again at some point and at least visit the man who'd found their daughter. "He was a part of her life, and obviously a warm and caring man." Beyond that, who knew what the true facts were?

Although this family came to China with no such expectations, some families return to China with the hope of locating the birth family, a hope that comes complete with the most optimistic scenario. But who can predict what will happen? And whatever the situation, an encounter, even a near-encounter, with a birth family can be an emotionally fraught undertaking for all concerned, say those who've dealt with such matters.

Hollee McGinnis, who has been there, cautions against expectations and advises families to think through all their motivations. Well aware of the fantasies that can be spun out about birth families, McGinnis asks, "Are you ready to confront the knowledge about your past? Are you prepared to meet strangers?"

Katy Robinson, another Korean adoptee and the author of *A Single Square Picture,* whose thoughts were included in a *New York Times* online discussion about adoption, reported, "It took twenty years to muster the courage to confront the most basic of questions: Who am I? Where did I come from?" She described her own trip back to Korea not as any final destination, but as a complex journey, "a picture in constant motion." She reestablished contact with her seventy-year-old birth father, who told her not a day had gone by that he didn't think of her.

After that, says Robinson, she settled into her dual history with more peace. "Today when I look in the mirror, I no longer see an image I want to change. I see a face with features I got from my Korean family, and expressions I got from my American one. At times, I feel deeply Korean; other times I feel all American. It's no longer important to be fully one or the other. I have the privilege to move between these two halves and still feel whole."

For McGinnis, it was a journey to self-acceptance, a journey of rejecting the labels and expectations placed on her by the outside world. McGinnis has strong feelings that such searches, if they are undertaken by older girls, should belong to the girls themselves, and not to the adoptive parents. "As adoptees we did not get to choose our adoptions," she writes. "We did not choose to be relinquished. We did not choose to be adopted. The decision to search is one of the few things adoptees get to choose. It is part of our adoption journey; it is not our adoptive parents' journey."

Ultimately, whether birth families are part of the journey or not, perhaps the most interesting trips of all will be those that the girls take on their own. Some have already occurred.

The Lee family of Albany, California, is unusual in several respects. Hanni Lee is Caucasian and speaks Mandarin well. Her husband, Alan, is Chinese American and speaks no Chinese. The Lees have three daughters adopted from China—Jiawen, age sixteen; Fang, age fifteen; and Qing Qing, aged eleven. All were adopted as older children, and all have kept up their Chinese. Hanni and her daughters have traveled back to China together half a dozen times. Jiawen has located some family members in China and visited them often.

In the summer of 2007, Fang, who was then fourteen, traveled to China for three weeks on her own, but supported by a network of family friends in China. She kept a blog, an enthusiastic account of her travels back to her home province of Yunnan, as well as other destinations. Completely bilingual, she worked for a week at her former orphanage and foster villages, translating for a team of physical therapists working with disabled children.

She went on to Hefei, the former home of her little sister, Qing Qing, where she visited the child Fang's family calls Little Yi, or sometimes, "Little Girl in Pink." Fang posted photos of herself holding the smiling child, who cried when she left.

As so often happens, once one life is touched by the red thread, others are drawn into the loop. The link to Little Yi had come about on an earlier trip to China, when Hanni Lee had taken Qing Qing back to visit the foster family who had cared for her. In the countryside near the foster care family's village, they saw a little girl sitting quietly in a chair. They learned that the child did not speak and had cerebral palsy. After they came home, they couldn't get her out of their minds. Hanni approached the charity Love Without Boundaries to see if they could help her, and they agreed. Lee herself raised some money from friends and family, and Little Yi started receiving treatments at a rehabilitation hospital. The child gradually learned to stand and began to speak. Though she still could not walk when Fang visited her, Little Yi was receiving further therapy to strengthen her legs. Eventually, the child's paperwork was submitted so that she could be eligible for adoption.

Traveling alone offered a very different experience from traveling with her adoptive mother, Fang said. "When we are together people always come up and ask, 'Who is this woman? Can you speak Chinese?' And it's ridiculous, but they always charge us extra."

"If you're not there," she told her mother, "it completely changes the nature of our experience. It changes how people see us." Fang especially loved going to the countryside. "That's where the real China is," she said. "I love the bird and flower market. If you just go to department stores, you could be anywhere. You can get a very American experience and stay very protected.

"Seeing China is kind of like seeing the other half of me," Fang told me. "I'm indulged in American culture all day long. To be in China is a nice feeling.

"Going back to see my orphanage every year has made me feel really lucky," she added. "Not that it's a bad place. But especially this time, visiting made me feel like I really have it made." At one orphanage she visited, Fang took packages of rice crackers, and when the children saw the treats, they swarmed over her. "Like ants on a sugar cube! They attacked me," she said, laughing. "They were pulling at me and pushing each other. It shows how little they have.

"Any adopted kid, no matter how old, should definitely go back to China," said Fang. "Taking a child back allows kids to see part of their past and their roots. But also, a child should be ready." And, she emphasized, "going back with your parents at age twelve is a very different experience than traveling on your own."

Fang was at the moment tutoring another adopted girl in Mandarin to help her get ready for a trip back to China. "One big thing we're working on is what to say when people ask her if she's Chinese. I told her it's better to say you're American. Otherwise, they'll expect you to speak Chinese."

"I say I'm American," said Fang. "But I also say I'm adopted from China. They say, 'So you're Chinese.' I say, 'I'm Chinese American.'"

After her solo journey, Fang had mixed feelings about leaving China. "Though it is nice to be home, I wish I could be in my two homes all at once. I think my sister Jiawen feels the same way. She would like to be in both places. We both have such a love for China," Fang told me. "But this is home. This is where my adoptive family is. I don't know where my Chinese family is."

"I feel saddened that my journey has ended," she wrote on her blog, "but knowing that life is composed of many treks and journeys comforts me."

Fang planned to go back to China again next summer, maybe to Tibet, and back to see Little Yi. Again, she wanted to find some helpful things to do, to work in an orphanage again, perhaps. And eventually, she says, she'd like to do something that helps build a bridge between the United States and China.

Such journeys will continue, each with its own timing, its own outcome. What lies ahead? Surprises, joy, sorrow, dilemmas—perhaps future revelations and experiences we can barely imagine. A picnic in a park someday with hundreds of adoptive families and a few honored guests—birth families from China? It could happen. Maybe we'll all share some potato salad and dumplings and marvel at how we have been drawn together, finally, through the strangest of circumstances, the most beautiful of children. Maybe by dessert, we'd all be baring our hearts.

China on the Move

The country where all our children began their lives has continued to be the most rapidly changing nation on earth—even before the 2008 Olympics fever shifted construction and modernization into even higher gear. On the outskirts of major Chinese cities now there are U.S.-style suburban housing developments with Spanish-style luxury homes and names like Belvedere and Orange County, hardly distinguishable from their counterparts in California or Arizona. The Beijing Olympics has picked up the pace of foreign investment, and major global corporations have paid hefty sums for exposure to the Chinese market. While China's poor continue to struggle, China's upscale consumers can afford German cars and French wines, and the urban masses are a profitable market for McDonald's and Coca-Cola. Hong Kong boasts a Disneyland, Shenzen a Swiss village.

Despite the boom in China, some things unfortunately have not changed quickly enough. China struggles with some of the biggest challenges on the planet—pollution, poverty, the underlying pressures of the world's largest population, and what seems to be more than its share of natural catastrophe.

In 2007, scientists reported that the *baiji*, the magical white dolphin—long considered a harbinger of rough weather—was "functionally extinct." Searches of the Yangtze that year revealed not a single creature, and researchers speculated that pollution and dense river traffic had finally killed off the dolphin—the first creature of its classification, "the great and ancient Order of Cetaceans," to be forever lost to the world.

If, when we adopted our first daughter, we could read about factories where young women were working unspeakably hard and long hours with little protection, a report ten years later in the *New York Times* underlined the same problems. While Americans were worrying about toys from China that contained high levels of lead, Chinese workers, often as young as sixteen, were facing far more serious hazards. In the Pearl River Delta region, our first daughter's first home, the *Times* reported that factory workers lost or broke forty thousand fingers on the job each year. In Franny's hometown, a chemical plant was making international headlines for its unsafe conditions.

After attention was drawn to the conditions in sweatshops in the 1990s, there were some improvements in some places. But there are still grievous abuses and abysmal conditions, especially for young women—any one of whom might have had to make that difficult choice to relinquish a child; any one of whom might be the birth parent of a child adopted from China. One of the companies singled out for committing abuses was Wal-Mart. According to the *Times* report, teenage workers were sometimes required to work fifteen hours a day, seven days a week, in factories that supply Wal-Mart's merchandise for the American consumer.

The one-child policy is now well into its third decade. Some of its long-term implications are still just becoming clear. The director of China's Family Planning Office has warned of a "population rebound" caused by the newly rich doing what they want in terms of having children, and by rural populations marrying earlier. Some demographers argue that the one-child policy has led to other problems—for example, too few children coming of age to care for a rapidly aging population.

Jasper Becker, author of a major book on the Chinese famine, said in 2005 that it was still hard in China to talk about why girls were abandoned. But it seemed the subject was being discussed more openly, though the messages were mixed. China's president, Hu Jintao, was reported to have publicly questioned the one-child policy. As has been the case since the beginning, enforcement of the policy is uneven. In some places it has been eased to the point of nonenforcement. In others, the harassing of women goes on. As late as August 2007, the Associated Press recounted the story of a woman forced to have a late abortion by injection. *The Economist* reported that some women were fleeing to Hong Kong to have their over-quota children.

The newest wrinkle is a crackdown on the affluent. The province of Zhejiang has threatened to "name and shame" rich families who were simply paying the fines to have more children. In Beijing, officials also threatened a crackdown aimed at over-the-limit families among the rich and famous, who were not only ignoring the law, it was charged, but also, through their high profiles, setting a bad example for the rest of the population. In January 2007, reports came from Hubei province in central China that members of the Communist Party who had violated the one-child edict had had their party memberships revoked.

During a news conference in February 2008, the vice-minister of China's Family Planning Office said that the Chinese government now recognized the need for adjustments in the policy, but that changes would come "incrementally." The next day, another official announcement threw that forecast into doubt, and in March 2008 China's top population official announced that the one-child policy would stay in effect for another decade, at least—"to ensure stable and balanced population growth."

"The one-child policy was the only choice we had, given the conditions when we initiated the policy," an official said, and added that while there could be some future changes to the policy, no one should expect it to come to a sudden halt.[8]

The gender gap, meanwhile, continues to yawn huge—the most extreme case on earth, says Judith Banister, an American demographer who has done in-depth studies on China's population. By 2007, the Chinese government was itself talking about the imbalance, 119 males to 100 females, according to the most recent national Chinese census—which translates to tens of millions of "extra" men. Discussions of what this means for China's future ensued. President Hu Jintao announced a goal of correcting the imbalance to 107:100 by the year 2010, a goal that most demographers see as unrealistic, if not impossible. The government has now offered in some cases to pay families with daughters, and provide incentives. In the countryside, it is now increasingly common to see billboards—"It is forbidden to discriminate against, mistreat, or abandon baby girls"—and slogans praising the virtues of girls and offering encouragement to rural couples to value their daughters.

In contemporary China, specifically Henan province, a new class of orphans has emerged—those rendered parentless by the AIDS epidemic that began when poor parents sold their blood and were infected with reused needles. The children who lost their parents were left to care for one another, living a hand-to-mouth existence, some of them infected with the HIV virus themselves. Many were ostracized. Half the Sky and other groups offered help to these children, building foster villages, getting the children to schools, providing badly needed medicines.

On World AIDS Day, December 1, 2007, Chinese premier Wen Jiabao visited orphans in Henan, including children living at Half the Sky's New Harmony Village at Shaodian. In a vegetable-growing area that had suffered because of public fear of AIDS, the Chinese press reported that the premier had his photo taken with a local farmer and announced, "You can [report] that the premier has eaten Wenlou's vegetables today." That same day, President Hu Jintao shook hands with HIV-positive people in Beijing and posed for photographs. A young girl from New Harmony Village spoke at the International AIDS conference and was the subject of a Chinese television program.

Perhaps the most stunning news of all came on Children's Day 2007, when the Chinese government announced ambitious plans for the children living in the nation's social welfare institutions. China's president Hu Jintao pledged that the nation would take steps to ensure that orphans and disabled children could live "under the same blue sky" as other children. In partnership with China's Ministry of Civil Affairs, Half the Sky was invited to create the first provincial-level Blue Sky/Half the Sky Model Center at a children's welfare institution in Hubei, making the foundation's education and nurture programs available to every welfare institution in that province. From there, the sky—literally—seemed the limit, as plans were put in place to build a Half the Sky Model Center and training facility in every one of China's thirty-one provinces and municipalities over the next five years, with no halt until every child in a Chinese institution had as much comfort, schooling, love, and support as it was physically possible to provide.

This coming year, Half the Sky is introducing its programs to five new provinces—Zhejiang, Guizhou, Liaoning, Sha'anxi, and Heilongjiang. The ultimate goal for Half the Sky—to change the face of orphan care in China, to make good on the foundation's stated aims of providing a caring adult in the life of every orphaned child—is growing closer. The foundation has already fulfilled that promise to thousands of children, from the tiniest frail, newly found infants who were now cuddled in a nanny's arms, to teenagers and older girls who were going out into the world with new skills and new confidence, thanks to the Big Sisters programs.

In March 2008, for Half the Sky's work in the children's institutions of China, Jenny Bowen was among the recipients of the prestigious Skoll Award for Social Entrepreneurship, presented by former president Jimmy Carter at Oxford University.

And always, there is more money needed, more work to be done. When China experienced its coldest winter in fifty years as the New Year holiday came in 2008, several orphanages in south and central China were hard hit by snowstorms and subzero temperatures. As travelers were stranded, trying to get home for the holiday, traffic and cities came to a standstill. Power failures occurred. Supplies, including furnace coal, ran short. In many places orphanage staff were running out of food, diapers, coal, or water. In Jiangxi, the heating had broken in the infant nurture rooms and the rooms were icy. The staff had bundled all the children into one big room to keep them warm. Other places desperately needed food and diapers and warm quilts and clothing. As supplies dwindled, prices rose, and orphanage staff in many places were using their own money to keep things going. Half the Sky immediately began raising emergency funds for the children and trying to get as much relief to as many places as possible.

"We as a community are going to take care of the children

through these critical days," wrote Jenny Bowen, asking the Half the Sky community to donate to a Little Mouse emergency fund (so named because it was the Year of the Rat).

The Chenzhou institution in Hunan province, where 150 infants were being cared for, was particularly hard hit. The facility was without electricity or running water for two weeks after snow destroyed the city's power source. A group from Half the Sky finally got through and managed to supply food, coal, blankets, and diapers. Richard Bowen—emeritus director of Half the Sky's board, father to two little girls from China, and a filmmaker—led an intrepid 300-mile expedition to Chenzhou, taking a truckload of supplies to the orphanage in extremely difficult conditions. Navigating bad weather, closed roads, and the challenges of finding what was needed, Bowen and his little band found amazing generosity among the Chinese who were told of the plight of the children. (Bowen posted a full account of the journey on Half the Sky's website, www.halfthesky.org.)

Afterward, as he thought about the babies waiting at the institution, nearly hidden under piles of blankets and snowsuits, Bowen wrote, "I can't shake the gnawing feeling that as the stars of this little drama, they remained blissfully unaware of the countless worldwide threads, the amazing generosity of donors abroad and their fellow Chinese who all contributed to this effort to make sure they would be okay now, so that someday they could thrive.

"Half the Sky's organizational culture has always stressed that, even though we care for children without families, at heart ours is an organization wholly about family. We're all about embracing that irony and widening the definition of family . . . beyond bloodlines, beyond nationalities. It's all about creating bonds of family where they once didn't exist.

"As I drove home to my daughters and wife, I [was] struck by the deeper meaning of this little adventure. Hidden from me till now, I realized how, in my own way, I became infected with the spirit of Chinese New Year. This holiday that puts family first, that says get home at all costs, your family's waiting . . . I'm sure that's what drove us up that mountain (even if those little family members didn't know they were awaiting our arrival)."

The orphanage director, Shi Xiangqun, responded with thanks: "In China we have an old saying: 'A friend in need is a friend indeed, and love can help us out of crisis'. . . . In front of natural disaster, there is no nationality difference in terms of love. True love can melt ice and snow and all difficulties can be overcome."

In the wake of the devastating Sichuan earthquake in May 2008, adoption groups and charities, including Half the Sky, went to work again. Sadly, there was now another group of orphaned children to care for—those who'd lost parents in the quake. Special funds were set up to get help for these children, including foster care.

In Berkeley, older girls held a bake sale to collect money, as did groups of adopted children elsewhere, who sent off what they earned to various charities doing relief work with the youngest victims of the earthquake.

And so the links to China continue to build, made stronger all the time by the adoption movement—families around the world who can't forget all the children in institutions who are also family, and people in China who will do what they can to help the children who wait in the orphanages, or who, like Kailee Wells, have been adopted and need some special help from people in their birth country.

That Matter of Identity

In 2008, the Chinese twelve-year calendar came full circle for Kelly, our older daughter, born in 1996 in the Year of the Rat in southern China. In 2008, when the Rat's turn came round again, we celebrated at the home of our daughters' Chinese "auntie." Betty Louie, a dynamic, beautiful woman, had taken our family under her wing and folded us all into her large Chinese American family.

We had found each other through luck. Carl Jung would have called it synchronicity, but given our experiences, it's also tempting to credit that old red thread. Long ago while waiting for Kelly, I had gone to Grant Avenue in San Francisco's Chinatown and paid a visit to one of my favorite stores, the Far East Flea Market. How could I have ever predicted that a few years later, another connection would lead us to the owner of that very store? But our dear friend Frances, after whom we named our second daughter, turned out to know a wonderful woman named Colette, who turned out to be the daughter of the store's proprietor: Betty.

"Amazing," I said, when I heard this connection. "That's where I got my favorite Buddha." When the next Chinese New Year came, Colette and her mother invited us to their annual celebration. Betty, in her ebullient and gracious way, swept up our girls, showering them with Chinese red envelopes filled with crisp bills every time they wished everyone Happy New Year: "*Gong hay fat choy!*" The table was laden with delectable Chinese food and the evening ended with a string of firecrackers. Betty told the girls to call her "Aunt," and invited them for a sleepover. "I think it's important that they have a connection to the Chinese community," said Betty. "I really want them to have a tradition that they can remember when they grow up." What rare good fortune for our daughters—and for us.

For the two Caucasians in our nuclear family, our daughters' connection to China and the Chinese American community has brought many unexpected gifts. Living in San Francisco, of course, makes it relatively easy to enjoy the riches of the Chinese American world, but our daughters led us to experience it on a different level. At the 2008 San Francisco Families with Children from China annual Between the Two New Years party, which was held at the Presidio this year, the Chinese consul general came to greet the adopted daughters of China, and San Francisco's Chinese American police chief, Heather Fong, came and mingled with the girls. "Wow, that's a pretty important job," said Kelly. Fong, it was said, has family members who have adopted from China. When the San Francisco Symphony put on its Chinese New Year Celebration concert this year, it featured Carolyn Kuan conducting, Weishan Liu playing the *gu zheng*, and Jiebing Chen playing Bach on the two-stringed Chinese *erhu*. "I don't think I'll try playing *that*," said Franny. It was a rich afternoon of East-West music, and presented several more great role models for our daughters.

The wider Chinese American community has also reached out specifically to the adopted children. Betty Louie was all for this. "Adoptive families visiting San Francisco with little girls from China come to my store all the time," she said with a laugh, "but I tell them that's not enough." The Alhambra, California, Chinese community invited two FCC San Diego families to ride on its float in the 2008 New Year parade, and FCC children and families also marched in the Holiday Bowl Balloon Parade. In New York City and Chicago, families and their adopted children have marched in the annual Chinese New Year's parades. In San Diego, the FCC group holds its annual Chinese New Year celebration at the Chinese Community Church facilities; members of the Chinese American community attend as honored guests. The Chinese Consolidated Benevolent Association sent a troupe of lion dancers to this year's party. "We feel very fortunate that so many of the Chinese community here have embraced us with open arms," said mother Marty Foltyn, mother of twelve-year-old Miranda, who came home from China in the group with Kelly. "It is so amazing, and an utterly unexpected connection that I never imagined when we went to China ten years ago," said Foltyn. Miranda, she added, now wants to be a lion dancer.

In New York, in the fall of 2008, the Museum of Chinese in America (MOCA) opened an exhibition on the Chinese American experience, a new permanent exhibition in a stunning skylit space designed by Maya Lin. It includes a section on children adopted from China and how families of such children have attempted to create a sense of cultural heritage and history for their children.

In San Francisco, the Chinese Historical Society of America was contemplating a party featuring storytelling and celebration for all the local adopted girls from China. Each year in San Francisco, too, the local Chinese Consulate has hosted a party for adoptive families of Chinese children.

This past year, the Organization of Chinese Americans (www.ocanational.org) invited representatives of Families with Children from China to meet with them to discuss common interests. Reported northern California FCC president Peggy Scott, "A tremendous feeling of fellowship and support was present in the room. . . . It was great to be . . . with so many Chinese American political activists, especially those who have been at it for such a long time. They are great role models for our kids. Many observed that while overt racism might be somewhat rare and easy to spot, subtle discrimination still infuses our society in insidious ways that, in the end, can be even more damaging for our children to encounter."

China, too, has been part of the move to reach out, organizing summer camps through the Chinese ministry in charge of adoption, for instance. One program, called About China, About Beijing, is intended to acquaint adopted children, twelve to sixteen years old, with China's culture, history, and people. The trips came about partly through Kenneth Yeung, a Chinese American from California who adopted his daughter Melissa, now thirteen, from China. So far, about one hundred children have gone back to China as part of this program, coordinated with Bay Area Adoption Services. Yeung said it all began because he wanted to give China the opportunity to show an interest in the kids. "Otherwise they may have a bitter feeling: 'My own country gave me away.'"

Just how this substantial wave of adoptive immigrants from China will fit into the broader historical context of Chinese immigration in the United States is a subject attracting the

interest of any number of scholars, including writer Ruthanne
Lum McCunn and others active in the Chinese Historical Society of America.

Ronald Takaki, a retired professor of Asian American Studies at the University of California, Berkeley, and a prominent
writer on the subject of multicultural America, told me recently, "These children are entering America at a time when the
Asian American population is the fastest-growing ethnic population in the U.S. In terms of the whole nation, we're about five
percent, and are projected to become ten percent in the lifetime
of your daughters. When you think about Chinese immigration
during the Gold Rush—the oppression, the discrimination, the
Exclusion Acts—you realize that these young Chinese Americans face a much brighter future. It's a different world they are
growing up in and maturing in. I think it's a hopeful world."

What's our daughters' place in this world? "That's a choice
they and their parents will have to make," said Takaki, the author of nearly a dozen books on multicultural issues, including
Strangers from a Different Shore: A History of Asian Americans and
A Different Mirror: A History of Multicultural America, which is
being made into a TV series. "It's important for parents to be
aware of the roots in America, and not just connecting to the
roots in China. China is no longer their country. It's important
to connect to their roots in America as Chinese Americans.
Their roots reach back to the Gold Rush. In terms of ancestry,
the Chinese were here earlier than a lot of others."

"The problem with connecting only with China is that it
continues to foreignize the children," Takaki said. "We have
parents who want to make sure their children understand Chinese culture and maybe even a Chinese language, but that is

shortchanging their children. The children are also Chinese American."

Takaki helped establish UC Berkeley's requirement that all undergraduates take a course aimed at broadening their grasp of racial and ethnic diversity within this country. "When I was growing up there were no books on Asian American history," he told me. "I had to write them. I didn't learn about my Asian roots in courses in elementary school or college. Your daughters will have that opportunity, especially if parents insist on Asian American history in the curriculum."

"We're all immigrants except for Native Americans," says adoptive mother and FCC–Northern California president Peggy Scott. "My grandparents were from the old country. They made it through the Depression in West Virginia and they felt like they owned America. My daughter Abby should get to feel the same way. I don't want Abby to ever think she is any less American or should have any fewer rights to her citizenship than any of the other immigrants in our family.

"But if the truth be known," Scott added, "Abby feels closer to the pandas in Chengdu than she does to the miners of the Gold Rush."

Emotional Geography

Some of the people who best understand what it feels like to grow up an ocean away from one's birthplace, often in a transracial family, remain the older Korean adoptees, who in the past decades have formed groups to explore their experiences and their issues of identity. Many from this community, and others who have experienced a similar adoptive journey, are now offering to mentor the girls adopted from China. The Korean Americans—with their national organizations, their many books and films on the subject—paved the way, but others have come forward to help.

Two University of California at Berkeley students, Andrea Lu and Leslie Sheu, studied in Beijing one summer. "We became rather concerned with the plight of orphans in China," said Sheu, and so they started a China Care chapter at Berkeley, along the lines of similar chapters at colleges such as Harvard, Duke, UCLA, and Brown, aimed at raising funds for orphanages and mentoring local children adopted from China. The two young women began meeting with other students and organizing guest lecturers to talk about such issues as the one-child policy and international adoption. They teamed up with Jennifer Jue-Steuck, who was born in Taiwan and adopted by "a transracial and multicultural family," who was also trying to start a group to mentor girls adopted from China.

Together, they formed the G2–China Care teen group in Berkeley. "We wanted to work with teens because we believe that this is a crucial time as children are growing up," said Sheu. "Identity issues start coming up and some might begin struggling with their often dual identities as Asian Americans." She said the teen group was a way for girls to get together, have fun, and bond with older Asian American girls. Rather than dig into the issues directly, said Sheu, "The idea is more to provide them role models or people to look up to or ask for advice as they start forming ideas about college and what they want to be."

The girls have also become involved in numerous fundraising efforts—selling red bracelets, holding bake sales and raffles aimed at sponsoring school fees for children in Chinese institutions. During Christmas 2007, the teen club worked at the local Barnes & Noble, wrapping gifts, and the bookstore donated a percentage of sales to China Care. The teens raised $1,000, then conferred on how to spend it. They chose to donate the money to provide surgeries for two specific orphaned children. Said one mother of a teen, "It shows how the girls see themselves as world citizens."

Jue-Steuck, a Harvard graduate in gender studies and now a doctoral candidate in the Department of Comparative Ethnic Studies at the University of California, Berkeley, has described her own adoptive experience as "floating down like a feather to an unmapped country between 'Chineseness' and 'Americanness.'" She has traveled around the world meeting with adoptive families groups, and also founded a group called Chinese Adoptee Links International (www.chineseadopteelinks.org) as well as a pen pal network, so that adoptees in different countries can correspond with one another. It's her belief that when girls hit the teen years, there are some things more comfortably discussed not with parents, but among themselves and with other young people who have shared a similar experience.

Ana Tanner, a bright, self-possessed eighth-grader, is one of the girls who joined the Berkeley teen club. Tanner, adopted as an infant from Jiujiang, Jiangxi province—the first child from her orphanage to come to the United States—had a number of interesting observations about life as a child from China. "As I grow older, people with similar experiences become more important," she said. When she was younger, she and her family often got together with other adoptive families, gathering in playgroups or gymnastics classes. "We didn't talk about adoption," she said, "We just played."

Now, when Tanner faces a comment at school or elsewhere that's racist or otherwise upsetting, she turns to other adopted girls to talk it over. "I'll think something is offensive, but I'm not sure if I am overreacting. There are things I notice that other people don't notice. The other kids in my class go, 'Huh?' These are things I talk to my adopted friends about.

"Racism is hard to deal with," she said. "It's a lot different when you're thinking about racism in theory than when you meet it in practice. I am always shocked when people say things that are not the nicest."

When we talked, she was applying to high schools, leaning toward those with diverse student bodies and Mandarin-language programs. Earlier in her schooling, she said, "The [Chinese] language thing kind of fell apart for me." Now she wanted to pursue it. She'd written an application essay on a turning point in her life—her adoption. "I have been thinking about that time when my life shifted, and could have gone either way," she said. She's been back to China a number of times with her family, including three visits to her orphanage. Now, during the summer before she started high school, she was hoping to travel to England and Ireland with Jennifer Jue-Steuck as a sort of ambassador, making contact with other families and talking to other girls adopted from China.

At the teen club, Tanner said she enjoyed just hanging out with other girls, and getting involved in fund-raising activities for the kids in China's orphanages. The teen group had just had a chocolate fondue party. Through the pen pal program, Tanner also corresponds with an adopted girl in England. Her pen pal's circumstances are very different from Tanner's—"she goes to a high school where she is one of the only Asian children." Yet while their experiences may have been different, said Tanner, "our outlooks are very similar."

For Ana Tanner, the link to other adopted girls has been a comfort. "I have enough opportunity to be around people with my same experience, but not pushed to the point where that's all I do," she said.

The Red Thread Winds Along

"In order to know who you are, you need to know something about where you came from; in order to move into the future, you have to be able to claim your past."
—Micky Duxbury

Who could have imagined a decade ago where we'd be at this point? Who can possibly predict what our daughters will be doing and thinking in another ten years?

How the time has flown. I looked out our window one day not long ago to see a mirror image of Kelly toddling down the sidewalk. Of course I rushed out the door. Our neighbors had come home with a child from China. To see little Olivia, with her light-up-the-world smile and her short dark hair, her gleeful and determined spirit, was to see Kelly all over again—and I was shocked by the lightning-quick passage of time. Where had the years gone? Kelly, an eleven-year-old on the verge of becoming a teenager, was upstairs hanging out with her pet gecko, while Franny had gone off to school just that morning to share her life story and photo book with her third-grade class for Valentine's Day. "It's all about love and opening your heart," her teacher told the class. "That's why Franny's story is important." Franny showed a great deal of presence and courage. And she got the inevitable question from a little boy: "What happened to your 'real' parents?"

"I don't know," said Franny. "I don't want to talk about that." Our daughters were growing up so quickly. At every stage, they have just become more interesting, more fully themselves. It has been an indescribable blessing and a privilege to share our lives with them, to watch them change and take on more of the world and come into their own. Every time I see another leap of growth, hear another unexpected question or fresh observation from one of them, I know that our family has reached another way station on the journey. And yet another. I have finally come to peace—I think—with the realization that we'll never catch up, that we'll always be figuring it out as we go.

It didn't take long after I wrote this book to figure out what the sequel should be—not another book by a parent, but a story told by the adopted children themselves. The next chapter, clearly, belongs to our daughters (and sons), and our role as adoptive parents will be to listen. Just to listen. The unfolding of the emotions and the stories involved in this adoptive movement may not be orderly or predictable or always to our liking. It may not be easy to hear the feelings that some of our children may have kept under wraps. It may be uncomfortable to hear the whole notion of transnational, interracial adoption questioned. And it may break through some of our illusions to realize that what we assumed was true for our daughters may in fact not have been. We may find that our efforts, no matter how well intended they've been, are up for review. Maybe, as one girl recently told me, some of us parents have "made way too much of this adoption stuff." At the very least there will always be more learning, more work ahead.

Soon the search for further answers will be Kelly's and Franny's to undertake, with all the help that we can give them. I hope the truth of whatever they find comes to them gently. I also hope that every birth family back in China will realize someday what a gift they have given to a family like ours; that they can know that their daughters are greatly loved and well cared for. I hope that changes within China help all its lost girls and all their lost family members. I hope the orphanages—if they must exist at all—get all the help they need. I hope the aunties and foster parents in China are numerous and good-hearted. I hope every little girl discovered on a bench, left in a field, found wandering alone, can be nourished, touched, smiled at, and given a home—if not in the land of her birth, then in another place where she'll be happy.

Two of my favorite writers on the subject, Betty Jean Lifton and Nancy Newton Verrier (*The Primal Wound: Understanding the Adopted Child*), both emphasize the necessary extra work that comes with the blessings of adoption, work that is a lifelong journey for everyone involved, children and adults alike.

Micky Duxbury, another wise voice on the subject, and the author of *Making Room in Our Hearts,* writes, "Adoption is often about stories, stories of how birth and adoptive families find one another; stories of loss and stories of reunion. Stories often make sense of what is not sensible; they give meaning to life events that are sometimes chaotic, and they plant us firmly in the realm of other humans that share our stories."

And, as a famous jazz musician once said, "We owe each other the truth of our journeys."

There are some hundred thousand stories out there, waiting to be told.

Girls, sharpen your pencils, start your computers.

World, hang on to your hats.

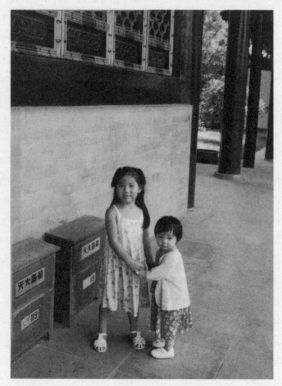

New sisters, Kelly and Franny, in Nanjing, China, 2001.

For All the Little
Girls from China

*Whenever I see one
I know there will someday be
this incredible sorority
of women brought here
as babies from China.*

*And their Great Wall
will always go all the
way through them to split
what happened in China/
what's happened here.*

*But they will help each other
over this wall all their lives
until those walls at their
centers are merely their
strong and flexible spines.*

*Maybe on the basis of
collective cultural hybrid
strength which they'll
find many ways to cultivate
(the strength of their stories!)*

*these women of the world's
first international
female diaspora
will inherit the earth.
And do something good with it.*

—*Penny Callan Partridge*

You Would Be Proud

I have returned
I looked for you
You were hiding in my heart
deep in my soul.
I am you and
you are me.
I am your grain of rice you've labored for.
I am your blueberry from Maine.
Mama.
Mum.
You would be proud
Proud to know that I am able to love
Proud to know that I have people who love me
and whom I love back
You would be proud to know that I journey alone
Proud to know
I would climb mountains just to glimpse your rice paddies
Proud to know
I would do anything to bring joy into your life.
You would be proud to know I don't blame you
You would be proud to know you gave me a chance
You would be proud to know I am your daughter
and you are my mama,
you are my mum.

—*Fang Fang Lee, age fifteen, lives with her adoptive parents in California. She wrote the poem after a summer trip to China and to Yunnan, the place of her birth.*

A Conversation
with Karin Evans

About her, her book, becoming a mother,
going back to China, adopting a second
child, and filling in the blanks of the past

The Lost Daughters of China *is your first book. Did your*
background as a journalist prepare you for the task of writ-
ing it?

All my training as a journalist went into writing the book—
being interested in getting to the bottom of things, interviewing people, researching. That being said, when you tackle your
first book, it's a huge undertaking. Updating it was a big job,
too, since so much had happened in the ten years since we traveled to China for our first daughter.

In a way, writing a book was very similar to writing a jour-
nalistic feature story—the same kind of research and interviewing, choosing a structure and a way to tell the story, balancing
points of view, interpreting facts, and trying to work it all into
a graceful whole. Chapter by chapter, a book can be structured
as a collection of smaller pieces.

Yet a book goes beyond, I think. You have to pay attention
to the cohesiveness of the whole, to the pacing, to the narrative

thread that will pull people through the various chapters and issues. And the scope of a book allows for more development, and, of course, both a broader and deeper reach. My book falls in the category of narrative nonfiction, I'd say, where the writer presents a factual story but also infuses it with storytelling and other literary devices. The scope of the book, and its nature, also allowed me to pose questions as well as answer them; to leave some things unsolved and open-ended. Every year, of course, I could write another epilogue.

It was a lot of work—more than I thought it would be when I started out—but I absolutely loved writing the book. I had to do it. I would have written it whether it found a publisher or not. I would have written it for me and for my daughters. It was a compulsion.

The book began as a series of letters to my daughter Kelly while we were waiting for our paperwork to be finished and to be approved to adopt. The book grew out of that journal. I was just writing, writing while I was waiting for her.

When did you decide to transform your letters into a book?

When I returned from China with my first daughter, the profound nature of what I had experienced really hit me. Here I'd been part of this extremely emotional and meaningful exchange. And yet I didn't know who was on the other side of it, and I probably never would.

But here was this beautiful little girl who would have questions someday about her birth parents and birthplace. I wanted to fill in as many of the missing pieces of her story as I could. I also wanted to know what was going on in China at that time, so I could tell her something about her homeland when she began asking questions.

So you continued working on the book when you were back in the United States?

Yes. But it was a big challenge. My writing time changed. I was totally naive about writing with a baby around. I thought, "She'll sit on a cushion next to me and play while I write." There was no writing while she was around!

So I got a wonderful part-time baby-sitter. She was a young college student, and she came in for four hours a day. My office was in the basement, and during those four hours, I'd put on Yo-Yo Ma and write big chunks at a time. While I was writing, I could hear Kelly's feet padding across the floor upstairs. It was a comfort, but it was still hard for me to be away from her.

I also wrote at night while Kelly was asleep or during the day while she was napping. And I always carried a notebook with me, so I could write in it in during whatever spare moments I had.

When did you start thinking about publishing your book?

I was in a writing group. It had dwindled to just two of us, me and a woman named Cynthia Kear. I showed her what I'd written, and she said, "I think you should really get this published."

I also had a good friend who is a literary agent, Barbara Moulton. She told me to come up with a proposal and sample chapters. Barbara sent it to publishers in New York, and Tarcher bought it.

At that point I began to do a lot of research. I read everything I could on China, by authors like Jonathan Spence, Jasper Becker, Susan Greenhalgh, Maxine Hong Kingston, Jung Chang, Betty Bao Lord, Orville Schell, Ronald Takaki, Arthur Waley, Jan Wong, Pearl S. Buck, Confucius. I had a friend who was a China scholar, working in China on her Ph.D. She told me the names of leading scholars on women in contemporary China. I got piles of books and papers by them.

I just kept reading, making notes. As I made notes, I kept footnotes about the sources. In the end, my notes file consisted of four hundred single-spaced pages!

Then I started interviewing people whenever and wherever I could. I talked with at least a hundred people. I interviewed Chinese women writers, women's studies scholars, cultural anthropologists, historians. I'd go to a symposium or a lecture on China, I'd meet someone, and one person would lead to another. Some people at a college in Arizona put me in touch with a woman who lived in the town where my daughter was born. We e-mailed back and forth, and she actually went and did some fieldwork, told me what things looked like in that town.

I also interviewed people within the adoption field, people who went back and forth to China, people who'd adopted in China very early on—that is, in the late 1980s and early 1990s.

There was a lot of serendipity and a lot of generosity on the part of people in China and people here. One person always led to another, to more ideas, to more opportunities.

*If you could go back and write this book all over again, would
you do anything differently?*

If I could have—and it just wasn't possible at the time—I would
have liked to spend a year in China and talk to everyone I could.
China is such a complex, ever-changing, vastly unknowable
country in so many ways. You could spend your whole life being
a China scholar and just know a pittance. I would have loved to
have had the opportunity to sink into the society and spend
time with Chinese women. That would have been ideal. Not
being able to do that, I consciously cast the book from the perspective of someone asking questions—and trying to answer
them—from afar.

I heard about birth mothers, I met people who had talked
with them, but I never got the opportunity to sit down and
talk with such a woman myself, and that was another thing I
very much wanted to do. There were sightings of birth mothers, and friends of mine were looking for birth mothers, too.
But partly because of the fear and the social structure there at the
time, it wasn't possible to find a birth mother who was willing
to talk to me.

By now, of course, there are Chinese birth families who have
talked to researchers and sociologists. There are other writers,
who have facility in the language, who have been at the right
place at the right time. These people have managed to find birth
mothers to talk to. So has filmmaker Changfu Chang, who not
long ago interviewed several families on camera.

As time goes by, I imagine more and more birth families
will be found and will add their stories to the information surrounding this fateful mixing of lives.

How much was China a part of your life before you adopted your daughters?

Certainly not as much as it is now. In my early twenties, I'd lived and worked in Hong Kong. The minute I got there, I felt at home. I just sank into the world of smells, sights, markets, the harbor, the temples, the people. I spent a lot of time just walking. I had a wonderful Chinese friend who took me to the out-of-the-way places few foreigners went.

My first job there was with *Newsweek*'s amazing old China hand, Sydney Liu. Whenever the editors needed to know what was happening in China, they'd send Sydney out for a long lunch. He'd come back and tell everybody in great detail what he'd learned, and I would condense it into a *Newsweek* file. I was his rewrite person. There were so many times when I was writing this book and some question would come up that I needed to answer, and I would think, Where is Sydney?

I'd always been attracted to Chinese art and Chinese brush painting in particular, and also Chinese music and literature. I also have many Chinese and Chinese American friends. I live in San Francisco, which is a very Asian city.

Do you speak Chinese?

I've taken some night-school Mandarin and listened to tapes, and I would love to learn. But no. When we adopted our second daughter, we knew she'd be speaking only Mandarin. She was three years old. I tried to learn phrases I'd need: "Are you hungry?" "Are you sleepy?" "Let's go here." But everything I said seemed incomprehensible to her. To be honest, anytime I'm asked this question, it motivates me to find another tutor, get us all started again. The girls have taken classes, but none of us has gotten very far. I would like the girls to have some facility with the language, and I would love to learn more myself. Last time we went to China the girls got a lot of mileage out of a few simple phrases. It would be wonderful for all of us to know more.

How did Kelly first react when you told her that she would be getting a little Chinese sister?

Kelly had been lobbying for the idea, asking, "Mom, can I have a sister?" She was wonderful on the trip to meet Franny, really helping her and watching out for her. It was a bit of a shock to her, though, that Franny had such a mind of her own. And Franny undoubtedly felt like a newcomer to a family that was already established. They moved on to the usual sibling rivalries, but I love it when I hear them giggling together.

You, your husband, and Kelly all went to China in the summer of 2001 to get Franny. How did Kelly react to being in China?

Kelly said it was very hot. She loved the hotel swimming pools best of all, and the dozens of kinds of dumplings. She liked the parks and watching all the activities.

Both girls were also such an object of attention everywhere we went. The Chinese tend to reach out to children—when you're in public places, when you're at the park, they come right up to you and start playing with the children. Kelly got a lot of attention that way, and so did Franny.

There was a hair salon at the hotel arcade. They do these incredible hairdos—butterflies and braids and so forth. Kelly and another girl wanted to get their hair done. While they did this, a huge crowd gathered around the hair salon, watching. The girls came out looking like Chinese opera stars.

How did Franny respond to Kelly?

Franny looked up to her immediately. Kelly had an empathic sense of what Franny was going through. There were times when I would try to talk to Franny in Chinese, and Kelly would say, "Mom, it's not working." Or Franny would cry, and Kelly would say, "I think she's missing her people." Franny had a hard time— she was three years old and trying to get used to strangers and a whole new life. It was a big, big transition for her. Also, she'd had heart surgery just four months before we adopted her.

Kelly was wonderful. It was great for Franny to have an older sister. Franny related to Kelly right away, way more easily than to us. Kelly was her comforter. Still, it was also a big adjustment for both girls.

Was it difficult for Franny to be three years old and not know any English?

Yes. Just imagine, not only are you picked up by people you've never seen before, but you can't understand most of what they are saying. And when you ask for something, they haven't a clue what you need. Fortunately, we had sign language and Chinese companions who could translate. After we got home, Franny learned English quickly. Children seem to learn faster than we do, of course, plus really young children seem to naturally know how to make do when they are trying to play with each other, even if they don't speak a common language.

What's been happening in Kelly's and Franny's lives since you wrote the book? How old are they now?

Kelly is eleven, Franny is nine. Kelly is in sixth grade, middle school, and loving it. Franny is in third grade. They are both just wonderful girls, and I could not imagine life without them. Kelly plays the flute and loves to read. Franny is taking several different kinds of dance—West African, ballet, modern. They both love animals, swimming, reading, art.

How aware is Kelly of her background, where she came from, how she came to be with you and your husband, and so forth? And Franny?

We made memory books for each girl, photos, souvenirs, laced together with a narrative of how we first heard about them, when we came to get them, the journey through various places in China before we came home. When Kelly was little, she'd bring the book to anyone who came to visit and show it to them, narrating her story, and saying things like, "I was born in China and then Mom and Dad came to get me and I was soooooo cute." As she has gotten older, she seems more matter of fact about it all.

Franny, from the beginning, has talked more about China. She was older and clearly remembered caregivers and another life before we came along. She talks about her Chinese mother frequently and has a lot of unanswered questions.

We have told each girl as much as we know about her story, and if we can help them later to find out more, we will. I think it helps that the girls have very close friends who are also adopted and that they have a Chinese "auntie" who has taken them under her wing. We keep ties with the families who were with us when we adopted each girl, and I think it helps the girls to know that they have close friends who have shared some of the same experiences.

The truth is, we don't really know what happened with either girl's birth parents. Individual circumstances can vary so wildly. All I can do is to tell the truth as I know it, with all the gaps in information, be open to their questions, and be as compassionate as possible toward everyone involved. But we also need to accept our daughters' feelings, whatever they are.

When it comes to this process, children often lead the way. When they're ready to know more, they bring it up. Or if they seem preoccupied with something, you try to create openings for discussion. You have to keep your antenna up. You can't ever assume that the kids are okay and their questions are all settled. There will always be new little pieces coming forth. You have to keep talking. And sometimes you all need help.

What sorts of reactions do you get from strangers on the street when they see you, a Caucasian woman, with two Asian-looking girls?

We live in northern California, which is very multicultural. In the San Francisco Bay Area, there are so many families like ourselves, or other combinations of transracially mixed families, that we hardly get a second glance.

But just when you are feeling comfortable, the questions pop up. Supermarket checkout lines seem to be particular minefields, when some curious adult starts looking at the children and looking at me and then fires comments or questions at us. "Well, aren't they just like little China dolls!" Or, "Are they *real* sisters?" Or, "Is their father Chinese?" I've learned over time to always think of the girls first, and how they are going to take what I say, rather than thinking I owe a stranger an explanation. If it persists, I get the girls out of there. You have to be prepared to handle such comments. Chinese restaurants can also present challenges. I've had curious waiters ask how much we paid, that sort of thing. Again, I always think, What would the girls want to hear me say? And I've gotten pretty skilled at shutting down such a line of questioning: "They're priceless. Now, can you tell me what kind of dumplings are on the menu?" That sort of thing. I've always admired the woman whose remark was passed around—and maybe it's an urban legend—but when some stranger asked whether her daughter's father was Chinese, she shot back, "I don't know. I didn't get a good look at him." But it's not always easy to have such a ready comeback. And you always have to think of your children's feelings first.

Do you worry about Franny and Kelly facing racism and discrimination?

Yes. There's racism out there, no question, and there's also a lot of insensitivity about adoption. Even in films made for children, the adoption theme seems such a popular plot device, and there are often remarks and assumptions that can be painful for an adopted child to hear.

It's good to be proactive at your children's schools, to do some gentle educating, about birth parents and adoption, all the while making sure that you are convincing others that your child is wanted and loved and special. Teachers still assign family tree projects and ask kids to write reports on their ancestors, often not realizing, I guess, that not every kid has this information. You have to be your child's advocate, and sometimes offer to help teachers come up with curriculum ideas that focus on different kinds of families.

These are real issues. As a parent who loves her kids, you want the world to be tolerant and loving, and you wish people didn't think and behave in cruel or ignorant ways, but they do.

We hope to give the girls enough self-esteem and the ability to speak for themselves, so that they're not dragged down by negative comments. As a parent who's not a minority, you don't really know what your child is going to go through out there in the world. But you want to help her and prepare her the best you can. You don't want her to be surprised or caught off guard by an insensitive remark. You want your children to feel comfortable and confident enough to shake off these sorts of comments and be proud of who they are. Sometimes I think it's good to role-play and let them practice some responses before they get blindsided on the playground.

Do you work full-time? What is your schedule like?

I work at home. I'm a freelance writer. And for the past two years, I've also been in an MFA program in poetry. I'm juggling my projects with the kids' schedules constantly. That means my workday is pretty broken up. I work at night a lot, and at other odd times. And I've learned a great secret to happiness is to do what I can, when I can, and let the rest go.

Did motherhood come pretty easily to you?

Yes and no. Kelly was pretty easy. When I first got her, we just fell into each other's arms. After a couple of days, I thought, "What did I ever do without her?" We were joined at the hip. We just kind of worked out the details. I talked to lots of other mothers.

With my second daughter, who was three years old when we adopted her, I was far more conscious of the gap we had to bridge, and we had to feel our way through lots of grief and anger, as well as cherishing the joyful moments. The transition can be so much harder for an older child. It took a lot more conscious work, and still does. I'll always have more to learn!

Are you working on another book?

I always have a couple projects going, but right now I have to complete my graduate thesis—on Chinese poetry—and finish a creative manuscript so I can earn my graduate degree. After that, I'd like to tackle another book.

When do you plan on showing Kelly and Franny The Lost Daughters of China?

Kelly's grown up knowing that I wrote a book and that it's largely about her. She's read portions, and over time we'll read more of it together. Early on, she used to come to some of the book signings I was asked to do. People would ask her if she was the little girl in my book. Kelly would say, "Yep. That's my mom, she's writing in books and giving them away." As I have been revising the book, I have talked a lot to both girls about their experiences and thoughts on the subject.

Do you plan to show Kelly the actual letters you wrote to her while you were waiting to adopt her?

Yes, though most of the sentiments and questions in them are included in the book. For both Kelly and Franny there is a bunch of stuff I've been keeping—clothes they came home in, notes from various people, all their paperwork, souvenirs from China, and so forth. Anything that's a piece of their past.

Do you consciously try to incorporate Chinese culture into your day-to-day lives? Do you think your daughters will feel a connection to China and Chinese culture when they grow up?

Yes, we all enjoy a lot of Chinese music, art, literature, festivals, whatever is available. It's important to feel connected to the Chinese American community, I think. The girls love to go to

San Francisco's Chinatown, and often on Sundays we go to Chinatown in Oakland for dim sum with friends. We have a number of friends who are Chinese American.

Whether my children will continue to feel the connection to China, I don't know. But the way we live, I know that the girls will at least have knowledge of China and the experience of going back and forth on trips. For six years I was on the board of Half the Sky Foundation, and we went to China in connection with that. It's given the girls an inside look that they might otherwise not have had.

My goal is to give the girls as much facility and knowledge and confidence as possible so they can make their own decisions about connections and identity. It would be wonderful if they felt a bit like world citizens, with a level of comfort in both America and China. We'll see.

Do you and your husband ever think about adopting another Chinese girl?

Realistically, no. But all it takes is walking into an orphanage and seeing the children. During one visit to China, I met this little twelve-year-old in an orphanage. She was a beautiful kid who couldn't walk. She was someone I knew I could open my heart and arms to. We have sponsored children like her, as well as infants, through Half the Sky.

More Food for Thought

*Ten Questions to Ask Yourself
(and Your Book Club Friends)
About* The Lost Daughters of China

1. Before you read this book, were you aware of the phenomenon of Americans adopting Chinese girls? What were your feelings and attitudes about it? Do you know any Americans who have adopted Chinese girls?

2. *If you are the adoptive parent of a Chinese daughter (or daughters):* How did Evans's book make you feel? Which of her anecdotes and insights resonated most for you? Did you find yourself strongly agreeing or disagreeing with anything she wrote?

3. *If you are thinking about adopting a Chinese daughter:* How did Evans's book make you feel? Do you feel more knowledgeable about what the future may hold for you and your family? Did anything in the book surprise you?

4. *If you are the adoptive parent of a non-Chinese child:* Did you find many points of similarity in your adoption experiences and Evans's adoption experiences?

5. What were your attitudes about China or Chinese culture before you read this book? Did your attitudes change at all after reading this book?

6. Discrimination against girls and women exists in many different countries and cultures. But the extreme favoritism of the Chinese toward boys—combined with the Chinese government's one-child policy and other factors—has resulted in a disturbing epidemic of "lost daughters," as well as orphanages overcrowded with girls. Is there anything the U.S. government can do to intervene in this situation? Or should America respect the laws, attitudes, and customs of the Chinese people, and leave the Chinese government to sort out its own problems?

7. Americans are adopting Chinese and other foreign-born children in increasing numbers. There are also more and more mixed-race families in the United States. How do these new types of families challenge your notions, if any, about the "traditional nuclear family"? When you see a light-skinned Caucasian woman strolling with a brown-skinned baby, for example, do you find yourself doing a double take or saying to yourself "I wonder if she's that baby's mother"?

8. In her book, Evans quotes the writer and family therapist Claire S. Chow on the subject of cross-cultural adoption: "Parents should realize that they aren't adopting just a child but an ethnically different child. Adoption itself carries a primal kind of loss. Add the loss of original country and culture, and you can see the magnitude of the problem." Do you agree with this statement? In what ways might an adopted Chinese girl have problems with self-identity and cultural identity, self-acceptance and social acceptance, as she grows up in the United States? Do you think a Caucasian orphan would have the same problems?

9. Some American couples who adopt Chinese girls choose to raise them with full knowledge about their Chinese backgrounds and attempt to give them a bicultural upbringing. Other couples choose to raise them with a "clean slate," with little or no acknowledgment of their Chinese heritage or past. Do you think one way is "better" than the other? Do you think this question applies to other types of international adoption as well?

10. Evans's book was born out of a series of letters she wrote to her daughter while she and her husband were waiting for her adoption to go through. The letters were very personal, and yet, in turning them into a book Evans created a work that was helpful and relevant to a wider audience. Do you have a similar collection of letters—to your children, to your mate or lover, to yourself, or to other important people in your life? Are there aspects of these letters that would be helpful or relevant to a wider audience?

Acknowledgments

Many people helped me with this book, beginning with my beloved and stalwart husband, Mark, and my extraordinary daughters, Kelly and Franny, who have graced my life more than I can say. Numerous friends helped also, by listening, advising, and listening some more: Frances Lana, Mary Adrian, Jeany Duncan, Kathy Page, Claire Ulam Weiner, Jodi Hoffman, Lucy Jelinek-Hays, Barbara Lane, Teo Furtado, Jozie Rabyor. Daryl Ryan led the way by showing, always, that all things are possible. Jerry Buchen built me the best writing retreat ever. My late father, Calvin (Kelly) Evans, showed me how loving and deep the ties of adoption could be. My late mother, Louise Evans, provided much help. My siblings, Gregory Evans, Douglas Evans, and Janet Evans Grunenwald, and their families, deserve thanks for showing me all along how good a family can be. My parents-in-law, Keith and Jo Humbert, were wonderful babysitters and cheerleaders, Keith Humbert helped, too, with research. My writing partners Cynthia Kear, Jane Meredith Adams, and Wendy Lichtman offered wise support, as did my agent, Barbara Moulton, and Tarcher's fine and thoughtful editor Sara Carder.

Any number of people who know far more about China and Chinese culture than I can ever hope to provided invaluable background: Ronald Takaki, Richard Effland, Jeanette Chu, Kay Ann Johnson, Zhang Zhirong, Susan Greenhalgh, Hong Ying, Amy Tan, Yvonne Rand, Belle Yang, Chen Mu Xian, Becky Guo, Stephen J. Roddy, Harry Wu, May Wong, Mary Hipp, Father Tom Wilcox, Sydney Liu, Chow Hai Lee, Vivian Chiang, Shirley Fong-Torres, Nona Mock Wyman, Min Sun Yee. China scholar Eileen Otis contributed valuable insights. Joyce McGuire Pavao, Val Free, Linda Grillo, Amanda Baden, and Claire S. Chow offered thoughtful observations on cross-cultural adoption.

Thanks, too, to all the members of our extended support group of families who have adopted from China, especially Jenny and Richard Bowen, Vic Schrader and Jill Touloukian, Peggy Scott, Lura Dolas and Darryl Brock, Hanni and Alan

Lee, and their daughters. Also: Patti Blumen, Michelle Green, Glenn and Linda Komatsu, Steve and Stephanie Chan, Mark Brown and Susan August-Brown, Kerry and Pauline Carlson, John and Naomi Cornwall, Jane Emmer and Sue Fink, Susan Lewis and Bob Taylor, Howard and Sharon Ogamori, Teri Tompkins and Lori Dick, Jim Wirt and Marty Foltyn, Steve and Amy Wolla, Susan Lakari and Ted Reiner, Steve Seeger and Victoria Ellison, Carole Sopp, Patricia Ng. My gratitude to Fang Fang Lee, Ana Tanner, Rebecca Hurdis, and Hollee McGinnis for generously sharing their experience. To foreign members of the adoption community for their support: Valerie Kaye in London, Jaume Josa in Spain, and Nicole Michaud in Montreal, who translated portions of this book into French. To adoptive parents Scott Novitsky and Linda Wells for their examples of courage and unwavering love. Our profound thanks to Betty Louie and Colette Fujimoto for sharing their family with us.

To Anchee Min for caring and telling the truth, my heartfelt thanks. I am also grateful to poet Penny Callan Partridge, and to poets Jia Jia, Luo Xioge, and Li Xiaoyu for their eloquent words, and to Julia Lin for introducing me to their work. To Greg Wolfe, Paul Mariani, Pete Fairchild, and Jeanne Murray Walker, my mentors at Seattle Pacific University, and to all my fellow MFA students for exceptional help with the writing craft. Any errors or lapses in judgment are, of course, my own.

Finally, my deepest thanks to Yo-Yo Ma for his recordings of the unaccompanied cello suites by Bach—my writing music.

Notes

Introduction

1. Numbers of Chinese children adopted by American citizens are based on U.S. Immigration and Naturalization visas issued. Of children adopted internationally by U.S. families in 2007, the largest number came from China—5,453 (down from 6,493 the previous year), followed by Guatemala with 4,728 and Russia with 2,310.
2. Betty Jean Lifton, *Lost and Found: The Adoption Experience* (New York: Harper & Row, 1988).

1. Journey to the East

1. Li Xiaoyu, "The Silk Dream," *Women of the Red Plain: An Anthology of Contemporary Chinese Women's Poetry,* trans. Julia C. Lin (New York: Penguin, 1992).
2. For text of the early adoption laws, see Laura A. Cecere's *The Children Can't Wait: China's Emerging Model for Intercountry Adoption.* China Seas, P.O. Box 391197, Cambridge, MA 02139. Copyright © Laura A. Cecere.
3. Ibid.
4. Jane Gross, "The Fight for Infertility Coverage," *New York Times*, December 7, 1998.
5. From the Evan B. Donaldson Adoption Institute.
6. Lisa Belkin, "Getting the Girl," *New York Times Sunday Magazine,* July 25, 1999.
7. "In Search of a Child" (series on adoption), *New York Times*, October 25, 1998.
8. "Chinese Orphanages: A Followup," published by Human Rights Watch/Asia, March 1996.

9. Our Chinese Daughters Foundation, Inc., 509 South Moore Street, Bloomington, IL 61701.

10. *The Dying Rooms* aired in the United States on January 24, 1996, on Cinemax; a portion aired subsequently on the CBS show *Eye to Eye*.

11. An account appears in the *Book of Songs*, the earliest anthology of poetry in China.

12. *Translations from the Chinese,* trans. Arthur Waley (New York: Alfred A. Knopf, 1941).

13. This Chinese version of "The Tortoise and the Hare," "A Lame Turtle's Conquest," comes from Zhang Ciyun, *The Chinese Idioms and Their Stories* (Beijing: Foreign Languages Press, 1996).

14. J. T. Condon, "Psychological Disability in Women Who Relinquish a Baby for Adoption," *Medical Journal of Australia*, February 3, 1986.

15. Name and other identifying details have been changed for this person as well as others involved in the China logistics.

2. From China with Love

1. Harry Wu, *Bitter Winds* (New York: John Wiley & Sons, 1995).

2. Pollution report from the *New York Times*, September 19, 1997.

3. Matt Forney, "Chinese Leader's Son Builds an Empire—In the Phone Business," *Wall Street Journal*, November 1, 1999.

4. Annie Dillard, *Encounters with Chinese Writers* (Middletown, CT: Wesleyan University Press, 1984).

5. Zhou Kaiya and Zhang Xingduan, *Baiji, The Yangtze River Dolphin and Other Endangered Animals of China* (Washington, D.C.: Stone Wall Press, 1991). Also "Demise of a Fabled River Runner," *San Francisco Chronicle*, March 22, 1998.

6. Orville Schell, *Mandate of Heaven* (New York: Simon & Schuster, 1994).

7. Janice E. Stockard, *Daughters of the Canton Delta, Marriage Patterns and Economic Strategies in South China, 1860–1930* (Stanford, CA: Stanford University Press, 1989).

8. Elisabeth Rosenthal, "Women's Suicides Reveal Rural China's Bitter Roots—Nation Starts to Confront World's Highest Rate," *New York Times*, January 24, 1999.

3. Down the River

1. Luo Xiaoge, "Drizzling Rain," in *Women of the Red Plain: An Anthology of Chinese Women's Poetry,* trans. Julia C. Lin (New York: Penguin, 1992).

2. From "Notice to Prospective Adoption Parents," issued by the United States Immigration and Naturalization Service. M-349 (05-09-91).

3. From "Report on Implementation of CEDAW (Committee on the Elimination of All Forms of Discrimination Against Women) in the People's Republic of China," published by Human Rights in China, December 1998.

4. Appeared in a fund-raising appeal published by Human Life International.

5. Quoted by Kay Johnson and subsequently in publications put out by Families with Children from China.

6. *The Book of Odes*, or *Songs*, is the oldest known collection of Chinese poetry, dating to 600 B.C. in the Chou dynasty, and is believed to have been compiled by Confucius. This English version is by Karin Evans.

7. Tsai Chin Chung, *Confucius Speaks: Words to Live By* (New York: Anchor Books, 1996).

8. Jia Jia, "Women of the Red Plain," *Women of the Red Plain: An Anthology of Chinese Women's Poetry,* trans. Julia C. Lin (New York: Penguin, 1992).

9. London *Telegraph*, April 11, 1997. Originally reported in *Theory and Time* (Shenyang, China).

10. Anne Behnke Kinney, ed., *Chinese Views of Childhood* (Honolulu: University of Hawaii Press, 1995).

11. Stockard, *Daughters of the Canton Delta.*

12. Hu Shih, "Women's Place in Chinese History," in *Chinese Women Through Chinese Eyes* (New York: M. E. Sharpe, 1992).

13. Ibid.

14. Robert Wyndham, ed., *Chinese Mother Goose Rhymes* (New York: Philomel, 1968).

4. The One-Child, Maybe-One-More Policy

1. Used first in Anhui province, later in Shaanxi, according to Susan Greenhalgh in "Evolution of the One-Child Policy in Shaanxi," *China Quarterly,* June 1990.

2. Jasper Becker, *Hungry Ghosts: Mao's Secret Famine* (New York: Free Press, 1997).

3. Alphonse L. McDonald, book review of *Hungry Ghosts, Population and Development Review*, October 23, 1998.

4. Professor Ma Yinchu, for instance, was subjected to "mass condemnation" after he published an essay warning of a looming population crisis, "The Relation Between the Population and the Productivity in Our Country," in *Daogong Bao*, May 9, 1957. At the same time that Thomas Malthus influenced Western thinking with his warnings about population outpacing resources, a similar theory was advanced by a Chinese scholar, Hong Liangji. For an in-depth discussion of China's population challenges, see chapter 24, "Levels of Power," in Jonathan D. Spence's *The Search for Modern China* (New York: W. W. Norton, 1990).

5. Inception of the policy is generally dated to September 1980, when China's Communist Party Central Committee issued an open letter calling for radical curtailment of population growth by limiting most couples to one child. The 1980 Marriage Law and 1982 Constitution underscored the approach as "basic national policy." From "Caught Between Tradition and the State," published by Human Rights in China. (HRIC is the largest independent organization focused on monitoring and promoting human rights in the People's Republic of China.) Materials cited are available on their website: www.hrichina.org.eap.

6. Early reports of coercive measures appeared in Steven W. Mosher's *Broken Earth: The Rural Chinese* (New York: Free Press, 1983), as well as subse-

quently in documents published by Human Rights in China, including "Caught Between Tradition and the State," released in 1995. Also reported by John Aird in *Slaughter of the Innocents: Coercive Birth Control in China* (Washington, DC: AEI Press, 1990).

7. Reported in Steven W. Mosher's *A Mother's Ordeal* (New York: HarperPerennial, 1993).

8. Bill McKibben, *Maybe One: A Personal and Environmental Argument for Single-Child Families* (New York: Simon & Schuster, 1998).

9. The story of Sun Lili appeared in Dele Olojede, "Chinese Woman Fights Family Planning Laws," *Newsday*, November 30, 1998.

10. Christine M. Bulger, "Fighting Gender Discrimination in the Chinese Workplace," *Boston College Third World Law Journal*, http://www.bc.edu/bc_org/avp/law/lwsch/journals.

11. "Caught Between Tradition and the State," published by Human Rights in China.

12. See note 14 below, on testimony of Gao Xiao Duan before the U.S. Congress.

13. Ted Koppel, "Executing Orders," *Nightline*, aired June 9, 1998.

14. Gao Xiao Duan, a former administrator of population control in the PRC, and Zhou Shiu Yon, who testified as a victim of coercive measures, appeared before the House Subcommittee on International Operations and Human Rights of the International Relations Committee, United States House of Representatives, June 9, 1998. An account of the proceedings was released by Chairman Christopher Smith's office. Dissident author Harry Wu also testified.

15. In 1985 the U.S. Congress passed the Kemp-Kasten Amendment, prohibiting U.S. birth control funds from going to any organization or nation that supported a program of forced abortion or sterilization. The Clinton administration later took steps to restore U.S. support to the United Nations Population Fund's Chinese program, resulting in a 1999 compromise to limit to $15 million aid to groups overseas that specifically advocate abortion rights. "Restrictions on Family Planning Money Waived," *New York Times*, December 1, 1999.

16. "Caught Between Tradition and the State," published by Human Rights in China.

17. Harry Wu interview with author, August 27, 1998.

18. Figure on abortion of female fetuses comes from Human Rights in China.

19. For text of old and new adoption laws, see Cecere, *The Children Can't Wait*.

20. According to Arthur Wolf and Chieh-shan Huang, authors of *Marriage and Adoption in China, 1845–1945* (Stanford, CA: Stanford University Press, 1980), adoption of girls and boys both was an integral part of the system of marriage and kinship.

21. Kwei-li, *Golden Lilies*, with an introduction by Eileen Goudge (New York: Viking, 1990).

22. Reports on the gender gap have been published in a number of sources, including *China Wakes*, by Nicholas Kristof and Sheryl WuDunn; "Caught Between Tradition and the State; Violations of the Rights of Chinese Women,"

China Rights Forum, Human Rights in China, winter 1993 and fall 1995; Betsy Hartmann in *Reproductive Rights & Wrongs* (Boston: South End Press, 1995); and the *South China Morning Post Sunday Magazine*, June 1995.

23. Bob Herbert, "China's Missing Girls," *New York Times,* October 30, 1997.

24. Ann Anagnost, "A Surfeit of Bodies: Population and the Rationality of the State in Post-Mao China," in *Conceiving the New World Order, The Global Politics of Reproduction*, ed. Faye D. Ginsburg and Rayna Rapp (Berkeley: University of California Press, 1995).

25. Reports on accident rates for rural women, conditions in U.S.–China joint ventures, published in Liu Ping, "Dying for Development," China Rights Forum, fall 1994.

26. "The Unofficial Report, Women Workers in China," China Labour Education and Information Centre, fall 1995.

27. Unemployment rate from Orville Schell, *San Francisco Examiner*, June 21, 1998.

28. Cases of abused, abducted women appeared in Kristof and WuDunn, *China Wakes*, and Human Rights in China documents previously cited.

5. The Taming Power of the Small

1. Robert Wyndham, ed., *Chinese Mother Goose Rhymes* (New York: Philomel, 1968).

2. Kwei-li, *Golden Lilies.*

3. Wang Fangyu, Richard M. Barnhart, and Judith G. Smith, eds., *Master of the Lotus Garden: The Life and Art of Bada Shanren (1626–1705)* (New Haven, CT: Yale University Press, 1990).

4. Figures from United States Immigration and Naturalization Service, 1997.

5. Peter Conn, *Pearl S. Buck: A Cultural Biography* (Cambridge: Cambridge University Press, 1996).

6. Maxine Hong Kingston, *The Woman Warrior: Memoirs of a Girlhood Among Ghosts* (New York: Alfred A. Knopf, 1975).

6. Matters of Life and Death

1. Information Office, PRC.

2. According to human rights groups, including Human Rights in China and Human Rights Watch/Asia.

3. RainbowKids International is on the Web at www.rainbowkids.com.

4. Early estimates of the number of state-run orphanages that dealt with foreign adoptions vary, from fifty to fewer than a hundred. China has over time opened more institutions to foreign adoption.

5. In one news report (Bob Herbert, *New York Times*, October 30, 1997), a young woman who had worked in an orphanage in Guangzhou was quoted as saying that she had seen tiny bodies carried out of the building in a wheelbarrow. The Asia/Pacific director of Amnesty International referred to orphanage conditions as "an area of darkness in Chinese institutional life." A German journalist used the term *Kindergulag.*

6. *Good Fortune: Families with Chinese Children Share Their Stories*, produced by Corky Merwin.

7. *The Dying Rooms* included footage from what the producers termed "China's showcase children's institute," Shanghai Orphanage. The little dying girl was filmed in Zhaoqing, just outside Guangzhou.

8. Refutations of the charges are included in material released by the Chinese government, including Facts/Sheet 1 on Orphanages in China, Chinese Embassy, United Kingdom, and "White Paper—the Situation of Children in China," presented by the Information Office of the State Council, PRC, April 3, 1996.

9. Angela Ki Che Leung, "Relief Institutions for Children," in *Chinese Views of Childhood,* ed. Anne Behnke Kinney, (Honolulu: University of Hawaii Press, 1995).

10. An account by Uli Schmetzer appeared in the *Chicago Tribune,* April 10, 1996.

11. Reports by pediatrician Nancy Hendrie, M.D., for instance, in the Boston-area Families with Children from China newsletter, or Michael Traister, M.D., in an FCC publication, and a study, "Health Status of U.S. Adopted Chinese Orphans," published by the Society for Pediatric Research, 1997.

7. East-West Lives

1. From "The Analects of K'ung Fu Tse," *Chinese Periodicals*, Beijing, 1986. English version by Karin Evans.

2. Richard Tessler, *West Meets East: Americans Adopt Chinese Children* (Westport, CT: Bergin & Garvey, 1999). Material used by permission of the author.

3. W. S. Tseng et al., "Transethnic Adoptions and Personality Traits: A Lesson from Japanese Orphans Returned from China to Japan," *American Journal of Psychiatry*, March 1990.

4. Kathy Kallick, "Use a Napkin (Not Your Mom!)," Sugar Beach, 1995.

5. Dick Lehr, "The Riddle of Julia Ming Gale," *Boston Globe*, October 8, 1996.

6. "The Korean Baby Boom Grows Up and Speaks Out," *Asia Week*, December 2, 1996.

7. An overview of opinion can be found in Felicia Laws, "Transracial Adoptions, A Case of Colorblind Love or Cultural Genocide?" *University of California McNair Journal* 93.

8. Pang-Mei Natasha Chang, *Bound Feet and Western Dress* (New York: Doubleday, 1996).

9. Chine Hui, "What Does It Take to Be an American?" *San Francisco Chronicle*, Open Forum, June 1996.

10. Nona Mock Wyman, *Chopstick Childhood in a Town of Silver Spoons* (Walnut Creek, CA: MQ Press, 1996).

8. In the Light of the Autumn Moon

1. Meng Jia, "Traveler's Song," *Maples in the Mist: Children's Poems from the Tang Dynasty,* trans. Minfong Ho (New York: Lothrop, Lee & Shepard, 1996).

2. Kay Ann Johnson and Amy Klatzkin, *Wanting a Daughter, Needing a Son* (St. Paul: Yeong & Yeong, 2004).

3. Robert Shaplen essay accompanying the photographs of Henri Cartier-Bresson in the collection *The Face of Asia* (New York: Viking, 1972).

9. The Search for Roots

1. Wang Wei, "News of Home," *Maples in the Mist: Children's Poems from the Tang Dynasty,* trans. Minfong Ho (New York: Lothrop, Lee & Shepard, 1996.)
2. *Time,* April 19, 1999.
3. Rainer Maria Rilke, *Letters to a Young Poet*, trans. Stephen Mitchell (New York: Random House, 1987).
4. Evan Eisenberg, "The Adoption Paradox," *Discover,* January 2001.
5. Nona Mock Wyman, *Chopstick Childhood* (Walnut Creek, CA: MQ Press, 1998).
6. The Mauser family website is at www.danielmauser.com.
7. Information on the Child Citizenship Act of 2001 is available online at www.ins.usdoj.gov/graphics/publicaffairs/factsheets/chowto.htm. Changes to the adoption laws have been made since this book was originally published, and more will come after this edition, both in U.S. procedures and in the Chinese protocols. The Families with Children From China website (www .fwcc.org) posts up-to-date information and points to other relevant resources.

11. Through the Chinese Looking Glass

1. Wang Zhi-Huan, "Climing Stork Tower," *Maples in the Mist: Children's Poems from the Tang Dynasty,* trans. Minfong Ho (New York: Lothrop, Lee & Shepard, 1996).
2. Helen Zia, "A Great Leap Forward for Girls," Ford Foundation Report, Winter 2000; online at www.fordfoundation.org. Also John Pomfret, "China's Losing 'War' on Births," *Washington Post* Foreign Service, May 3, 2000.
3. Chinese Academy of Social Sciences. Also Henry Chu, "7 Brides for 14 Brothers," *Los Angeles Times,* February 14, 2001.
4. Elisabeth Rosenthal, "Without 'Barefoot Doctors,' China's Rural Families Suffer," *New York Times,* March 14, 2001.
5. Orville Schell, www.salon.com, accessed March 13, 1999.
6. Marsha Ginsburg, "Crisis Inflames Bias Against Asians," *San Francisco Chronicle,* April 14, 2001. William Wong, "A Great Wall of Unease," *San Francisco Chronicle,* April 18, 2001.
7. Among the explorations of future tensions: Richard Bernstein and Ross H. Munro in *The Coming Conflict with China* (New York: Alfred A. Knopf, 1997); Julia Bloch speaking before the World Affairs Council, June 7, 1999; and Orville Schell writing in www.salon.com, June 8, 1999. On the Chinese side, Liu Ji, vice president, Chinese Academy of Social Scientists, and an adviser to Jiang Zemin, noted in June 1998 that China, if pushed the wrong way, could easily become an anti-American force, as reported by Reuters.
8. Reports on obesity from the *New York Times,* November 15, 1998.
9. Pomfret, "China's Losing 'War' on Births."
10. *New York Times,* November 1, 1998. According to China Population Information Center, the fertility rate had dipped to 1.8 children per family by 1997.

11. *China Rights Forum* (Winter 1995).
12. Helen Zia, "Open Forum: Why I Will Carry the Olympic Torch," *San Francisco Chronicle,* April 9, 2008.
13. Howard W. French, "Chinese Single Moms Struggle: Significant Social Obstacles Greet Those Who Defy Convention," *New York Times,* April 5, 2008.
14. The *Washington Post* story on Xie Lihua appeared August 5, 1997.
15. Henry Chu, "A Bumper Crop of Self-Esteem in China," *New York Times,* September 19, 1997.
16. *Washington Post,* October 24, 1998.
17. See Hong Ying's remarkable *Daughter of the River* (New York: Grove Press, 1998).
18. *Letter to Maya,* produced by Nancy Brown, Blue Dog Productions, 373 Waverley St., Palo Alto, CA 94301.
19. Todd Crowell and David Hsieh, *Asia Week,* July 13, 1996.
20. Jan Wong, *Red China Blues: My Long March from Mao to Now* (New York: Doubleday/Anchor Books, 1996).
21. George Koo, "The Real China: A Firsthand Perspective on Human Rights in Today's China," *Harvard International Review* (Summer 1998).
22. See, among other accounts, Medea Benjamin, Global Exchange, a human rights organization based in San Francisco. Also Liu Ping, "Dying for Development," *China Rights Forum* (Fall 1994).
23. Also-Known-As, started by a group of adult Korean adoptees and friends, seeks to serve those on their adoption life journey and open the possibility of intercountry and interracial adoptions for future generations. The group offers a mentorship program, a speakers' bureau, language and cultural programs, motherland visits, and community service with other ethnic minority communities. For more information, visit www.alsoknownas.org.

Epilogue

1. Meng Haojan (Tang dynasty poet), "Night-Mooring on the Chien-te River," translated by Karin Evans.
2. One collection of China adoption stories is posted at www.tussah.com/lara/chinasto.htm.
3. Elizabeth Bartholet, "International Adoption: Current Status and Future Prospects," *Adoption* 3, no. 1 (spring 1993).
4. John M. Glionna, "Two Lives Emerged from the Ashes," *Los Angeles Times,* December 12, 2007.
5. Elizabeth Fitzsimons, "In the Eyes of a Baby Girl, My First Lesson in Motherhood," *New York Times,* May 13, 2007.
6. Lindy Washburn, "A Sister Act," *Oberlin Alumni Magazine,* Spring 2006.
7. You may find additional information at the a-China DNA Project website, www.achinadnaproject.org.
8. Jim Yardley, "China Says One-Child Policy Will Stay for at Least Another Decade," *New York Times,* May 11, 2008.

Bibliography

Aird, John S. *Slaughter of the Innocents: Coercive Birth Control in China*. Washington, D.C.: AEI Press, 1990.

Angier, Natalie. *Woman: An Intimate Geography*. New York: Houghton Mifflin, 1999.

Becker, Jasper. *Hungry Ghosts: Mao's Secret Famine*. New York: Free Press, 1997.

Bernstein, Richard, and H. Ross Munro. *The Coming Conflict with China*. New York: Alfred A. Knopf, 1997.

Bowen, Richard. *Mei-Mei, Little Sister: Portraits from a Chinese Orphanage*. San Francisco: Chronicle Books, 2005.

Buck, Pearl S. *The Good Earth*. New York: Pocket Books, 1958.

Bumiller, Elisabeth. *May You Be the Mother of a Hundred Sons: A Journey Among the Women of India*. New York: Ballantine Books, 1990.

Cecere, Laura A. *The Children Can't Wait: China's Emerging Model for Intercountry Adoption*. Cambridge, Mass.: China Seas, 1998.

Center for Remote Sensing. *Tourist Atlas of Guangdong Province*. Zhongshan University and Guangzhou Municipal Tourism Bureau, Cartographic Publishing House of Guangdong Province, 1990.

Chan, Wing-Tsit. *A Source Book in Chinese Philosophy*. Princeton, N.J.: Princeton University Press, 1973.

Chang, Pang-Mei Natasha. *Bound Feet and Western Dress*. New York: Doubleday, 1996.

Cheng, Nien. *Life and Death in Shanghai*. New York: Grove Press, 1987.

Chow, Claire S. *Leaving Deep Water: The Lives of Asian American Women at the Crossroads of Two Cultures*. New York: Dutton, 1998.

Conn, Peter. *Pearl S. Buck: A Cultural Biography*. Cambridge: Cambridge University Press, 1996.

Conway, Jill Ker. *True North: A Memoir*. New York: Vintage Books, 1995.

Dawkins, Richard. *River Out of Eden: A Darwinian View of Life.* New York: Basic Books, 1995.

Dillard, Annie. *Encounters with Chinese Writers.* Middletown, Conn.: Wesleyan University Press, 1984.

Djao, Wei. *Being Chinese: Voices from the Diaspora.* Tucson: University of Arizona Press, 2003.

Duxbury, Micky. *Making Room in Our Hearts: Keeping Family Ties Through Open Adoption.* New York: Routledge, 2007.

Edelman, Hope. *Motherless Daughters: The Legacy of Loss.* New York: Dell Publishing, 1994.

Ehrlich, Gretel. *Questions of Heaven: The Chinese Journeys of an American Buddhist.* Boston: Beacon Press, 1997.

Fairbank, John King. *The Great Chinese Revolution 1800–1985.* New York: Harper & Row, 1987.

Gammage, Jeff. *China Ghosts: My Daughter's Journey to America, My Passage to Fatherhood.* New York: William Morrow, 2007.

Gifford, Rob. *China Road: A Journey into the Future of a Rising Power.* New York: Random House, 2008.

Gilmartin, Christina K., Gail Hershatter, Lisa Rofel, and Tyrene White. *Engendering China: Women, Culture, and the State.* Cambridge, Mass: Harvard University Press, 1994.

Ginsburg, Faye D., and Rayna Rapp, eds. *Conceiving the New World Order: The Global Politics of Reproduction.* Berkeley: University of California Press, 1995.

Goldstein, Sidney. "Urbanization in China, 1982–87: Effects of Migration and Reclassification." *Population and Development Review* 16, 4 (December 1990).

Gong, Rosemary. *Good Luck Life: The Essential Guide to Chinese American Celebrations and Culture.* New York: HarperCollins, 2005.

Greenhalgh, Susan. "The Evolution of the One-Child Policy in Shaanxi, 1979–88." *China Quarterly* (June 1990).

———, Chug Zhu, and Nan Li. "Restraining Population Growth in Three Chinese Villages, 1988–93." *Population and Development Review* 20, 2 (June 1994).

Hackin, J., et al. *Asiatic Mythology: A Detailed Description and Explanation of the Mythologies of All the Great Nations of Asia.* New York: Crescent Books, 1965.

Hall, Christine. *Daughters of the Dragon: Women's Lives in Contemporary China.* London: Scarlet Press, 1997.

Hartmann, Betsy. *Reproductive Rights and Wrongs: The Global Politics of Population Control.* Boston: South End Press, 1995.

Hertsgaard, Mark. *Earth Odyssey: Around the World in Search of Our Environmental Future.* New York: Broadway Books, 1998.

Hessler, Peter. *Oracle Bones.* New York: HarperCollins, 2006.

Him Mark Lai, Genny Lim, and Judy Yung. *Island: Poetry and History of Chinese Immigrants on Angel Island, 1910–1940.* Seattle: University of Washington Press, 1980.

Hirshfield, Jane, ed. *Women in Praise of the Sacred: 43 Centuries of Spiritual Poetry for Women.* New York: HarperPerennial, 1995.

Hong, Ying. *Daughter of the River.* Translated by Howard Goldblatt. New York: Grove Press, 1998.

Johnson, Kay Ann. "The Politics of the Revival of Infant Abandonment in China with Special Reference to Hunan." *Population and Development Review* 22, 1 (March 1996).

———. *Women, the Family and Peasant Revolution in China.* Chicago: University of Chicago Press, 1983.

———, and Amy Klatzkin. *Wanting a Daughter, Needing a Son: Abandonment, Adoption, and Orphanage Care in China.* St. Paul: Yeong and Yeong, 2004.

Johnson, Kay Ann, Banghan Huang, and Liyao Wang. "Infant Abandonment and Adoption in China." *Population and Development Review* 24, 3 (September 1998).

Jung Chang. *Wild Swans.* New York: Simon & Schuster, 1991.

Kingston, Maxine Hong. *The Woman Warrior: Memoirs of a Girlhood Among Ghosts.* New York: Vintage, 1989.

Kinney, Anne Behnke. *Chinese Views of Childhood.* Honolulu: University of Hawaii Press, 1995.

Klatzkin, Amy, ed. *A Passage to the Heart: Writings from Families with Children from China.* St. Paul: Yeong and Yeong, 1996.

Kristof, Nicholas D., and Sheryl WuDunn. *China Wakes: The Struggle for the Soul of a Rising Power.* New York: Vintage Books, 1995.

Kwei-li. *Golden Lilies.* Adapted by Eileen Goudge. New York: Viking, 1990.

Li Yu-ning, ed. *Chinese Women Through Chinese Eyes.* Armonk, N.Y.: M. E. Sharpe, 1992.

Lifton, Betty Jean. *Lost & Found: The Adoption Experience.* New York: Perennial Library, 1988.

Lin, Julia C., trans. *Women of the Red Plain: An Anthology of Contemporary Chinese Women's Poetry.* New York: Penguin, 1992.

Lindqvist, Cecilia. *China: Empire of Living Symbols.* Translated by Joan Tate. New York: Addison-Wesley, 1991.

Lord, Bette Bao. *Legacies: A Chinese Mosaic.* New York: Fawcett Books, 1991.

———. *Spring Moon.* New York: Harper, 1994.

Lu Hsun. "Idle Thoughts at the End of Spring," *Selected Works.* Beijing: Foreign Languages Press, 1927.

McKibben, Bill. *Maybe One: A Personal and Environmental Argument for Single-Child Families.* New York: Simon & Schuster, 1998.

Min, Anchee. *Katherine.* New York: Berkley Books, 1996.

———. *Red Azalea.* New York: Berkley Books, 1995.

Mosher, Steven W. *Broken Earth: The Rural Chinese.* New York: Free Press, 1983.

———. *A Mother's Ordeal: One Woman's Fight Against China's One-Child Policy.* New York: HarperPerennial, 1993.

Pfaelzer, Jean. *Driven Out: The Forgotten War Against Chinese Americans.* New York: Random House, 2007.

Pipher, Mary. *Reviving Ophelia: Saving the Selves of Adolescent Girls.* New York: Ballantine Books, 1994.

Pomfret, John. *Chinese Lessons: Five Classmates and the Story of the New China.* New York: Henry Holt, 2006.

Qi Xing. *Folk Customs at Traditional Chinese Festivities.* Translated by Ren Jiazhen. Beijing: Foreign Languages Press, 1988.

Roberts, Moss, ed. and trans. *Chinese Fairy Tales & Fantasies.* New York: Pantheon Books, 1979.

Rojewski, Jay, and Jacy Rojewski. *Intercountry Adoption from China: Examining Cultural Heritage and Other Postadoption Issues.* Westport, Conn.: Bergin & Garvey, 2001.

Schell, Orville. *Mandate of Heaven: A New Generation of Entrepreneurs, Dissidents, Bohemians, and Technocrats Lays Claim to China's Future.* New York: Simon & Schuster, 1994.

Scheper-Hughes, Nancy. *Death Without Weeping: The Violence of Everyday Life in Brazil.* Berkeley: University of California Press, 1992.

Shlain, Leonard. *The Alphabet Versus the Goddess: The Conflict Between Word and Image.* New York: Viking, 1998.

Spence, Jonathan D. *The Gate of Heavenly Peace: The Chinese and Their Revolution, 1895–1980.* New York: Penguin, 1982.

———. *The Search for Modern China.* New York: W. W. Norton, 1990.

Steinberg, Gail, and Beth Hall. *Inside Transracial Adoption.* Indianapolis: Perspectives Press, 2000.

Stockard, Janice E. *Daughter of the Canton Delta: Marriage Patterns and Economic Strategies in South China 1860–1930.* Stanford, Calif.: Stanford University Press, 1989.

Sunee, Kim. *Trail of Crumbs: Hunger, Love, and the Search for Home.* New York: Grand Central Publishing, 2008.

Takaki, Ronald. *A Different Mirror: A History of Multicultural America.* Boston: Back Bay Books, 1993.

Tan, Amy. *The Joy Luck Club.* New York: G. P. Putnam's Sons, 1989.

———. *The Opposite of Fate.* New York: Penguin, 2003.

Tessler, Richard, Gail Gamache, and Liming Liu. *West Meets East: American Adoption of Chinese Children.* Westport, Conn.: Bergin & Garvey, 1999.

Tom, K. S. *Echoes of Old China.* Honolulu: Hawaii Chinese History Center, 1989.

Trenka, Jane Jeong, Julia Chinyere Oparah, and Sun Yung Shin, eds. *Outsiders Within: Writing on Transracial Adoption.* Cambridge, Mass.: South End Press, 2006.

Tsai, Chih Chung. *Confucius Speaks: Words to Live By.* Translated by Brian Bruya. New York: Anchor Books, 1996.

Tsao Hsueh-Chin. *The Dream of the Red Chamber: Hung Lou Meng.* New York: Pantheon Books, 1958.

Verrier, Nancy Newton. *The Primal Wound: Understanding the Adopted Child.* Baltimore: Gateway Press, 1997.

Verschuur-Basse, Denyse. *Chinese Women Speak.* Westport, Conn.: Praeger Publishers, 1996.

Volkman, Toby Alice, ed. *Cultures of Transnational Adoption.* Durham, N.C.: Duke University Press, 2005.

Waley, Arthur. *Translations from the Chinese*. New York: Alfred A. Knopf, 1941.

Wang, Fangyu, Richard M. Barnhart, and Judith G. Smith, eds. *Master of the Lotus Garden: The Life and Art of Bada Shanren (1626–1705)*. New Haven, Conn.: Yale University Press, 1990.

Watson, Burton, ed. and trans. *The Columbia Book of Chinese Poetry: From Early Times to the Thirteenth Century*. New York: Columbia University Press, 1984.

Wolf, Arthur, and Chieh-shan Huang. *Marriage and Adoption in China 1845–1945*. Stanford, Calif: Stanford University Press, 1980.

Wolf, Margery. *Revolution Postponed: Women in Contemporary China*. Stanford, Calif.: Stanford University Press, 1985.

Wong, Jan. *Red China Blues: My Long March from Mao to Now*. New York: Doubleday/Anchor Books, 1996.

Wu, Harry. *Bitter Winds*. New York: John Wiley & Sons, 1995.

Wyman, Nona Mock. *Chopstick Childhood in a Town of Silver Spoons*. Walnut Creek, Calif.: MQ Press, 1997.

Yang, Belle. *Baba: A Return to China upon My Father's Shoulders*. San Diego: Harcourt, Brace, 1994.

Yen Mah, Adeline. *Falling Leaves: The True Story of an Unwanted Chinese Daughter*. New York: John Wiley & Sons, 1997.

Zha, Jianying. *China Pop: How Soap Operas, Tabloids, and Bestsellers Are Transforming a Culture*. New York: New Press, 1995.

Zhou, Kaiya, and Xingdun Zhang. *Baiji: The Yangtze River Dolphin and Other Endangered Animals of China*. Washington, D.C.: Stone Wall Press, and Nanjing, China: Yilin Press, 1991.

Zia, Helen. *Asian American Dreams: The Emergence of an American People*. New York: Farrar, Straus & Giroux, 2001.

Resources

For detailed information on adoption from China, an excellent source is the Families with Children from China website, offering background for prospective parents, guidelines and answers to frequently asked questions, travel and health information, updates on new rules or legislation—in both the United States and China—that affect adoption, personal stories from families who have adopted, guides to Internet sources, and a listing of local FCC chapters on the Web at www.fwcc.org.

The China Center of Adoption Affairs maintains a website at www.china-ccaa.org, which offers extensive information on Chinese adoption protocols, including recent updates and changes in the laws, and information on required paperwork.

For extensive background, research, and current information on adoption in general, the Evan B. Donaldson Adoption Institute is a valuable resource. Contact the organization at 120 Wall Street 20th floor, New York, NY 10005-3902; telephone 212-269-5080 or on the Web at www.adoptioninstitute.org.

Pact, an adoption alliance based in the San Francisco Bay Area, is an excellent, well-grounded source of lifelong education and support for adoptive families, particularly on issues of race and cross-cultural parenting. The organization offers seminars and other programs specifically designed for adoptive families. For more information write: Pact, 4179 Piedmont Avenue, Suite 101, Oakland, CA 94611; telephone 510-243-9460; or on the Web at www.pactadopt.org.

Teaching Tolerance is a wonderful and necessary program—offering a magazine, videotapes, and school presentations—produced by Morris Dees and staff at the Southern Poverty Law Center. For information, write: Teaching Tolerance, 400 Washington Avenue, Montgomery, AL 36104.

Charitable Initiatives

The Foundation for Chinese Orphanages, with support from adoptive families, provides help to numerous institutions in China. The address is 8 Berkeley Street, Cambridge, MA 02138-3464.

The Amity Foundation, an experienced China-based humanitarian aid organization based in Nanjing, has been working in orphanages for more than a decade. Among the projects: rehabilitation for disabled children, grandmothers' programs, providing special attention to infants and young children. Fund-raising by Families with Children from China–New York benefits these and other projects. Donations may be sent to Families with Children from China, Fund-raising Appeal, Box 865, Ansonia Station, New York, NY 10025.

Half the Sky Foundation is a joint endeavor by American adoptive families, Chinese officials, and child development specialists in both countries to establish early childhood education, infant nurture programs and Big Sisters programs in orphanages, plus Family Villages foster care. On the Web at www.halfthesky.org. Or write to Half the Sky Foundation, 740 Gilman Street, Berkeley, CA 94710.

Love Without Boundaries provides medical help, nutrition, and other support to children in China's institutions. Visit www.lovewithoutboundaries.com, or write to Love Without Boundaries, 306 South Bryant, Suite C, PMB 145, Edmund, OK 73034.

For a more extensive listing, see the Families with Children from China website (www.fwcc.org).

Permissions

About the Author

Karin Evans has worked as a writer and editor for numerous publications, including *Outside*, *Rocky Mountain Magazine*, the San Francisco *Examiner Sunday Magazine*, *Health*, and *Hippocrates*. She spent two years as a stringer for the Hong Kong bureau of *Newsweek*. She has edited a number of books, and her writing has appeared in such publications as *More*, *The Boston Globe*, *The New York Times*, the San Francisco *Examiner*, *The Denver Post*, and the *Los Angeles Times*. Evans served for six years on the board of Half the Sky Foundation and, with Amy Tan, coauthored the text for *Mei-Mei—Little Sister: Portraits from a Chinese Orphanage*, by Richard Bowen. An avid hiker and cyclist, she lives with her husband, attorney Mark Humbert, and their daughters Kelly Xiao Yu and Franny Yi Xuan in northern California. She is currently studying toward an MFA degree in poetry at Seattle Pacific University.